Technocracy Inc, A Who's Who of Global
Control

Technocracy Inc, A Who's Who of Global Control

Will Stickle

CONTENTS

Technocracy is often presented as progress - a sign that humanity has matured beyond tribalism, politics, and ideology. But stripped to its core, technocracy means rule by engineers, systems, and "experts," where authority flows not from consent but from claimed competence. It is a governance structure where equations, algorithms, and technical expertise are treated as substitutes for collective decision-making, where political leaders gradually surrender control to specialists in the name of efficiency and precision. This shift didn't happen overnight; it evolved alongside industrialization, automation, and the growing belief that society could be managed like a machine - predictable, measurable, and optimized.

The roots of technocracy can be traced back to the early 20th century when engineering and systems theory collided with political thought. The industrial revolution had already proven that machines could replace human muscle; now the same philosophy was applied to human judgment itself. If production lines could be optimized, why not economies? If traffic systems could be modeled, why not entire cities? And if people were just another set of variables in a complex network, why shouldn't they be governed like one? This was the seductive promise: eliminate the chaos of human politics, reduce uncertainty, and let the "best minds" run the world.

On the surface, this sounds logical - rational even. But logic has owners. Algorithms do not create themselves, and expertise does not exist in a vacuum. Every system reflects the priorities, values, and assumptions of the people who design it. When engineers are elevated to the role of policymakers, their worldview becomes the framework for everyone else's reality. And when those frameworks are encoded into technology, the choices they make are largely invisible to the public. Decisions once debated in the open become buried in code, protocols, and statistical models that no ordinary citizen can challenge.

Technocracy thrives on this invisibility. It creates an architecture where control hides behind complexity. When a government claims "the model shows we must act," it closes the door to debate. When an algorithm determines loan approvals, parole decisions, or vaccine mandates, accountability disappears into mathematical abstractions. Even when predictions fail - when the models are wrong, when the experts are mistaken - there is no recourse. The system adjusts itself, blames faulty data, and continues forward, unchallenged.

This also shifts the very definition of expertise. Under technocracy, power no longer belongs to those who represent the people but to those who control information. Scientists, engineers, and data analysts become de facto rulers - not through direct authority but through shaping the frameworks within which authority operates. Elected officials become figureheads reading from scripts written by specialists, their decisions justified by reports and projections few understand and fewer can refute. The appearance of democracy remains, but its substance quietly dissolves.

The most dangerous element is how technocracy manufactures consent. It doesn't rule through brute force; it rules through the illusion of objectivity. When a politician makes a decision, you can question motives and ideology. When a system produces an answer, it's presented as neutral and beyond dispute. "The data says" becomes a new form of divine authority. People stop arguing about whether a policy is right or wrong and start debating whether they've "interpreted the data correctly." This shifts the battleground from ethics to metrics, reducing human values to technical parameters.

The deeper consequence is cultural. When society begins to equate intelligence with expertise and expertise with authority, individuality is diminished. People become users, not citizens - inputs rather than participants. Governance becomes less about human flourishing and more about systems management. A citizen's role narrows to compliance within parameters they didn't set and can't meaningfully influence. In such an environment, personal freedom exists only to the extent it doesn't interfere with optimization.

Technocracy is also inherently expansionist. Once established in one domain, it naturally seeks others. A system built to regulate energy consumption soon feeds into economic models predicting productivity, which in turn integrate with surveillance networks tracking individual behavior. Each layer justifies the next in the name of efficiency, security, or sustainability. Over time, governance becomes less about leadership and more about administration - steering a vast machine where no single individual appears to be in control, yet power concentrates silently in the hands of those who build and maintain the machine.

This quiet centralization produces a paradox: technocracy promises decentralization by claiming to distribute decision-making across systems and experts, but in practice, it funnels control upward. The more data a system collects, the more decisions are made at the top. The more predictive models influence policy, the less room there is for local context or human judgment. What looks like democratized access to information is often the opposite - it's a narrowing of acceptable narratives enforced by the architecture of technology itself.

Technocracy also breeds fragility. Systems optimized for maximum efficiency are highly vulnerable to disruption. When everything is connected, when control flows through a few centralized channels, any failure - technical, economic, or political - cascades rapidly. In such an environment, resilience is sacrificed for precision, and the illusion of control masks the reality of systemic vulnerability. History shows repeatedly that over-engineered systems fail spectacularly, yet technocracy doubles down, convinced that better models, better data, and better tools will solve the problems created by its previous designs.

But perhaps the most insidious aspect of technocracy is cultural dependency. Over time, populations begin to internalize the belief that ordinary people cannot be trusted to make meaningful decisions. Agency is surrendered voluntarily because people are conditioned to defer to "those who know better." Citizens stop expecting transparency, stop questioning authority, and eventually lose the vocabulary to articulate alternatives. Control no longer requires coercion; compliance becomes self-reinforcing because people genuinely believe there is no other way to manage complex societies.

By the mid-20th century, this mindset had already begun shaping the global order. Post-war reconstruction didn't just rebuild cities and economies; it restructured governance itself around managerial expertise. New institutions emerged - financial, political, and scientific - that presented themselves as neutral arbiters of progress. But the foundational logic remained the same: rule by specialists, centralized control masked as collaboration, and authority justified by metrics and models rather than public consent. The world became a laboratory, and entire populations became experimental variables within it.

Technocracy isn't the replacement of politics; it's the perfection of politics under another name. It removes the messy, visible conflicts of ideology and replaces them with quiet, systemic decisions that shape the boundaries of what's politically possible. It hides power where few people can see it and fewer can reach it. And once established, it rarely reverses itself - because the very systems that enable technocracy are the ones that define its legitimacy.

The Industrial Revolution reshaped civilization with a speed and violence unmatched in history. It created vast new wealth but concentrated that wealth into the hands of a small elite, transforming the balance of power across continents. Factories, railways, and mechanized production generated fortunes on a scale unimaginable a century earlier, but this economic transformation also created instability. The explosion of urban populations, the breakdown of traditional social structures, and the rise of a newly empowered working class terrified the ruling elite. What followed was a quiet counter-revolution - the birth of modern ideologies of social control designed to manage populations, channel dissent, and preserve concentrated power under the guise of progress.

The first wave of industrial capitalists saw clearly that mass production required mass compliance. Factories didn't function if workers refused to show up, organize, or demand higher wages. The elite response was to engineer systems that could manage labor indirectly without relying on brute force. Education was redesigned not to liberate thought but to discipline it. Compulsory public schooling, introduced under the promise of literacy and opportunity, became a tool to train obedient workers who could follow instructions and accept hierarchy. The industrial model didn't stop at machines; it extended to people. Human beings became another form of input to be standardized, optimized, and controlled.

Simultaneously, new ideologies emerged that reshaped how societies understood freedom, morality, and governance. Utilitarianism, born in the salons of the wealthy, reduced human value to productivity and output, framing the individual as secondary to the "greater good." Eugenics followed, cloaked in scientific language, proposing that populations could be improved by managing reproduction and selecting traits deemed desirable by the elite. These ideas were not fringe; they were mainstream among industrial magnates, government planners, and academic institutions. The common thread was always the same: a belief that progress required management, and management required control.

The working class was not left out of this equation - it became its central focus. As industrial wealth expanded, so did the fear of revolt. Marxism and early socialist movements grew rapidly in response to brutal labor conditions, threatening to destabilize the very system that created industrial wealth. For the elite, the challenge became dual: suppress radical uprisings while co-opting reform movements to maintain legitimacy. Welfare programs, labor laws, and workplace reforms emerged not purely from compassion but as strategic concessions designed to prevent rebellion while preserving ownership and hierarchy. Social stability was manufactured, not earned.

Behind these ideological shifts came the rise of new institutions built to shape thought and behavior. Philanthropic foundations, often funded by industrial fortunes, played a central role. Organizations like the Rockefeller Foundation and the Carnegie Endowment presented themselves as altruistic forces advancing education, science, and public health. In reality, they were instruments of soft power, steering academic research, shaping curricula, and embedding elite values into the very framework of public life. By funding universities, scientific research, and media outlets, they exerted control over which ideas gained legitimacy and which were buried. The narrative of progress was carefully curated, and dissenting voices found themselves marginalized.

The Industrial Revolution also transformed government itself. States recognized that sustaining economic growth required predictability, and predictability required managing human behavior on a mass scale. Bureaucracies grew, census systems expanded, and surveillance began to evolve from a military function into a civilian one. Statistical modeling, population studies, and early social sciences became tools to predict and influence trends before they threatened stability. "Scientific management" - pioneered by thinkers like Frederick Winslow Taylor - turned workplaces into laboratories of efficiency, where every movement was measured, every decision optimized, and every deviation eliminated.

This fusion of wealth, governance, and ideology laid the groundwork for what followed in the 20th century: an era where the appearance of freedom masked increasingly subtle forms of control. Individuals were conditioned to believe they were free to choose while the range of acceptable choices narrowed. Public discourse was guided by experts and institutions whose authority came not from democratic mandate but from their claimed mastery of knowledge. The individual was reframed as a participant in systems they didn't design, while collective identity was reshaped around productivity, conformity, and managed aspiration.

By the time the world entered the early 1900s, the foundation was set for the systems of control that dominate modern life. The same industrial fortunes that built factories and railroads also built schools, research institutions, media networks, and public policy frameworks designed to perpetuate their influence. Ideologies of social control weren't imposed through overt tyranny but through normalization - the gradual integration of centralized authority into the routines of daily life. Control became cultural, embedded in habits, expectations, and institutional trust. People were conditioned to see their role not as sovereign individuals but as components of an economic engine, expected to work, consume, and obey.

The wealth generated by the Industrial Revolution didn't just transform economies; it reshaped human psychology and societal structure. It created a managerial class whose power was defined not by birthright but by expertise, a class that believed it had the right - even the obligation - to design society according to its own ideals. From there, the leap to modern technocracy was inevitable. Once control could be justified in the name of efficiency, public health, or stability, the logic extended endlessly. The tools became more sophisticated, the data more precise, and the ideologies more subtle, but the underlying premise remained the same: power was safest when distributed upward, and populations were safest when guided, monitored, and managed.

This was not accidental or inevitable; it was deliberate design. The narrative of progress was written to obscure the transfer of agency from individuals to institutions. Industrial wealth built more than machines; it built systems - systems that trained generations to equate obedience with stability and dependence with security. What began as an economic transformation evolved into an architecture of control, one that survives today not through overt coercion but through shaping perception itself.

Democracy sells the story that power flows upward from the people, that consent forms the foundation of governance, and that leaders serve at the pleasure of those they represent. It promises a system where citizens shape laws, hold authority accountable, and steer the course of their collective future. But beneath this familiar ritual lies a different reality - one where unelected elites wield disproportionate influence, steering policy, shaping narratives, and deciding outcomes long before the public ever casts a vote. The illusion is sustained through ceremony and spectacle, but the substance of decision-making has been quietly removed from public hands.

The appearance of choice is central to this illusion. Citizens are presented with candidates preselected by party machines funded by corporate wealth, lobbied by powerful interests, and filtered through media narratives owned by the same few conglomerates. By the time the public enters the conversation, the boundaries of debate have already been drawn. Elections function less as moments of genuine decision and more as mechanisms of validation, ratifying paths already chosen by entrenched networks of power. Voters believe they are influencing outcomes, yet the machinery of policy - regulatory frameworks, economic strategies, and geopolitical positioning - operates largely outside democratic reach.

Unelected elites don't announce themselves. They operate through institutions designed to appear neutral: central banks, intelligence agencies, trade bodies, think tanks, and international organizations. These entities set agendas, draft treaties, and manage crises with little transparency and virtually no direct accountability to the public. Decisions affecting billions - interest rates, financial bailouts, climate policy, military alliances - are made in boardrooms and closed-door summits, not parliaments or town halls. By the time such decisions reach elected officials, they are often framed as necessities rather than options, presented as technical matters beyond the understanding of ordinary citizens.

The media amplifies this divide, shaping perception rather than providing clarity. Narratives are curated, debates constrained, and public outrage carefully channeled into safe directions that leave core power structures untouched. The illusion of diversity in opinion masks the reality of a unified consensus among ruling classes on key economic and political priorities. Whether under conservative or progressive branding, the policies that sustain financial monopolies, perpetual debt, and globalized control remain largely unchallenged. Even when governments change hands, the deeper architecture of governance persists untouched, immune to electoral shifts.

This creates a form of managed participation where people are encouraged to engage just enough to validate the system but never enough to meaningfully disrupt it. Dissent is absorbed into controlled opposition, grassroots movements are co-opted or discredited, and radical alternatives are dismissed as unrealistic or dangerous. The public is conditioned to see complex governance as requiring specialized knowledge, reinforcing dependency on "experts" and "authorities" who are neither elected nor easily removed. Power consolidates upward while citizens are pacified with symbols - flags, anthems, campaigns, and slogans - designed to maintain emotional loyalty to institutions that no longer serve them.

This model thrives on invisibility. The real levers of influence - finance, intelligence, surveillance, technological infrastructure - operate beyond public scrutiny, embedded within bureaucracies that rarely change regardless of electoral outcomes. As the gap between perception and reality widens, trust in democratic systems erodes, but the alternatives are intentionally obscured. People are told that without these systems, chaos would reign, ensuring compliance through fear rather than genuine consent. In this way, democracy becomes less a mechanism of governance and more a performance - a story people are encouraged to believe while the true decisions are made elsewhere.

This erosion did not happen suddenly. It evolved alongside industrial capitalism, technocracy, and global integration, with each stage pushing more authority into the hands of those least accountable. Today, as automation, data-driven policy, and centralized financial systems deepen, the distance between voter and ruler has grown to the point where participation often feels symbolic rather than substantive. The paradox is sharp: citizens are freer than ever to express themselves, yet less able than ever to influence outcomes.

Democracy endures as a brand, a reassuring label attached to systems that no longer embody its original promise. The ceremonies continue, the campaigns grow louder, and the narratives more polarized, but behind the noise, the decisions that shape the future remain insulated from public reach. What emerges is not governance by the people, but governance through their consent to stories carefully designed to keep them in their place.

The framework of this book rests on a simple directive: follow the engineers, follow the money, follow the code. It's not a slogan; it's a map of power. Everything else - the institutions, the politics, the narratives - flows from these three converging forces. Where engineers design the systems, where money funds and directs them, and where code locks those decisions into permanence, you find the architecture of control shaping the modern world. This is not a conspiracy in the traditional sense; it's a structural evolution. Power moves through infrastructure now - not speeches, not campaigns, but networks, protocols, and algorithms invisible to the public eye.

Following the engineers means understanding who builds the machinery of society, both physical and digital. The world runs on systems most people neither see nor comprehend - energy grids, logistics networks, communication satellites, data centers, and now artificial intelligence models that interpret and act upon reality at speeds humans can't match. Engineers hold more influence than politicians because they design the rules inside which politics operates. A line of code can decide who gets a loan, whose posts are censored, or which supply chains collapse. Governments often implement policies constrained by what engineers deem possible, and yet these technologists are rarely accountable to voters or bound by democratic process. Their priorities - efficiency, optimization, and scalability - inevitably shape the limits of public freedom.

Following the money reveals the motives behind these systems. While engineers build, capital directs. Funding decides which technologies are developed, which remain experimental, and which are buried. Global finance prioritizes control, predictability, and returns on investment. If an innovation threatens entrenched interests or redistributes power downward, it is starved of capital and confined to obscurity. Conversely, technologies that centralize authority - surveillance tools, algorithmic management platforms, predictive analytics - receive nearly unlimited funding because they serve the interests of those who already hold influence. Corporations and financial institutions operate above borders, shaping national policies through lobbying, trade agreements, and debt structures, ensuring that control aligns with profit at every stage.

Following the code exposes how these priorities become permanent. Once decisions are embedded into software, protocols, and digital infrastructure, they are extraordinarily difficult to reverse. Code executes silently, enforcing policies automatically at scale. Algorithms make millions of decisions every second without oversight, interpreting human behavior through data and acting upon it without negotiation. Governance migrates from laws written on paper to rules embedded in systems, where consent becomes irrelevant because participation itself implies compliance. Opting out of these frameworks is nearly impossible - the modern individual relies on platforms and services designed not to be bypassed, where access to information, finance, and even identity depends on technological integration.

These three vectors - engineers, money, and code - converge into a new locus of power, one that is distributed enough to seem invisible but coordinated enough to dictate outcomes. Politicians debate symptoms while infrastructure shapes reality. Policy documents are drafted after the systems are already operational, long after the real choices have been made. Voters believe they are electing leaders, but the framework they live within has already been set by the engineers who designed the tools, the financiers who funded them, and the coders who wrote their logic into permanence.

The result is a quiet inversion of sovereignty. Where the industrial age was defined by control over labor and resources, the digital age is defined by control over information and access. The terrain of power is no longer land or factories but data, algorithms, and protocols. Whoever sets the parameters sets the boundaries of freedom, and those parameters are rarely debated in public forums. People are conditioned to see innovation as neutral and inevitable, yet every innovation encodes someone's priorities, values, and worldview. The illusion of choice persists while the deeper architecture of decision-making hardens beneath it.

This framework is how we dismantle the illusion of randomness and chaos. By tracing the engineers, the financiers, and the code itself, patterns emerge - not abstract theories, but direct causal chains that show who benefits, who loses, and why. It reveals the subtle migration of power away from parliaments, courts, and town halls into systems most people do not control and cannot fully understand. It also exposes the continuity across eras: the same industrial wealth that birthed social control ideologies has now evolved into digital networks where governance is outsourced to algorithms and institutions insulated from public accountability.

To understand where we are, we must follow these threads relentlessly. The engineers are not neutral. The money is not benevolent. The code is not passive. Each carries intent, shaping the world silently while the public debates symbols. By studying how these forces intertwine, we reveal the deeper structure behind events that otherwise appear disconnected: economic crises, censorship battles, resource wars, and policy shifts that seem sudden but are anything but.

This is not about predicting the future; it's about decoding the present. The levers of power no longer announce themselves. They operate through technical systems, private networks, and institutional consensus masked as objectivity. By following the engineers, following the money, and following the code, the architecture of control stops being invisible. Once seen clearly, it cannot be unseen.

PART I - SEEDS OF CONTROL (1750–1920)

How the machine age birthed the technocratic mindset.

Dawn of the Machine Age
(1750–1820)

The First Industrial Revolution marked the opening act of a transformation that would rewrite the relationship between power, production, and society. It began in Britain during the late 18th century and radiated outward, reshaping economies, dismantling traditional livelihoods, and concentrating authority into the hands of those who controlled machines and resources. At its core, this revolution was about energy and control - energy harnessed through steam and coal, and control achieved through mechanization, patents, and systems that turned human labor into another component of industrial machinery.

The rise of the steam engine sits at the heart of this shift. James Watt, often celebrated as an innovator, perfected the design but also secured patents that effectively gave him dominance over an emerging energy economy. Steam power transformed not just industry but society itself, unlocking an unprecedented capacity to move goods, people, and information faster than ever before. Yet Watt's story reveals the deeper undercurrents driving the revolution: intellectual property laws became weapons, ensuring that control over innovation meant control over markets. Watt's patents didn't merely protect his ideas; they created monopolies that throttled competition and concentrated wealth into fewer hands, setting a precedent for the industrial age.

Richard Arkwright extended this transformation by pioneering the factory system. His vision wasn't just about building machines but designing entire environments optimized for production. By centralizing labor, materials, and technology under one roof, Arkwright created a model where workers became extensions of the machines they served. Individual craftsmanship - once the foundation of economic independence - was dismantled in favor of uniformity and scale. The factory system extracted autonomy from artisans and farmers, pulling them into regimented routines where every movement was dictated by the demands of machinery. This shift fundamentally altered the human relationship to time, labor, and survival, tethering millions to industrial schedules and corporate dependency.

Eli Whitney added another layer to this transformation through his development of interchangeable parts. At first, this seemed a democratizing innovation - simplifying manufacturing, reducing costs, and accelerating production. But interchangeable parts carried within them the seeds of early automation. They eliminated the need for highly skilled craftsmen, replacing individual expertise with standardized processes that could be replicated by less-trained labor or, eventually, by machines entirely. Whitney's system laid the groundwork for a new philosophy of production: efficiency above all else, with human variability treated as a flaw to be engineered out of existence.

Together, these innovations shattered centuries-old patterns of life. The First Industrial Revolution didn't simply create new industries; it restructured society around centralized systems of production, ownership, and control. Power flowed not to those who worked but to those who patented, financed, and scaled technology. The entrepreneurs and financiers of this period understood quickly that mastery of energy, infrastructure, and mechanization meant mastery over markets and populations alike. Steam, coal, and steel became tools of empire, enabling nations like Britain to dominate global trade and impose industrial models across continents.

Yet the most profound impact wasn't just economic; it was psychological. For the first time, vast numbers of people became dependent on systems they neither understood nor controlled. Survival hinged on wages rather than land, and communities that had once sustained themselves through local production found their autonomy stripped away. The promises of industrial progress - wealth, convenience, modernity - came at the cost of independence, identity, and agency. Behind the celebrated ingenuity of Watt, Arkwright, and Whitney lay the birth of a new form of power: control achieved through technology, protected by law, and scaled by finance.

This period was the blueprint for every industrial wave that followed. It established patterns that still define modern life: monopolies cloaked in innovation, centralized systems shaping human behavior, and an ever-tightening integration between technology and governance. The First Industrial Revolution didn't just change how people worked; it changed what it meant to be free within a system designed to manage and extract human potential at scale.

Company towns emerged in the 19th century as industrial wealth collided with the need to manage growing workforces, producing one of the most effective systems of social control the modern world had seen to that point. On the surface, these towns were marketed as benevolent - model communities built by forward-thinking industrialists to provide workers with housing, schools, stores, and entertainment. In reality, they were laboratories of paternalism, designed to keep labor disciplined, dependent, and compliant, while ensuring that every aspect of workers' lives - from wages to rent to morality - remained under the company's control.

At the heart of the company town was the promise of stability. Industrialists framed their creations as utopian solutions to overcrowded cities and chaotic urban poverty, offering workers a carefully managed environment where their basic needs would be met. But the design was deliberate: company-owned housing kept workers geographically tethered to the workplace, while company-owned stores captured the wages they paid out. It wasn't uncommon for employees to be paid in "scrip" - currency valid only at company stores - effectively eliminating their ability to participate in the broader economy. A man could work sixty hours a week and find himself perpetually indebted to the same employer who issued his wages. Debt became a silent tool of control, binding families to corporations as securely as any chain.

These towns didn't just regulate the economy of their residents; they shaped their culture, habits, and values. Management often dictated acceptable behavior, policing morality through rules about drinking, gambling, and church attendance. Some towns imposed curfews. Others banned labor organizing outright, surveilling workers and punishing dissent. In many cases, the company acted as landlord, judge, employer, and sheriff, collapsing civil society into a single authority. This blurring of corporate and civic power left workers with little recourse when exploitation occurred, as any attempt to challenge conditions meant risking not just a job but one's home, community, and reputation.

Industrialists justified this paternalism by claiming to act in the workers' best interests. Figures like George Pullman - whose railcar company built one of the most infamous company towns in Illinois - argued that controlling employees' living conditions improved productivity and public morality. Pullman's model town boasted manicured lawns, libraries, and neatly planned streets, but workers paid high rents for the privilege of living there and had no ownership of their homes or neighborhoods. When economic downturns forced wage cuts, Pullman refused to lower rents, triggering the 1894 Pullman Strike, a violent confrontation that exposed the underlying reality of the system: beneath the rhetoric of care lay pure economic dominance.

The company town also served as a powerful tool against collective action. By isolating workers and entwining every aspect of their existence with their employer, corporations fragmented solidarity and suppressed organizing efforts. Strikes became riskier when losing a job meant immediate eviction and financial ruin. And when workers did resist, companies often called on local or federal forces to maintain "order," blurring the lines between private interests and state power. This merging of economic and political authority created a model of corporate sovereignty - small-scale experiments in governance where citizens were subjects first and employees second.

Despite their decline in the 20th century, the company town established patterns that persist in modern forms. Today's corporate campuses, employer-controlled healthcare systems, and digital platform economies carry echoes of the same logic: intertwining livelihood, community, and identity in ways that erode independence while deepening dependency. Where the Pullmans of the 19th century controlled housing and groceries, today's corporations control data, connectivity, and access to opportunity. The tactics evolved, but the underlying strategy remains unchanged: concentrate authority, manage behavior, and create environments where opting out feels impossible.

The birth of company towns revealed an enduring truth about industrial capitalism: control was never just about labor performed inside the factory. It extended outward into every facet of life, weaving economic dependence, cultural conformity, and moral discipline into a single framework. These towns were not accidents of history; they were deliberate architectures of power designed to secure profits by managing people as tightly as machinery. The lesson is clear: whenever an institution claims to provide for every need, it rarely does so without expecting something greater in return - not just labor, but submission.

The First Industrial Revolution laid the groundwork, but it was in the 19th century that the first truly data-driven society began to emerge. For the first time in history, human activity was quantified, measured, and optimized at scale, transforming labor and production into a mathematics of control. Logistics, productivity, and profit became the metrics around which entire societies were reorganized. What began as a response to industrial complexity evolved into a philosophy: everything that could be measured would be managed, and everything that could be managed could be exploited.

Factories became laboratories of precision. Owners and engineers tracked every variable that influenced production - hours worked, units produced, machine downtime, material costs, and shipping speeds. The worker was no longer viewed as an individual but as a statistical unit, a variable in an equation designed to extract maximum output for minimum cost. Time-and-motion studies analyzed each gesture, each tool placement, each break between tasks. Frederick Winslow Taylor's "scientific management," developed in the late 1800s, epitomized this shift: break every job into discrete motions, measure each one, and eliminate anything deemed inefficient. Human judgment was no longer trusted; optimization became a mechanical imperative.

This obsession with measurement extended beyond the factory walls into the movement of goods and resources. Railroads became the arteries of industrial society, and their efficiency depended on unprecedented coordination. Companies tracked schedules, distances, tonnage, and costs down to fractions of a cent. Standardized time zones - once irrelevant to daily life - were introduced not for social convenience but for logistical necessity. Coordinating massive flows of coal, textiles, steel, and food required centralized planning supported by meticulous data collection. Information became power, and those who controlled it gained leverage not just over production but over entire economies.

Governments followed suit, adopting similar methods to manage growing populations in increasingly urbanized environments. Census-taking became more sophisticated, recording not just counts of citizens but occupations, earnings, literacy, and housing conditions. Bureaucracies expanded to analyze these datasets, translating them into policies that shaped everything from tax systems to military conscription. Industrial wealth depended on a steady, predictable labor force, and measuring people became a prerequisite for controlling them. A society that once moved at the pace of seasons now moved at the pace of schedules, deadlines, and output quotas.

The link between data and profit grew inseparable. Companies learned that the more they measured, the more they could extract. Logistics systems evolved to minimize waste and maximize margins, while supply chains stretched across continents to chase lower costs and greater returns. Business records became more detailed and standardized, enabling corporate empires to manage thousands of workers and millions of transactions with unprecedented precision. Efficiency became a moral imperative, and profitability its measure of virtue. What wasn't measured didn't matter, and what couldn't be quantified was treated as irrelevant.

Yet this data-driven order also created new hierarchies. Those who gathered, analyzed, and controlled information occupied positions of growing authority, while those being measured were stripped of agency. Decisions were increasingly made by distant managers and financiers who never set foot on the factory floor but dictated how every second, every shipment, and every resource would be used. The early industrialists realized something profound: control over data meant control over people, not through direct coercion but by designing the systems within which their lives unfolded.

This period marks the beginning of a deeper cultural shift - the belief that society could be engineered through measurement and feedback loops. Once people accepted that efficiency was synonymous with progress, they also accepted its demands: tighter schedules, greater surveillance, and reduced autonomy in exchange for stability and growth. The first data-driven society didn't simply produce goods faster; it produced new forms of dependency, locking populations into systems where survival depended on compliance with rules they had no part in creating.

The logic of this transformation would only accelerate in the decades that followed. The techniques refined in factories and railroads became templates for managing entire nations, corporations, and eventually global economies. By turning human activity into data points, industrial society created the tools for control that would later evolve into the algorithmic governance of the modern era. What began as ledgers and schedules became the foundation of systems that would decide, invisibly and automatically, who thrives and who is left behind.

The Luddite rebellions were among the first organized uprisings against the power structures born of industrialization - an early revolt against what we would now call machine elites. Beginning around 1811 in

Nottinghamshire and spreading through other parts of England, these weren't random riots or ignorant acts of "anti-technology hysteria," as later narratives framed them. They were deliberate, targeted, and deeply political responses to a system that was rapidly dismantling centuries-old ways of life. The Luddites understood, perhaps more clearly than anyone else at the time, that the Industrial Revolution was not simply about technological progress - it was about control.

The rebellion was driven by textile workers, skilled artisans whose livelihoods were being erased by mechanized looms and automated processes. For generations, these craftsmen had operated within a system where mastery of a trade meant independence, dignity, and the ability to negotiate directly for the value of their labor. But with the rise of machines - like those deployed by innovators such as Richard Arkwright and his imitators - the bargaining power of individuals collapsed. Owners could hire unskilled workers, often women and children, to operate machines at a fraction of the cost, replacing artisans entirely. The machine wasn't just a tool; it became an economic weapon wielded by elites to centralize profits and control labor.

What the Luddites rebelled against was not the existence of technology but its deliberate use as a mechanism of displacement and domination. Factories weren't simply introducing efficiency; they were reshaping society into a hierarchy where decisions about work, wages, and survival were made far from the communities they affected. This was understood by the rebels, who targeted machines strategically - smashing the frames and looms in workshops and factories that had displaced their trades. Their actions were coordinated and disciplined, governed by clandestine groups sworn to secrecy under the name "General Ludd," an almost mythical leader invoked to unify resistance and confuse authorities.

The British state's response revealed exactly whose interests were being defended. Parliament passed harsh laws criminalizing machine-breaking, punishable by imprisonment, transportation, or even death. Thousands of troops were deployed - more soldiers than Britain stationed against Napoleon at the same time - to suppress what the government portrayed as an existential threat to "progress." The elite narrative reframed the Luddites as backward, irrational, and dangerous, embedding a caricature of them into cultural memory as anti-technology fanatics. This distortion persists even today, where "Luddite" is synonymous with ignorance rather than resistance.

In reality, the Luddites were some of the first to grasp how industrialization concentrated power. They understood that machines were not neutral objects but embodied the intentions of their owners. Control over technology meant control over labor, and control over labor meant control over society. By mechanizing production and erasing autonomy, the elites of the era forced people into dependency on wages while extracting greater profits with fewer obligations to their workforce. The Luddites saw where this led and acted before the transformation was complete.

Their defeat was decisive and brutal. By 1816, the rebellion had been crushed through mass arrests, executions, and propaganda campaigns that painted resistance as futile. The factory system expanded without constraint, and with it came the very conditions the Luddites feared: workers reduced to interchangeable parts, entire communities dependent on centralized employers, and the steady erosion of local self-sufficiency. Yet their warning echoes louder today than it did two centuries ago.

Seen through the modern lens, the Luddite rebellions were not a rejection of progress but a fight over who controls it. They were the first collective stand against a new ruling class - one that derived its authority not from land or bloodlines but from its command over technology and capital. It was an uprising against early technocrats and financiers who, shielded by the state, reshaped economies without consent and dismantled entire ways of life in the name of efficiency and profit.

The tragedy of the Luddites is not just their defeat but their erasure from the narrative of industrial history. Their struggle was buried under the myth that technological advancement is inevitable and apolitical, a narrative designed to keep populations compliant as new systems of control emerge. But if we strip away the propaganda, their fight marks the opening chapter in a conflict that continues today: who governs - the people themselves, or the owners of the machines they depend on to live?

2

The Height of the Industrial Revolution

The railroad-steel-coal trinity formed the backbone of the 19th-century industrial order, reshaping nations, accelerating empire-building, and rewriting the balance of global power. This wasn't just technological progress - it was the creation of a system where infrastructure became synonymous with control. Whoever commanded rail lines controlled trade. Whoever controlled steel controlled industry. Whoever owned coal controlled energy itself. Together, these forces created the foundations of modern geopolitics, binding entire economies to the demands of extraction, production, and movement on an unprecedented scale.

Coal was the starting point - the black fuel that powered everything. It drove steam engines, fired furnaces, and lit cities, turning geological deposits into empires. The hunger for coal reshaped landscapes and societies alike. Entire towns sprang up around mines, producing communities entirely dependent on extraction for survival. As demand grew, so did the consolidation of ownership, with a handful of industrialists controlling vast reserves and dictating prices across entire regions. Control over coal wasn't just economic; it meant dominance over energy flows, making it the first true lever of industrial power. Without coal, steel could not be forged, and without steel, railroads could not be built.

Steel transformed coal's potential into infrastructure. The Bessemer process, developed in the 1850s, revolutionized steel production, reducing costs and scaling output to levels previously unimaginable. This innovation fed directly into industrial expansion, enabling bridges, factories, ships, and most critically, railroads. Steel magnates like Andrew Carnegie recognized that dominance in this sector meant leverage over entire economies. Those who controlled steel determined the pace and direction of modernization itself. More than a commodity, steel became a political force, shaping both domestic policies and international relations. Nations without steel industries were relegated to dependency, while those with robust production became global players.

Railroads tied it all together, transforming steel and coal into instruments of empire. They connected remote mines to urban centers, linked industrial hubs to ports, and bound emerging markets to centralized power. Rail networks didn't just move goods; they reorganized society. Regions that had once been self-sufficient were drawn into industrial economies, their agricultural and resource outputs redirected toward urban factories and global trade. By controlling the railways, industrialists and governments could dictate where cities flourished, where populations migrated, and which territories rose or fell in strategic importance.

The power of this trinity became most visible in geopolitics. Industrial nations competed fiercely for access to coal reserves and strategic rail corridors, sparking conflicts that redrew borders and reshaped alliances. In the United States, the railroad barons amassed fortunes and influence rivaling governments themselves, wielding monopolistic control over transport and trade. In Britain, rail networks extended imperial reach, enabling extraction from colonies at scale. Across Europe, industrial competition fueled militarization, as steel-fed armies and coal-powered navies became measures of national strength. Infrastructure wasn't neutral; it was weaponized, forming the skeleton of economic and political dominance.

But the integration of rail, steel, and coal also produced a new hierarchy of power at home. Industrial tycoons leveraged their control over infrastructure to dictate labor conditions, manipulate markets, and pressure governments into favorable policies. Towns, industries, and entire populations became dependent on a few corporate empires whose interests increasingly diverged from those of the people they ruled over. In many regions, the state itself bent to the priorities of industrial capital, blurring the line between public authority and private power.

The railroad-steel-coal nexus shaped more than economies - it reshaped time itself. Journeys that once took weeks became possible in days, collapsing distance and accelerating the tempo of commerce, communication, and war. But this speed came with dependence: as societies reorganized around centralized infrastructure, autonomy dwindled. Communities could no longer control their own outputs or set their own rhythms; survival became tethered to systems they neither designed nor governed.

This trinity also set the stage for future industrial transformations. By creating the first truly interconnected economic networks, it provided the blueprint for globalization - resource extraction feeding centralized production, feeding distribution systems designed to maximize efficiency and profits. It created both the conditions for technological acceleration and the vulnerabilities of systemic interdependence. Empires rose on these rails and furnaces, but they also became hostage to them, reliant on continuous growth to sustain the infrastructure that defined their power.

The railroad-steel-coal system didn't just fuel the industrial age; it created its logic. It taught elites that dominance depended on control over flows - of energy, materials, and people - and that building the frameworks of movement meant owning the future. Every empire that followed, from the colonial networks of Britain to the corporate superstructures of the United States, built on this foundation. The tools evolved, but the principle remained: infrastructure determines sovereignty, and whoever commands the arteries commands the body.

Isambard Kingdom Brunel embodied the ambition, audacity, and contradictions of the 19th-century industrial elite. A visionary engineer, he became one of the central figures in Britain's transformation into an empire defined by steel, steam, and speed. His work on railways, bridges, tunnels, and ports didn't just modernize transportation - it restructured landscapes, reorganized cities, and reshaped the patterns of human life itself. Brunel wasn't simply building infrastructure; he was designing systems of control disguised as progress, creating the frameworks within which society would operate for generations.

Brunel's most enduring legacy lies in his work on railways, where he transformed Britain's economic and geographic realities. As chief engineer of the Great Western Railway, he envisioned a seamless network connecting London to the industrial west and beyond, reducing vast distances to manageable spans and making speed the new measure of power. He introduced broad-gauge track, a technical innovation that allowed for smoother rides and faster travel but also served a strategic purpose: by creating a nonstandard gauge, Brunel locked competing railways out of his network, centralizing control under the Great Western and ensuring a near-monopoly on critical routes. Behind every celebrated achievement in engineering lay a calculated move to control flows - of people, goods, and capital.

The bridges and tunnels Brunel built were feats of audacity that symbolized this power. The Clifton Suspension Bridge, the Thames Tunnel, and his massive iron steamships all reflected an industrial mindset that treated nature as an obstacle to be conquered and bent to human will. These structures didn't just connect cities and regions; they integrated economies and bound populations into centralized systems. The Great Western's routes dictated where industries could thrive, where towns would rise, and where labor would migrate. Infrastructure wasn't neutral - it determined destiny. Those who commanded it shaped entire social and economic hierarchies, and Brunel understood this better than anyone.

Brunel also represented a new kind of authority: the technocratic planner whose influence extended beyond construction into urban design and economic policy. By determining the placement of stations, ports, and transport hubs, he effectively dictated the rhythm of urban life and commerce. Cities reorganized themselves around the demands of his networks, adapting marketplaces, residential zones, and industrial hubs to align with the flows his railways created. Municipal governments deferred to his expertise, and financial backers trusted his vision to maximize returns on their investments. In this way, Brunel stood at the intersection of engineering, finance, and governance - a technocrat before the term existed, shaping cities not through political debate but through the hard realities of steel and stone.

His grand projects also reveal the growing entanglement between technology and empire. Brunel's designs enabled Britain to project power across its colonies by accelerating the movement of troops, goods, and resources. Steamships like the SS Great Eastern - among the largest vessels of its time - extended Britain's reach across oceans, reinforcing global trade dominance. Rail networks strengthened internal cohesion at home while linking ports to extractive industries abroad, integrating Britain into an early prototype of globalized logistics. Where military conquest had once been slow and resource-intensive, Brunel's systems offered speed, scalability, and efficiency, making empire cheaper to maintain and harder to resist.

But embedded in Brunel's brilliance was the central paradox of industrial modernity: these systems empowered nations while disempowering individuals. Railways standardized time, collapsing local rhythms into schedules dictated by centralized timetables. Towns dependent on his routes prospered, while those bypassed withered into irrelevance. By tying survival to integration within his infrastructure, Brunel inadvertently demonstrated how technological networks could override local autonomy and impose a new hierarchy of access and opportunity. Freedom of movement became less about choice and more about compliance with the systems someone else designed.

Brunel's career also illustrates the rise of engineering as a political force. His authority rested not on election or legal mandate but on mastery of technical knowledge and the ability to manifest visions that few others could comprehend, let alone challenge. He answered primarily to financiers and industrialists who saw infrastructure as both profit and leverage, bypassing traditional democratic structures entirely. This fusion of expertise, capital, and centralized planning was the early template for technocracy: a new ruling class emerging not from aristocratic bloodlines but from control over systems so complex that most of society simply trusted the experts to manage them.

Brunel's world was one of ambition and relentless expansion, but its consequences extended far beyond his lifetime. His railways, bridges, and ports didn't just move goods and people; they redefined the relationship between state, market, and individual. They foreshadowed the rise of modern urban planning, where entire populations are organized according to logistical imperatives rather than human needs. In celebrating his genius, Britain also celebrated a quiet surrender - the handover of collective sovereignty to a small class of engineers, financiers, and industrialists whose decisions shaped the structure of society without requiring its consent.

Brunel's legacy isn't just technological; it's structural. His work illuminates how infrastructure became an instrument of governance, where the placement of a railway line could determine the prosperity of a city, and the specifications of a bridge could influence the flow of empire. By following his tracks, we see the emergence of a new paradigm: power shifting from kings and parliaments to those who control the frameworks through which life is organized. The technocratic age didn't begin in laboratories or data centers - it began on the rails, under the bridges, and in the stations Brunel built.

Cornelius Vanderbilt and Andrew Carnegie stood at the pinnacle of the 19th-century transformation, two men whose fortunes reshaped the meaning of power in America and laid the groundwork for a new age of corporate sovereignty. They didn't simply build businesses - they built private empires. Their railroads, steel mills, and shipping lines became instruments of authority rivaling the federal government itself, creating corporate fiefdoms where entire regions, industries, and populations lived under their influence. In their world, wealth wasn't just a measure of success; it was leverage, the capacity to dictate the terms of modern life.

Vanderbilt began his rise on the water. Starting with a single ferry boat, he expanded into steamships at a time when control over trade routes meant control over economic opportunity. But it was the railroads where his influence became imperial. By consolidating fragmented lines into a seamless network, Vanderbilt transformed the northeastern United States into his domain. His New York Central Railroad didn't just move goods and people; it decided which towns thrived and which withered. By controlling access to markets, Vanderbilt shaped the geography of wealth, bending entire regions to the needs of his empire. Political leaders deferred to him, financiers courted him, and competitors feared him. Where the state built roads to connect citizens, Vanderbilt built rails to concentrate power.

Andrew Carnegie approached empire differently but no less decisively. Where Vanderbilt dominated transport, Carnegie dominated steel, the material upon which industrial society was built. Through relentless innovation and ruthless cost-cutting, he scaled production to unprecedented levels, flooding markets and undercutting rivals until he controlled the backbone of American infrastructure. Carnegie's steel built the rails Vanderbilt relied on, the bridges spanning America's rivers, and the skyscrapers rising in its cities. In an age defined by expansion, Carnegie controlled the substance that made expansion possible. By the 1890s, his operations produced more steel than entire nations, giving him influence over industries, labor markets, and political agendas alike.

These men built more than businesses - they created corporate fiefdoms where economic power translated into social dominance. Vanderbilt's control over shipping rates determined the success or failure of entire industries dependent on his tracks. Carnegie's command of steel prices shaped construction, manufacturing, and transportation simultaneously. Their fortunes insulated them from accountability, while their philanthropy crafted narratives of benevolence that softened public resistance. Foundations, libraries, and universities bore their names, but these were not acts of charity detached from strategy. By embedding their influence into education and culture, they secured a legacy that outlived their companies, ensuring future generations would continue to operate within systems they designed.

Their methods were often brutal. Vanderbilt cornered markets, crushed competitors, and manipulated stock prices with precision. Carnegie drove workers to their limits while keeping wages low, relying on managers like Henry Clay Frick to suppress strikes and break unions with force when necessary. The Homestead Strike of 1892 - where armed guards opened fire on protesting steelworkers - revealed the raw violence underpinning Carnegie's empire. Corporate authority extended beyond the workplace into law enforcement, with private militias and hired detectives acting as enforcers of industrial discipline. When governments did intervene, it was usually to protect property, not people, reinforcing the fusion of private wealth and public power.

These corporate fiefdoms revealed the structural shift underway in America. Political democracy continued on the surface - elections, legislatures, and courts - but economic sovereignty migrated upward into private hands. The scale of Vanderbilt's and Carnegie's operations allowed them to bypass traditional constraints, negotiating directly with states and leveraging their monopolies to influence policy. Where landowners once ruled through titles and armies, industrialists now ruled through infrastructure and capital. They built systems so large and indispensable that governments themselves became dependent on them, a quiet inversion of authority that laid the foundation for technocratic governance in the decades ahead.

What set Vanderbilt and Carnegie apart from their peers was not just the size of their fortunes but the systems they left behind. Vanderbilt's rail networks became the veins through which the country's economic lifeblood flowed, eventually merging into the broader logistics architecture of the modern age. Carnegie's steel empire evolved into U.S. Steel, the first billion-dollar corporation, institutionalizing corporate dominance at a scale unimaginable a generation earlier. These weren't personal empires anymore; they became permanent structures, codified in law, finance, and infrastructure, shaping the trajectory of the nation long after their founders' deaths.

By the early 20th century, Vanderbilt and Carnegie had helped create a reality where economic power and political sovereignty diverged. Their corporate fiefdoms operated like parallel states, with their own rules, enforcement mechanisms, and spheres of influence. Workers, communities, and even governments were subordinated to industrial priorities, often without realizing it. The wealth they amassed didn't just buy influence - it rewrote the framework within which society operated, leaving behind systems designed to favor the consolidation of power and the minimization of resistance.

Their legacies illuminate a larger truth about the industrial era: the story wasn't just about invention and progress but about who gained control over the structures those inventions created. Vanderbilt and Carnegie didn't merely ride the wave of industrialization - they directed it, leveraging infrastructure, finance, and labor into a new kind of sovereignty. Their world foreshadowed ours, where corporations don't just participate in economies; they define them, governing without ever appearing to rule.

The telegraph marked the beginning of a new kind of empire - not built on land, steel, or coal, but on information. Before its arrival, communication moved at the speed of horses, ships, and printed letters. Distance shaped power; geography dictated strategy. But with the first successful telegraph lines in the 1830s and Samuel Morse's code standardizing the language of transmission, time itself collapsed. Messages that once took weeks to arrive could now travel hundreds of miles in minutes. This shift didn't just connect economies and governments - it transformed the architecture of control, birthing the first networks where information could be centralized, managed, and weaponized.

The telegraph rewrote the tempo of commerce. For traders and financiers, real-time updates on prices, shipments, and markets meant profits could be extracted at a scale never before possible. Stock exchanges transformed overnight as data began to flow faster than goods themselves, decoupling finance from geography. Investors in London could manipulate commodity prices in New York or Calcutta based on instant transmissions, widening the gap between those who controlled information and those dependent on it. Economic power began migrating upward, concentrating in hubs where telegraph lines converged, giving financial elites a vantage point above entire markets.

Governments understood immediately what the telegraph made possible - and what it threatened. Control of information became synonymous with control of the state. Britain, with its global empire, raced to build undersea cables linking its colonies, ensuring London could coordinate military, trade, and administrative decisions with unprecedented speed. Wars were fought and treaties negotiated based on messages relayed through thin copper threads. The ability to move information faster than armies could march or ships could sail gave those who controlled the lines a strategic advantage so profound it reshaped geopolitics. Territories no longer mattered simply for resources; they mattered for their position in the network.

But the telegraph didn't just connect; it concentrated. The infrastructure required massive investment, placing ownership largely in the hands of corporations with state backing. Companies like Western Union in the United States and the Eastern Telegraph Company in Britain created monopolies over the flow of information, deciding who gained access, at what cost, and on what terms. These were not neutral carriers. By controlling infrastructure, they shaped perception, directing which messages moved, which markets thrived, and which voices disappeared into silence. A new kind of power emerged: the authority not to own territory but to govern information itself.

This transformation also redefined warfare. Armies began relying on telegraph lines for coordination, enabling larger and more complex operations across vast distances. But reliance created vulnerability. Cutting cables became a tactic of sabotage, while securing telegraph stations became a strategic priority. Whoever could intercept or manipulate transmissions gained leverage over enemies and allies alike. The telegraph made speed decisive but also introduced an unprecedented fragility - networks could be weaponized, and the first contests over information dominance were born.

Beyond politics and finance, the telegraph reshaped human perception. It standardized time, collapsing distances into near-simultaneity. News no longer belonged to local communities; it became centralized, disseminated through wire services that decided what stories mattered and in what order they reached the public. Information became less about truth and more about distribution, giving early media gatekeepers disproportionate influence over collective understanding. The capacity to shape narratives at scale emerged alongside the technology that delivered them.

The telegraph foreshadowed the systems of information control that define the modern age. It introduced the logic of networks: whoever owns the infrastructure controls the flow, and whoever controls the flow shapes reality. It created dependencies, embedding economic survival, military strategy, and social cohesion within systems managed by a small number of actors. It demonstrated, for the first time, how power could be exercised invisibly - not through armies or legislation but by determining what information moves, how fast, and to whom.

By the late 19th century, the telegraph had become the nervous system of empire, stitching together distant economies and political centers into a single web. But this integration came at a price: autonomy diminished as regions fell into synchronization with global financial and political priorities dictated from the top. Local knowledge became secondary to centralized data, and decision-making moved further away from the communities it affected. The telegraph promised connection and delivered control - an early prototype of the algorithmic governance to come. The rise of the industrial working class reshaped the foundations of society in the 19th century, creating vast populations dependent on centralized systems of production and capital for their survival. As factories multiplied and rural populations migrated to cities, entire communities were uprooted from traditional forms of self-sufficiency and thrust into tightly managed industrial economies. This dependency was not an accident - it was the inevitable outcome of a system designed to concentrate resources, control labor, and maximize profit. But dependency breeds volatility, and volatility threatens power. To contain unrest and stabilize the new industrial order, the ruling elite began constructing a framework of social engineering - tools, institutions, and ideologies aimed at shaping human behavior, conditioning compliance, and manufacturing consent.

Before industrialization, most people lived within localized economies where survival depended on access to land, craft, or community. Autonomy came from knowing how to sustain oneself and one's family without reliance on distant systems. The factory system dismantled this balance almost overnight. As mechanized production scaled, independent artisans were replaced by wage laborers, and agricultural families abandoned their land to chase jobs in urban centers. Once severed from self-sufficiency, these new industrial workers were locked into an economic structure where food, housing, and security depended entirely on access to wages controlled by employers. For the first time in history, millions of people had no alternative but to sell their labor to survive.

This dependency made the working class both indispensable and dangerous. Industrial growth required a steady supply of compliant labor, yet the very conditions of that labor - long hours, meager wages, unsafe environments, and job insecurity - created fertile ground for dissent. Strikes, riots, and organizing efforts erupted across Europe and America, threatening not only profits but also the stability of entire governments. The elite quickly realized that sheer force could suppress uprisings temporarily but could not solve the structural problem: an industrial economy concentrated masses of workers in the same spaces, under the same pressures, giving them both the grievances and the numbers to resist. If control was to be maintained, it would have to move beyond factories and into the minds of workers themselves.

Social engineering became the quiet solution. Education was redesigned, particularly for the children of the working class, not to cultivate critical thought but to instill discipline, punctuality, and obedience
- traits valued by industrial employers. Schools mirrored factory routines: fixed schedules, standardized curricula, and hierarchical authority
structures conditioned students for life on the production line. Lessons
emphasized loyalty to the state and trust in institutional authority, discouraging independent thinking that might challenge existing power
dynamics. Literacy was taught not to empower but to integrate; reading
became a tool to consume state-approved narratives and corporate messaging rather than question them.

At the same time, governments and industrialists invested heavily in
shaping cultural norms. Propaganda campaigns reframed dependence
on wages and centralized production as progress, casting industrial labor as a moral duty and a patriotic contribution to national strength.
Religious institutions were co-opted to preach humility, hard work,
and submission to authority, blending spiritual identity with economic
compliance. Leisure activities were increasingly designed and controlled
by employers, from company-sponsored festivals to sporting events,
providing carefully curated outlets for frustration while reinforcing
communal loyalty to corporations rather than solidarity among workers.

Philanthropy, too, became a weapon. Industrialists like Andrew
Carnegie and John D. Rockefeller funded libraries, universities, and
foundations that positioned themselves as benefactors of the working
class. In reality, these institutions acted as tools for shaping acceptable
behavior and embedding elite values into society. By controlling the
frameworks through which knowledge and opportunity were distributed, the ruling class reinforced narratives that equated upward mobility with personal morality, placing blame for poverty on individual
failure rather than systemic exploitation.

At the heart of this social engineering was a deeper objective: to neutralize collective resistance by fragmenting the working class and embedding trust in the very systems that exploited it. Labor unions were often undermined through infiltration or outright criminalization, while immigration policies were manipulated to pit ethnic and cultural groups against one another, diverting anger away from elites and toward fellow workers. Surveillance expanded, both overt and covert, with factory managers monitoring behavior inside workplaces and police tracking organizing efforts beyond them. Resistance wasn't simply discouraged - it was predicted, contained, and redirected before it could gain momentum.

By the late 19th century, industrial society had constructed an architecture of control that reached far beyond economics. Dependency on wages created leverage; education and culture molded behavior; philanthropy and propaganda manufactured trust; and law enforcement provided the teeth when persuasion failed. The population had been reorganized into a system where survival required compliance and where questioning that system became increasingly difficult. The shift from self-sufficient individuals to managed populations marked a turning point in human history, setting the stage for modern technocratic governance where behavior could be shaped not by force but by design.

This was the quiet bargain of industrial modernity: stability in exchange for autonomy, order in exchange for agency. The working class gained access to new forms of prosperity but at the cost of control over the structures shaping their lives. Dependency became normalized, embedded so deeply into the rhythms of daily existence that it ceased to be recognized as dependency at all. And beneath it all, social engineering refined itself into an invisible art - a set of systems and institutions calibrated to maintain equilibrium while ensuring power continued to flow upward.

The 1851 Great Exhibition in London was more than a celebration of innovation - it was a declaration of dominance. Organized under the patronage of Prince Albert and housed within the vast glass-and-iron Crystal Palace, the event symbolized the self-confidence of an elite class convinced it had mastered not only industry but the future itself. The exhibition displayed 100,000 objects from across the world, representing what Britain framed as humanity's march toward progress, but beneath the pageantry lay something else entirely: a carefully curated showcase of mechanized power, designed to cement hierarchy and announce Britain's supremacy in an industrial world it intended to rule.

For the British elite, the Great Exhibition was political theater. Britain stood at the apex of global power, its empire sprawling across continents, fueled by coal, steam, and steel. The Crystal Palace became the altar of industrial modernity, where visitors were invited to witness the miracles of mechanization - precision looms weaving textiles at unmatched speed, steam engines driving pistons with relentless force, and intricate tools producing standardized goods that would dominate global markets. Yet this wasn't simply a celebration of creativity; it was a demonstration of control. By flaunting technological dominance, Britain reinforced its authority not only over its own working class but over colonies, competitors, and potential challengers.

The displays reflected a clear hierarchy. British inventions and industries occupied the central exhibits, presented as the pinnacle of human achievement, while colonial contributions were pushed to the periphery, framed less as innovations and more as raw materials - resources to be extracted and refined by British industry. Cotton from India, timber from Canada, tea from Ceylon, and gold from Australia were positioned as trophies of empire, reminders that the wealth driving Britain's mechanized ascendancy came from global exploitation. Colonized peoples were simultaneously erased and displayed - stripped of agency while their lands and labor were recast as evidence of imperial benevolence.

Equally significant was how the exhibition communicated with Britain's own population. For the industrial working class, whose lives were dominated by the grueling schedules of factories and the dependence on wages, the event became a spectacle designed to inspire awe and compliance. The machinery on display was not just impressive - it was overwhelming, presented as inevitable. Progress was framed as a natural, unstoppable force, beyond politics or debate. In this narrative, industrialization wasn't a choice but a destiny, and the only rational role for the masses was to accept their place within it. By overwhelming visitors with scale and complexity, the elite created a subtle form of psychological conditioning: if you cannot comprehend the machinery, how could you ever hope to control it?

At the same time, the exhibition served as a hub of elite networking and coordination. Industrialists, financiers, scientists, and state officials from across Europe and America gathered under the same roof, forging alliances and sharing strategies for consolidating influence. Deals were struck behind closed doors while the public wandered the galleries, unaware that the real power of the event lay in the relationships being built between governments and corporations. It was an early template for the technocratic summits of the future - gatherings where the public spectacle serves as a distraction while policy and infrastructure are quietly aligned at the top.

The Crystal Palace itself embodied this ideology. A vast cathedral of glass and steel, it stood as both an architectural triumph and a symbolic gesture: transparency for the public, but control for those who built it. Its design reflected industrial Britain's core values - standardization, modularity, scalability - principles that would come to define not only manufacturing but governance itself. The building, like the machines inside it, represented the capacity to bend nature and society to the demands of centralized systems. Its sheer scale announced Britain's mastery over material, labor, and knowledge, projecting an image of inevitability that made resistance seem futile.

But behind the celebration, cracks were already forming. While the exhibition promised a unified vision of progress, the realities outside its walls told a different story. The same mechanization displayed as marvels of modernity had displaced artisans and fueled unrest among the working class. Child labor powered many of the industries being glorified, and colonial extraction left entire regions impoverished while Britain amassed unprecedented wealth. These contradictions were not hidden by accident; they were deliberately obscured beneath spectacle. By dazzling the public with inventions and narratives of benevolence, the exhibition transformed structural inequality into a celebration of British identity and destiny.

The Great Exhibition also marked the beginning of a new kind of soft power - the global staging of technological dominance to establish political leverage. Nations left the event not just inspired but pressured, fully aware that competing with Britain required matching its industrial capacity. It triggered an acceleration of mechanization elsewhere, driving rivals like France, Germany, and the United States to expand their own steelworks, rail systems, and manufacturing empires. But Britain had set the tone: the future would belong to those who controlled machines, energy, and infrastructure, and the rest of the world would either adapt or fall behind.

In retrospect, the 1851 Great Exhibition wasn't merely a world's fair; it was the opening ceremony of a new era. It celebrated technological achievement while masking the dependencies and exploitations underpinning it. It dazzled the public while facilitating elite coordination. It framed industrialization not as a contested process but as a natural law, discouraging resistance and shaping cultural expectations around progress. The Crystal Palace became both monument and message: the machine had arrived, and those who controlled it would shape the world's destiny.

3

Masters of Capital, Masters of Men (1870–1900)

The Second Industrial Revolution, spanning roughly from the 1870s to the early 20th century, accelerated the transformation of society into a system of interlocking infrastructures, corporations, and financial empires. Where the First Industrial Revolution was defined by steam, coal, and mechanization, the second was powered by electricity, petroleum, and chemistry - forces that extended industrial control into every aspect of daily life while consolidating wealth and authority at unprecedented scales. If the first wave centralized production, the second centralized power, creating corporate empires that rivaled states and reshaping the geopolitical order around energy and innovation.

Electricity became the defining catalyst of this new age, unlocking a level of flexibility and precision impossible under steam. It illuminated cities, powered factories, and enabled machines to operate continuously, untethered from fixed energy sources like coal-fired boilers. Thomas Edison's direct-current systems and Nikola Tesla's alternating-current innovations did more than fuel inventions - they created entire markets, industries, and dependencies. Street lighting transformed urban life, extending working hours and redefining productivity. Electric motors replaced human and animal labor at scale, accelerating mechanization while deepening the dependence of workers on centralized grids they did not control. Power generation required massive investment in infrastructure, placing control of electricity - and by extension, the pace of industrial growth - into the hands of financiers and corporations with the capital to build it.

Petroleum was the second pillar of this transformation, fueling a new era of mobility and mechanized warfare. The internal combustion engine revolutionized transport, replacing horses and steam with cars, trucks, and ships powered by refined oil. Control over petroleum reserves became synonymous with strategic dominance. Industrialists like John D. Rockefeller understood this early, using Standard Oil to build one of the most formidable monopolies in history. Through aggressive acquisitions, predatory pricing, and exclusive contracts, Rockefeller secured near-total control over refining, transport, and distribution. Standard Oil didn't just sell energy; it dictated the pace of global industrialization. Nations dependent on oil imports found themselves subordinated to corporate decisions, while Rockefeller's empire leveraged its dominance to influence legislation, manipulate markets, and steer U.S. foreign policy toward protecting resource access.

Chemistry, the third pillar, extended industrial control into the very fabric of life. Advances in chemical engineering gave rise to synthetic dyes, fertilizers, explosives, pharmaceuticals, and plastics, embedding industrial products into the essentials of agriculture, medicine, and war. German conglomerates like BASF, Bayer, and Hoechst pioneered chemical empires, their research feeding not only consumer industries but state militaries. Fertilizer and pesticide production reshaped global food systems, tying agricultural outputs to industrial supply chains. Pharmaceuticals began shifting medicine toward corporate dependence, while chemical explosives redefined warfare's scale and lethality. These developments blurred the boundary between civilian life and militarized economies, locking entire nations into industrial cycles dictated by the corporations producing the technologies they relied upon to compete and survive.

Together, electricity, petroleum, and chemistry produced unprecedented interdependence. Cities could no longer function without power grids; transportation systems were chained to oil distribution networks; agriculture and medicine depended on chemical manufacturing. The infrastructures enabling modern life were so capital-intensive and technologically complex that only a handful of corporations and financiers could build and maintain them. These entities - General Electric, Standard Oil, DuPont, Siemens, and others - became more than companies. They became institutions, shaping policy and wielding influence over governments, research agendas, and public perception. As they consolidated, their priorities dictated not just market trends but the trajectory of entire nations.

This consolidation fundamentally altered the relationship between capital and sovereignty. The Second Industrial Revolution created a new breed of elites: technocrats backed by financiers, operating on scales larger than governments and often with greater efficiency. Infrastructure itself became political power. Whoever controlled the grids, pipelines, and manufacturing chains controlled society. Public governance increasingly yielded to private interests, as policymakers relied on corporate expertise to manage technological complexity they neither understood nor controlled. Regulation followed behind innovation, rarely ahead of it, ensuring that systems were built to serve those who created them rather than those who depended on them.

The geopolitical consequences were immense. Access to petroleum reshaped military strategy and foreign policy, pushing nations toward securing resource-rich territories through colonization, trade dominance, and war. Electricity and chemical technologies accelerated arms races and industrial competition between powers like Britain, Germany, and the United States, laying the groundwork for global conflict in the 20th century. Infrastructure became both weapon and prize: pipelines, refineries, and chemical plants were strategic targets, and controlling supply lines became as critical as controlling territory itself.

By the dawn of the 20th century, the world was wired, fueled, and synthesized into an industrial system far larger than any one government could command. What began as technological innovation evolved into an architecture of dependence, where entire populations relied on systems designed by private elites. The Second Industrial Revolution didn't just change economies; it engineered a new social order, one where the flows of energy, information, and material were tightly bound to corporate interests operating above democratic oversight.

The foundations laid during this period still shape the modern world. Every electrical grid, every global shipping route, every petrochemical complex traces its roots to this era - an age when the commanding heights of industry merged with financial power to create institutions so vast they became inseparable from the state. In celebrating progress, society surrendered agency, exchanging autonomy for access and security for scale. The result was a world no longer organized around self-sufficiency but around systems too complex to escape and too profitable to dismantle.

John D. Rockefeller stands as one of the most consequential figures in the history of industrial power - not just because he built Standard Oil into one of the largest and most ruthless monopolies the world had ever seen, but because he understood something deeper: control over energy was only the beginning. To consolidate influence, you had to shape the frameworks through which people learned, healed, and understood the world. Through oil, he built an empire; through education and medicine, he embedded his values into society itself, creating structures so deeply rooted that their influence persists to this day.

Standard Oil was the foundation. Beginning in the 1860s, Rockefeller moved aggressively into the petroleum industry just as the internal combustion engine and mass electrification were set to transform economies. He recognized early that refining, not drilling, was the key to dominance. By controlling the middle of the supply chain - processing crude oil into usable products like kerosene, lubricants, and eventually gasoline - he could dictate terms to both producers and consumers. Through vertical integration, Rockefeller acquired pipelines, refineries, shipping routes, and distribution networks, creating a system so efficient and far-reaching that competitors had little chance of survival. Efficiency, however, was paired with ruthless strategy. Standard Oil engaged in predatory pricing, temporarily slashing rates below cost to bankrupt rivals before absorbing their assets. Exclusive contracts with railroads secured favorable shipping rates, making it nearly impossible for competitors to move their products to market. Lobbying efforts quietly influenced legislation, and allies were placed in key financial and political institutions to protect Standard Oil's dominance. By the 1880s, Rockefeller controlled around 90% of U.S. oil refining, making his company one of the most powerful private entities in the world. Governments increasingly depended on Standard Oil's infrastructure to keep economies running, shifting the balance of authority from public institutions to private empires.

But Rockefeller's ambitions extended beyond energy. He understood that real power required shaping culture and knowledge itself. Through the Rockefeller Foundation, created in 1913, he began funding universities, research centers, and public policy initiatives. On the surface, this philanthropy was framed as altruistic - a benevolent gesture to advance science, education, and public health. In practice, it aligned institutions with corporate and technocratic priorities. Universities like the University of Chicago and Rockefeller University became hubs for research serving industrial and economic agendas. By funding academic disciplines and shaping curricula, the foundation influenced which ideas gained legitimacy and which disappeared into obscurity.

Nowhere was this influence more profound than in medicine. At the turn of the 20th century, Rockefeller saw the opportunity to industrialize healthcare the same way he had industrialized oil. He poured millions into the transformation of medical education, most notably through his funding of the Flexner Report in 1910. Ostensibly designed to improve medical standards, the report recommended closing hundreds of smaller, independent medical schools - particularly those teaching alternative practices like homeopathy, naturopathy, and holistic care - while consolidating power in elite, university-affiliated programs focused on pharmaceutical and surgical interventions.

The result was the creation of a standardized, centralized model of medicine aligned with corporate interests, particularly the burgeoning pharmaceutical industry, which itself grew out of the chemical empires of the Second Industrial Revolution. Rockefeller's funding flowed heavily into biomedical research and drug development, creating a system where treatments became commodities controlled by industrial supply chains. Preventive and natural approaches, which offered fewer opportunities for profit, were systematically delegitimized. By shaping the medical establishment, Rockefeller effectively merged healthcare with industrial capitalism, ensuring that future generations would rely on products and institutions his foundations helped design.

Rockefeller's influence on education mirrored this strategy. By funding teacher colleges, curricula reforms, and education boards, he helped shape a model of schooling designed not to foster critical thought but to produce compliant, disciplined workers for an industrial economy. Students were trained to adapt to schedules, hierarchies, and standardized tasks - habits directly transferable to factory floors and corporate offices. Knowledge became curated, streamlined, and filtered through institutional gatekeepers whose funding tied them to elite priorities. What appeared to be progress was, in reality, the construction of a framework for managing populations from childhood to adulthood.

By embedding himself in energy, education, and medicine, Rockefeller built something far more enduring than wealth: a system. His corporate empire provided the infrastructure; his philanthropy shaped the narratives and institutions that justified it; his influence ensured that the next generation of scientists, doctors, and policy-makers would operate within boundaries he had helped define. This was control exercised not through visible coercion but through design - an early prototype of technocratic governance where private institutions set the agenda while governments administered it.

The dismantling of Standard Oil in 1911 under antitrust laws did little to diminish Rockefeller's reach. The company splintered into entities that would become Exxon, Chevron, and Mobil - corporations that remain among the most powerful in the world. His foundations continued to expand their influence in education, healthcare, and public policy, funding everything from the creation of the World Health Organization to the development of standardized testing in schools. Through these mechanisms, Rockefeller's priorities outlived him, shaping systems so deeply that most people today operate within them without knowing their origin.

Rockefeller didn't simply build an oil empire; he helped architect a new societal order. By consolidating energy, engineering dependency, and embedding influence into cultural institutions, he exemplified how private wealth could redesign entire civilizations under the guise of progress. Where governments once ruled by decree, Rockefeller demonstrated that control over infrastructure and knowledge could achieve the same outcome more quietly - and more permanently.

J.P. Morgan emerged at the center of a transformation that redefined power in the late 19th and early 20th centuries. Where Rockefeller consolidated energy and Carnegie commanded steel, Morgan mastered finance itself - the lifeblood of industrial society. He understood that the new industrial order wasn't just built on oil, coal, and steel but on the flows of capital funding them. By controlling those flows, he could shape entire sectors, influence governments, and engineer stability or crisis depending on his priorities. Morgan wasn't merely a banker; he was one of the first true financial technocrats, orchestrating consolidation on a scale that permanently rewired the relationship between corporations, the state, and the public.

Morgan's power came from his position as an intermediary between industrialists, investors, and governments. While others fought over production and markets, he built leverage by financing both sides. Railroads were his entry point. By the 1890s, the chaotic expansion of rail infrastructure across the United States had led to destructive competition, bankruptcies, and inefficiencies. Morgan stepped in as a "stabilizer," restructuring debts, merging competing companies, and centralizing management under his control. What appeared to be rescue was also conquest: by consolidating railroads into tightly managed systems, Morgan dictated freight rates, supply chains, and ultimately the economic fate of entire regions. Towns lived or died by his decisions, and his influence over transportation made him indispensable to the nation's industrial growth.

His methods extended far beyond railroads. In 1901, Morgan orchestrated the creation of U.S. Steel, buying Carnegie's empire and combining it with several other firms to form the first billion-dollar corporation. It was more than a merger; it was the formalization of a new model of corporate governance where power flowed upward to centralized entities operating beyond meaningful public oversight. Through similar maneuvers, Morgan's banking house financed and effectively controlled industries from shipping to electricity, from manufacturing to mining. His reach was so vast that the term "Morganization" entered the language - the process of reorganizing and consolidating industries under his system of control.

Morgan's role during financial crises solidified his position as the de facto central banker before one existed in the United States. In the Panic of 1907, when markets collapsed and credit froze, it was Morgan - not the federal government - who summoned the nation's leading financiers to his library in New York and forced them to pool resources to stabilize the banking system. He dictated which institutions would be saved, which would fail, and on what terms. Congress watched from the sidelines while one private individual effectively steered the national economy. This moment laid bare a truth the public was slow to recognize: in the absence of a central bank, Morgan had become one.

This power didn't emerge in isolation. Morgan operated within a tightly connected elite network of industrialists, financiers, and policymakers, blurring the line between private wealth and public governance. His influence over government was subtle but decisive, leveraging his role in stabilizing markets to push policies favorable to centralized banking and corporate consolidation. When the Federal Reserve Act passed in 1913, establishing a permanent central banking system, its structure reflected Morgan's model - private banks controlling the levers of monetary policy under a veneer of public oversight. The Federal Reserve institutionalized the role Morgan had played personally, embedding financial technocracy into the architecture of the U.S. economy.

Morgan also understood the strategic value of information. His firm cultivated deep relationships with journalists, lobbyists, and politicians, managing narratives to protect confidence in the financial system while shielding his operations from scrutiny. Through quiet alliances, he shaped public perception of crises and solutions alike, ensuring that his actions were framed as stabilizing necessities rather than power grabs. Where Rockefeller and Carnegie built visible empires of steel and oil, Morgan built one of influence - subtler, harder to see, but ultimately more enduring.

Yet Morgan's control came with a cost: growing public distrust. His domination over banking and industry fueled progressive-era backlash against monopolies and corporate concentration. Congressional hearings like the 1912 Pujo Committee investigated the "Money Trust" - a small network of financiers, with Morgan at its center, who controlled enormous shares of national wealth and credit. The hearings confirmed what many suspected: a handful of institutions, led by Morgan's firm, determined the allocation of capital across the economy. The outcry pushed reforms, but none truly dismantled his framework. If anything, it legitimized it by formalizing federal systems designed to stabilize finance while preserving elite control.

By the time of his death in 1913, J.P. Morgan had become more than a financier; he was an architect of modern economic governance. His model - centralized, networked, and insulated from public accountability - remains embedded in today's financial systems. The institutions he shaped still define policy, credit flows, and industrial priorities. Where earlier elites ruled through land or physical infrastructure, Morgan ruled through abstraction: by mastering debt, liquidity, and the mechanisms of trust, he gained authority over resources without owning them directly.

Morgan's legacy reveals the deeper trajectory of industrial capitalism. As production scaled, so did its financial superstructure, and control migrated upward to those who managed the complexity. His era marked the transition from visible empires of steel and oil to invisible empires of finance, where decisions made in private boardrooms cascaded across entire nations. This was the dawn of technocratic capitalism - a system where governance flowed not through democratic deliberation but through financial instruments designed and managed by unelected elites.

Andrew Carnegie's rise was the story of steel, but his legacy is far larger than industrial dominance. He didn't just build factories; he helped build the architecture of modern power. Carnegie mastered the logic of scale, turning his steel empire into one of the most formidable monopolies in history. Yet just as important was what he did with that wealth - using philanthropy not as charity but as a tool to shape institutions, control narratives, and embed elite priorities deep into society. Carnegie understood that raw economic power creates influence, but shaping culture and knowledge sustains it across generations.

Carnegie began as a poor Scottish immigrant, working his way up through the Pennsylvania Railroad before founding the Carnegie Steel Company in the 1870s. His genius lay in relentlessly optimizing production and aggressively reinvesting profits into technological innovation. He embraced the Bessemer process early, slashing the cost of steel production and outpacing competitors by scaling capacity at unprecedented levels. By vertically integrating every stage of production - from mining iron ore and coal to controlling transport routes and steel mills - Carnegie built an empire immune to disruption. He reduced prices until rivals collapsed or sold out, consolidating the industry into his control. By the 1890s, Carnegie Steel was producing more steel than all of Great Britain, making Carnegie one of the richest men in the world and setting the foundation for U.S. industrial supremacy.

Yet Carnegie's monopoly came at a human cost. His relentless pursuit of efficiency demanded longer hours, lower wages, and relentless discipline from his workforce. The infamous Homestead Strike of 1892 exposed the brutality underlying his empire. When workers at the Homestead plant protested wage cuts, Carnegie's lieutenant, Henry Clay Frick, brought in private Pinkerton guards to crush the strike. The confrontation turned violent, leaving several dead and many injured. The strike's failure dealt a blow to organized labor and signaled a new reality: corporations like Carnegie Steel wielded power greater than governments, using private armies to enforce industrial discipline while the state largely stood aside or intervened on behalf of capital.

Carnegie justified his methods through his philosophy of the "Gospel of Wealth." In essays and speeches, he argued that extreme inequality was not only inevitable but beneficial. According to Carnegie, society advanced when the most capable individuals accumulated wealth and then redistributed it in ways that uplifted the public. But this was not altruism in the pure sense; it was social engineering. Carnegie believed that ordinary people lacked the judgment to manage large sums and that elites like himself were best suited to determine which institutions deserved support. Through this lens, philanthropy became a mechanism of control, a way to shape public values, steer education, and mold the intellectual framework of society.

Nowhere was this strategy clearer than in his investments in education and culture. Carnegie funded more than 2,500 public libraries, believing access to curated knowledge would "elevate" the working class - but the collections were carefully selected to reflect mainstream industrial values rather than challenge them. He financed the creation of institutions like the Carnegie Institute of Technology (now Carnegie Mellon University) and the Carnegie Institution for Science, directing research priorities toward areas aligned with industrial and national interests. He also funded teacher training programs, music halls, and civic centers, embedding elite influence into the cultural infrastructure of entire cities.

Carnegie also played a significant role in shaping the research ecosystem, funding foundations and grants that prioritized scientific and technical studies over broader liberal education. This served both his own industrial priorities and those of a growing corporate class eager to align education with economic production. Universities that accepted Carnegie's funding often adopted curricula designed to supply industries with a steady pipeline of compliant workers trained to fit emerging corporate systems rather than challenge them. As with Rockefeller, philanthropy provided the appearance of generosity while entrenching frameworks that benefited elites.

Carnegie's approach also extended into global influence. He financed the construction of the Peace Palace at The Hague and invested heavily in international arbitration initiatives, framing himself as a champion of global stability. Yet these efforts often aligned with the strategic interests of American industrial and financial elites, promoting legal and trade systems favorable to U.S. corporations abroad. His philanthropy advanced ideals of modernization, integration, and "progress," subtly tying global development to the structures of Western industrial power. By 1901, Carnegie sold his steel empire to J.P. Morgan, creating U.S. Steel, the world's first billion-dollar corporation and a monument to corporate consolidation. Having exited industry, Carnegie spent the rest of his life refining his philanthropic model, channeling his fortune into foundations that would continue shaping education, science, and culture long after his death. These foundations didn't just hand out grants - they acted as strategic levers, steering institutional priorities and embedding industrial values within the very framework of public life.

Carnegie's dual legacy - monopolist and benefactor - illustrates a deeper reality about elite power in the industrial age. His steel empire gave him unprecedented economic leverage, but his philanthropy ensured cultural dominance, manufacturing consent through the soft power of education and research. By controlling the production of knowledge and directing the paths of intellectual development, Carnegie and his peers created systems where generations would inherit institutions already aligned with elite interests. The working class may have gained libraries and schools, but they inherited narratives designed to keep them within the machinery of industrial capitalism.

In this, Carnegie's story is less about wealth than architecture. He built frameworks - economic, cultural, and educational - that persist today, shaping values and priorities under the guise of progress. Where his steel created the literal skeleton of modern infrastructure, his philanthropy laid the psychological foundations of compliance, creating populations conditioned to trust institutions already captured by elite influence. His empire may have dissolved, but his systems endure, quietly defining the limits of thought, opportunity, and dissent in ways few people recognize.

The late 19th and early 20th centuries marked the deliberate emergence of planned monopolies - not as accidents of industrial growth but as conscious strategies engineered by a small class of elites who understood that total control over production, distribution, and markets required vertical integration. This was not simply the natural outcome of technological innovation or competition; it was the systematic consolidation of power into structures designed to dominate entire sectors of the economy while minimizing risk, suppressing resistance, and insulating profits from disruption.

The model was simple but revolutionary: own everything. Control the raw materials, the factories, the transportation networks, and the retail outlets - every link in the chain from resource to consumer. By centralizing these functions within a single corporate framework, industrialists eliminated dependency on outside suppliers, neutralized competitors, and maximized efficiency. Vertical integration transformed industries into empires, where decision-making flowed upward, competition collapsed, and wealth concentrated in fewer and fewer hands. What emerged was a new form of sovereignty - one where corporations didn't just operate within markets but designed and controlled the markets themselves.

John D. Rockefeller perfected the model with Standard Oil. By controlling oil extraction, refining, transportation, and distribution, he engineered one of the first and most enduring monopolies in history. Standard Oil's dominance was not achieved solely through innovation;

it was planned through an intricate web of contracts, acquisitions, and alliances. Railroads offered Rockefeller preferential shipping rates in exchange for exclusive access to his freight, shutting competitors out of vital networks. Independent refiners were bought, bullied, or bankrupted. By the 1880s, Standard Oil controlled roughly 90% of U.S. oil refining, setting prices at will and bending entire economies around its priorities. The courts eventually ordered its breakup in 1911, but the monopoly survived in fragments, with offshoots like Exxon, Chevron, and Mobil retaining enormous power - proving that regulatory "reform" often preserves dominance by decentralizing it cosmetically rather than dismantling it structurally.

Andrew Carnegie deployed the same logic in steel, building a supply chain so tightly integrated that Carnegie Steel became untouchable. By controlling iron ore mines, coal fields, limestone quarries, railroads, and mills, Carnegie could produce steel faster and cheaper than any rival. His plants ran on relentless optimization, reinvesting profits into technological upgrades and constantly squeezing inefficiencies out of the system. Competitors unable to match his scale collapsed or were absorbed. Carnegie's sale to J.P. Morgan in 1901 created U.S. Steel, the world's first billion-dollar corporation and a lasting monument to the planned monopoly model. U.S. Steel operated not as a competitor within an open market but as the market itself, setting prices and production levels across an entire sector.

J.P. Morgan, meanwhile, applied vertical integration beyond industry and into finance itself. His banking empire didn't just fund monopolies; it engineered them, orchestrating mergers and reorganizations that concentrated control in fewer hands. Morgan's "Morganization" strategy restructured railroads, manufacturing, and infrastructure networks into tightly controlled hierarchies under his influence. By financing both industrial growth and its consolidation, Morgan effectively dictated the pace and direction of American capitalism. When crises hit, like the Panic of 1907, Morgan stepped in as a stabilizing force - but his "rescues" always strengthened the very institutions that deepened dependency on centralized financial power.

Planned monopolies reshaped labor dynamics as well. The rise of integrated corporate systems meant workers were no longer employed by individual firms competing in open markets but by vast networks with no meaningful alternatives. A steelworker might labor in a Carnegie mill, live in a company-owned town, shop at a company store, and depend on company railroads for basic goods. This architecture turned entire regions into corporate fiefdoms where economic survival depended on loyalty and compliance. Attempts to organize unions or resist exploitation were met not just by private security and strikebreakers but by coordinated strategies spanning multiple corporations, backed by the courts and often enforced by federal troops.

Vertical integration also embedded corporate power into governance itself. As industries consolidated, so did their influence over policy and regulation. Legislators were lobbied, judges were persuaded, and state agencies increasingly deferred to "expert" recommendations provided by the very monopolies they were supposed to oversee. Infrastructure projects, tariffs, and trade agreements were tailored to favor the largest players, further entrenching their dominance. Public institutions became dependent on private capital to maintain growth and stability, blurring the boundary between government and corporation. The planned monopoly wasn't just tolerated - it became the foundation of national economic strategy.

This architecture also redefined global power. Corporations controlling vital industries wielded influence over foreign policy as access to resources like oil, rubber, and steel became matters of state interest. Rockefeller's oil empire shaped U.S. interventions abroad to secure petroleum markets, while Carnegie Steel and U.S. Steel supplied the raw materials that armed America's rise as a global military power. Multinational integration emerged early, as corporations extended their reach into colonies and resource-rich territories, locking developing economies into dependency and tying imperial expansion to industrial consolidation.

By the early 20th century, the framework of planned monopolies was complete. Through vertical integration, a handful of corporate empires controlled the fundamental flows of energy, materials, and capital, leaving individuals and governments alike tethered to systems they neither designed nor governed. These structures created the conditions for technocracy to emerge, where unelected elites and private institutions dictated the limits of economic and political possibility. Even when antitrust laws attempted to curb excesses, the response wasn't to dismantle power but to reorganize it, ensuring continuity while pacifying public outrage.

The strategy worked because it was subtle. Planned monopolies were justified in the language of efficiency, modernization, and progress, making their dominance appear natural and inevitable. By controlling both the infrastructure and the narratives surrounding it, industrial elites insulated their power from democratic challenge. The appearance of competition remained - multiple brands, multiple companies - but beneath the surface, ownership and decision-making were centralized, producing the illusion of choice within structures designed for control. The vertical integration of industry was more than a business strategy; it was the construction of an invisible architecture of power. Once built, these systems became self-reinforcing, embedding dependency into the daily lives of entire populations. Railroads, pipelines, factories, and refineries formed the skeleton of modern civilization, but the real innovation lay in the consolidation behind them. Planned monopolies created economies where freedom was constrained by infrastructure, autonomy replaced by systemic reliance, and sovereignty quietly surrendered to networks too vast to escape.

The rise of industrial monopolies in the late 19th and early 20th centuries did not simply shape markets - it reshaped the law itself. Figures like John D. Rockefeller, Andrew Carnegie, J.P. Morgan, and their contemporaries understood early that dominating industries was only half the battle. To make their power permanent, they needed to institutionalize control through legislation, regulation, and judicial precedent.

This wasn't a chaotic or accidental process; it was deliberate, coordinated, and highly strategic. Monopolists didn't just operate within the legal framework of the United States - they influenced its creation, embedding their priorities into the very architecture of governance.

The industrialists' approach combined direct lobbying, political financing, and subtle narrative manipulation. At the federal level, laws that appeared to constrain corporate excess were often drafted in ways that ultimately protected monopolistic interests. Regulatory agencies created in response to public outrage became tools of capture, providing the illusion of oversight while institutionalizing frameworks favorable to elite priorities. These strategies evolved in response to growing public resentment toward "robber barons" and their sprawling empires, allowing monopolists to deflect criticism while tightening control.

One of the earliest examples was the Sherman Antitrust Act of 1890. At face value, it was a populist victory - a law designed to dismantle corporate monopolies and restore open competition. In practice, enforcement was weak and inconsistent. Federal courts, often sympathetic to corporate arguments about "efficiency" and "progress," interpreted the statute narrowly, making it difficult to apply effectively against industrial giants. Ironically, the Sherman Act was initially used more aggressively against labor unions than monopolies. Strikes and collective bargaining were framed as "restraints of trade," weaponizing antitrust law against workers rather than against concentrated capital.

Rockefeller's Standard Oil became the centerpiece of antitrust battles. By the early 1900s, public outrage over its predatory practices - price-fixing, secret railroad rebates, and aggressive buyouts - forced the government to act. The 1911 Supreme Court decision ordering Standard Oil's breakup is often remembered as a triumph against monopoly power, but the reality was far more complex. Standard Oil was divided into 34 entities, yet Rockefeller retained substantial ownership in each, and many recombined into the modern energy giants Exxon, Chevron, and Mobil. The effect was not the destruction of dominance but its reorganization under a less politically vulnerable structure. The ruling placated public anger while preserving Rockefeller's influence and embedding his business model deeper into U.S. energy policy.

The creation of the Interstate Commerce Commission (ICC) in 1887 offers another revealing example. Established to regulate railroad monopolies and protect consumers from abusive freight rates, the ICC quickly became an instrument of industry itself. Railroad barons like Vanderbilt and Morgan leveraged their financial networks and political connections to shape ICC policy, ensuring that "regulation" formalized their dominance instead of dismantling it. The commission standardized rates in ways that locked smaller competitors out of the market, effectively turning a public oversight body into a cartel enforcer operating under federal authority.

The banking elite followed a similar playbook. The Panic of 1907 - a financial crisis triggered by reckless speculation - paved the way for the creation of the Federal Reserve System in 1913. J.P. Morgan, who personally intervened to stabilize markets during the panic, became the model for a centralized banking authority. The Federal Reserve was framed as a mechanism to prevent future crises, but its design embedded private banking interests directly into monetary governance. Member banks controlled significant policy decisions, and Wall Street financiers gained extraordinary influence over currency, credit, and interest rates. What was presented as a public safeguard institutionalized private control at the heart of the U.S. economy.

Monopolists also shaped corporate law at the state level, particularly in Delaware and New Jersey, which pioneered permissive incorporation statutes. These laws allowed businesses to merge freely, issue multiple classes of stock, and shield directors from liability, creating legal vehicles perfectly suited for consolidation. Corporations flocked to these jurisdictions, and Delaware eventually became the dominant hub for U.S. corporate registration - a position it maintains today. Far from constraining monopolies, the legal framework evolved to facilitate them, normalizing centralized ownership and protecting executives from accountability.

Education and philanthropy were deployed strategically to reinforce these legal and regulatory victories. Rockefeller and Carnegie funded law schools, universities, and policy think tanks that trained future judges, attorneys, and regulators to view industrial consolidation as natural and even desirable. Legal theories of "efficiency" and "market rationality" became mainstream, creating ideological alignment between courts and corporate priorities. This soft power embedded pro-monopoly assumptions into the intellectual foundations of U.S. law itself, ensuring future legal challenges would play out within boundaries set by the very elites being challenged.

By the early 20th century, the monopolists' influence had been institutionalized across multiple levels:

- Legislation created the appearance of accountability while entrenching corporate dominance.
- Regulatory agencies became tools of capture, managing markets to protect the largest players.
- Judicial precedents interpreted laws in ways favorable to industrial elites.
- Monetary policy centralized financial power under private banking influence.
- State incorporation laws enabled consolidation and insulated executives from liability.
- Educational pipelines produced legal and economic frameworks aligned with elite priorities.

What emerged was not a competitive free market but a managed system designed from the top down, where monopolies operated under the legitimacy of federal authority. Ordinary citizens were told they were protected from corporate abuse, but in reality, the architecture of control had simply been legalized, normalized, and made permanent.

This case study demonstrates a broader truth about U.S. governance during the industrial era: laws and regulations rarely dismantled concentrated power. Instead, they formalized it, embedding elite influence so deeply into the state that challenging it became nearly impossible. The monopolists didn't just win in the marketplace - they rewrote the rules of the game, ensuring future generations would inherit systems built to maintain their advantage.

4

Scientific Management and Human Engineering

F rederick Winslow Taylor reshaped work and, with it, the relationship between humans and machines. At the turn of the 20th century, as industrialization accelerated and production scaled to unprecedented levels, Taylor introduced a system he called "scientific management" - a method designed to eliminate inefficiency by reducing labor into measurable, controllable parts. Behind the language of progress and productivity was a deeper transformation: the systematic dismantling of human autonomy within the workplace. Taylor's ideas didn't simply make factories more efficient; they redefined workers as extensions of machines, breaking their movements, decisions, and identities into discrete, standardized components optimized for output.

Taylor began developing his theories in the 1880s and 1890s while working as a foreman at the Midvale Steel Company in Philadelphia. There, he observed what industrialists called "soldiering" - the tendency of workers to slow their pace deliberately to avoid being overworked. From the perspective of management, this was wasteful; from the perspective of workers, it was survival, a way to preserve energy and protect jobs in an economy where productivity gains often led to layoffs or pay cuts. Taylor's response was radical: measure every motion, every tool placement, every second spent on each task. By timing and analyzing repetitive actions, he sought to design the "one best way" to perform every job.

His experiments at the Bethlehem Steel plant became infamous. Taylor studied laborers loading pig iron and concluded that the optimal daily workload was 47 tons per man - significantly higher than the average output. To enforce this, he selected workers he considered physically suitable, trained them in the precise motions he prescribed, and paid them slightly higher wages to comply. Those who failed to meet his standards were demoted or replaced. The human body became a variable in an equation, its value measured by efficiency and endurance, not skill or creativity. In Taylor's view, individuality was an obstacle to progress.

Taylorism fundamentally reframed the role of the worker. Before industrial standardization, many laborers - artisans, craftsmen, and machinists - maintained control over their methods and pace. They drew on experience, judgment, and improvisation. Scientific management stripped this away, transferring knowledge and authority from workers to managers and engineers. Decisions about how work should be performed were centralized, codified, and enforced from above. Workers no longer designed their labor; they executed instructions derived from data, becoming interchangeable components within systems designed to maximize output.

Taylor positioned his ideas as neutral science, but their social and political implications were profound. By reducing work to quantified routines, he created a framework where management wielded absolute control over production, while workers were discouraged - even punished - for deviation. Efficiency became an ideology, and compliance a moral expectation. Companies adopted "time and motion" studies across industries, from steel plants and textile mills to clerical offices and assembly lines. As Taylorism spread, it imposed a new culture: productivity as virtue, individuality as inefficiency, and labor as a mechanical process governed by expert-designed systems.

The broader impact extended beyond factories. Taylor's methods influenced education, military training, and even government administration. Schools adopted rigid schedules and standardized curricula designed to mimic industrial discipline, conditioning children to follow routines rather than question them. In the military, Taylorist principles informed drills and logistics, treating soldiers as units to be coordinated with machine-like precision. In government, bureaucratic workflows were reorganized to prioritize measurable "outputs" over human judgment. Across institutions, Taylor's obsession with efficiency became embedded in the DNA of modern society.

But the cost was significant. Scientific management stripped meaning from work, replacing skill and craft with monotonous repetition. Workers rebelled, forming unions and resisting the relentless pressure to meet quotas. Strikes erupted in industries where Taylorism was adopted most aggressively, and critics accused Taylor of dehumanizing labor, treating people as tools rather than participants in production. Even within management circles, debates emerged over whether chasing efficiency at all costs undermined innovation and morale. Yet despite resistance, the logic of Taylorism endured, largely because it served the priorities of industrial elites: standardized labor meant predictable profits, scalable systems, and tighter control over growing workforces.

Taylor's influence reached its apex in the early 20th century when Henry Ford integrated his principles into the moving assembly line. Ford's factories achieved unprecedented productivity, reducing the time to build a car from 12 hours to under two. But this "progress" came by locking workers into rigid, repetitive tasks that maximized output while minimizing autonomy. The worker became inseparable from the machine, a living mechanism synchronized to industrial rhythms. Fordism combined Taylor's theories with mechanization, completing the transformation of labor into an extension of technology rather than its master.

Scientific management also paved the way for the modern technocratic mindset. By framing human behavior as data to be measured, optimized, and controlled, Taylor anticipated the rise of algorithmic governance in the digital era. Today's productivity tracking software, algorithm-driven scheduling, and workplace surveillance systems are direct descendants of Taylor's principles. The dream of "one best way" to organize human activity has evolved from stopwatch-and-clipboard studies to automated metrics and predictive analytics, but the core philosophy remains unchanged: autonomy is inefficient, and systems designed from above are presumed superior to decisions made from below. Taylor died in 1915, but his influence permeates the world he helped create. His vision reduced human labor to inputs in a machine, shifting power from individuals to centralized managers, engineers, and ultimately corporations. Scientific management redefined the purpose of work - not as a source of dignity or creativity but as a resource to be optimized for productivity and profit. By breaking humans into machine components, Taylor laid the groundwork for a social order where control could be exercised invisibly, not through force but through design.

Time-and-motion studies began as a blunt industrial tool but evolved into the blueprint for algorithmic control of labor - a transformation that replaced human judgment with systems designed to optimize every gesture, every decision, and every second of work. Emerging in the early 20th century alongside Frederick Winslow Taylor's scientific management, these studies extended his obsession with efficiency by breaking human activity into quantifiable fragments. Engineers armed with stopwatches and notebooks shadowed workers, recording every motion in meticulous detail, dissecting even the simplest tasks into smaller and smaller components. The goal was clear: find the "one best way" to perform any action, codify it, and impose it universally.

Frank and Lillian Gilbreth - pioneers of motion study - carried Taylor's work further by photographing and filming workers to analyze movements frame by frame. Using early cameras and chronophotography, they charted hand motions, body angles, and tool placements, searching for wasted effort. They developed elaborate charts to map "therbligs" - their term for the smallest measurable units of human motion. Where Taylor focused on speed and throughput, the Gilbreths emphasized minimizing strain, fatigue, and "inefficiency," but the outcome was the same: human labor reduced to a dataset, a process to be engineered rather than lived.

The studies promised productivity gains, and industries adopted them widely - steel plants, textile mills, railroads, automotive factories, even clerical offices. Each environment became a laboratory where workers were measured, timed, and reorganized according to expert prescriptions. Nothing was left to intuition; managers dictated the sequence of actions, the tools to use, the posture to maintain, and the speed to sustain. Under this framework, a worker ceased being an independent agent and became an interchangeable component designed to fit seamlessly within an optimized system.

But the real transformation came when these studies were codified into mechanical systems. As industries scaled, reliance on direct human supervision became impractical. To enforce standardization, factories redesigned workflows around machinery and assembly lines that embodied time-and-motion principles directly into their mechanics. Henry Ford perfected this with his moving assembly line, integrating Taylorist data into the production system itself. Workstations were fixed, tasks segmented, and timing controlled by the pace of the line. The system dictated labor's rhythm, and deviation became impossible. Human adaptability - once a strength - was reframed as inefficiency to be eliminated.

This mechanization of control set the stage for its next evolution: algorithmic management. As computing power advanced, time-and-motion principles migrated from clipboards to software. Where early engineers observed individual workers, modern systems track entire workforces in real time. Sensors, cameras, productivity apps, and performance dashboards now collect streams of data far beyond anything Taylor or the Gilbreths imagined: keystrokes, scan rates, idle times, eye movements, even biometric indicators like heart rates and stress levels. Tasks are assigned, monitored, and evaluated by systems that continuously calculate optimal throughput. In warehouses, retail environments, and digital workspaces, algorithms set schedules, route orders, and flag deviations automatically - transforming supervisors into executors of policies generated by machines.

Amazon's warehouse operations are the most visible example of this shift. Algorithms determine how workers move, how quickly items are picked, and how long breaks can last. Every step is tracked, every second accounted for, and every worker benchmarked against constantly updated performance models. "Time off task" metrics are enforced automatically, producing terminations without managerial input. The software decides when to pressure, when to penalize, and when to replace - extending Taylor's stopwatch into a 24/7 digital overseer. The system no longer merely measures behavior; it shapes it directly.

This model has seeped into the broader economy. Rideshare platforms monitor driver location, acceptance rates, and customer feedback, using dynamic pricing and ratings to manipulate behavior without direct orders. Food delivery apps track couriers' routes and reward compliance with algorithmic incentives, gamifying efficiency while quietly extracting maximum labor. In offices, keystroke monitoring, webcam surveillance, and productivity dashboards replicate the same control mechanisms for remote workers. Across industries, the core premise remains unchanged: individual autonomy is subordinated to system-optimized performance.

The shift from manual time-and-motion studies to algorithmic management has deeper social consequences. In Taylor's era, workers understood they were being observed and could resist collectively. In today's systems, control is invisible, embedded in code and infrastructure. There's no stopwatch to protest, no foreman to confront - only algorithms making decisions in real time, enforced by software that claims objectivity while quietly encoding corporate priorities. Unlike Taylor's engineers, algorithms don't negotiate, and they don't explain. Resistance becomes fragmented because each worker's interaction with the system is individualized, tailored, and isolated.

This automation of oversight also creates new forms of dependency. As metrics determine schedules, pay rates, and career opportunities, workers are incentivized to optimize themselves to match the system's logic. The human adapts to the machine, not the other way around. Data collected over time trains predictive models that anticipate performance, allowing companies to shape not just what workers do but what they're likely to do next. Autonomy is not only constrained but preempted.

Yet beneath the promise of efficiency lies the same dynamic that defined Taylorism over a century ago: control. The language has evolved - "optimization," "real-time analytics," "smart workflows" - but the logic is identical. Systems designed to maximize output simultaneously concentrate power, shifting decision-making away from individuals and communities into centralized, opaque infrastructures. The result is a workplace where humans are no longer measured against the machine; they are measured as machines, valued by the metrics they generate rather than the knowledge they possess.

What began with stopwatches and motion charts has become a sprawling architecture of algorithmic governance. Time-and-motion studies broke the body into units; modern systems extend this logic into cognition, emotion, and identity. The worker of the 21st century is quantified in ways Taylor could never have imagined, their choices constrained by systems they neither control nor fully understand. Where Taylorism required obedience, algorithmic management demands integration. The system doesn't just organize labor anymore - it organizes the worker.

The early 20th century marked a cultural and political turning point - an era when the ruling class embraced a sweeping ideology centered on efficiency, progress, and the supposed scientific management of society itself. This "efficiency craze" emerged as industrialization scaled beyond anything previously imaginable, creating systems so vast, interconnected, and fragile that elites began to see themselves not merely as business leaders or policymakers but as engineers of civilization. Underneath the rhetoric of modernization and rational governance was something more profound: a belief that society could, and should, be redesigned from the top down, using data, technology, and "expertise" as tools of control.

This ideology drew heavily on Social Darwinism, a distorted application of Charles Darwin's theories of evolution to human society. Elites interpreted "survival of the fittest" as proof that inequality was natural, inevitable, and even desirable. Wealth and power were recast as signs of superior ability, while poverty, illness, and social instability were framed as consequences of individual weakness rather than systemic exploitation. Within this framework, industrialists, financiers, and technocrats positioned themselves as evolutionary "winners" - the most capable custodians of progress - and used this logic to justify shaping society according to their priorities. Social Darwinism became the moral foundation for policies that concentrated power, rationalizing not just economic dominance but the creation of hierarchical systems in which human beings were managed like resources.

Paired with this ideology was the growing faith in scientific progress as an organizing principle for society. Technological breakthroughs in electricity, petroleum, chemistry, and communication fueled the belief that human ingenuity could solve any problem - provided the right people were in charge. Scientific knowledge was framed as inherently neutral, yet its applications were tightly bound to elite priorities: increasing industrial efficiency, expanding imperial control, and managing populations. Inventions weren't just celebrated for what they enabled but for what they symbolized - proof that the future could be designed, optimized, and predicted if humanity submitted to the leadership of those who "understood the science."

The rise of engineering schools and technocratic professions institutionalized this ideology, producing a new class of "experts" trained to administer complex systems. As industrial infrastructures grew more sophisticated, universities began establishing dedicated programs in mechanical, electrical, and civil engineering to produce graduates capable of managing vast networks of factories, railroads, energy grids, and urban planning projects. Schools like MIT, Carnegie Institute of Technology, and Stanford became pipelines into the emerging technocratic elite, grooming engineers not only as problem-solvers but as overseers of society's physical, economic, and social frameworks.

This professionalization of expertise created a cultural shift: authority migrated away from politics and toward engineering. Where previous generations debated policies in terms of morality or ideology, the efficiency craze recast governance as a technical problem requiring technical solutions. Urban development was framed in terms of traffic flows and infrastructure loads. Agricultural systems were reorganized according to yield metrics and soil chemistry. Public health was redesigned around data-driven population management, laying the groundwork for centralized medical institutions like those Rockefeller would later dominate. Expertise became synonymous with legitimacy, giving engineers, managers, and economists increasing influence over decisions that had once been reserved for elected representatives.

Technocratic professions flourished far beyond traditional engineering. Industrial psychologists emerged to study worker behavior and design "optimal" environments for productivity, often erasing individuality in the process. Management sciences formalized Taylorist principles into reproducible systems taught in business schools, embedding control theories directly into the education of corporate leaders. The legal and policy sectors followed suit, creating administrative institutions and regulatory frameworks staffed by credentialed "experts" rather than representatives accountable to the public. A new elite class formed around specialized knowledge, operating above democratic institutions while claiming neutrality through the language of science.

But beneath this veneer of objectivity, the efficiency craze was deeply ideological. By framing elite control as the natural outcome of evolutionary fitness and technical competence, it delegitimized popular participation and masked structural inequality. Decisions affecting entire populations - from wage policies to city planning to health regulations - were justified as "scientifically necessary," not politically contested. Dissent was recast as ignorance, inefficiency, or even pathology, while compliance became synonymous with rationality and progress.

This mindset also aligned perfectly with the interests of industrial monopolists and financiers. The same elites funding engineering schools and research institutes also steered their priorities, ensuring that technological development served corporate strategies. By shaping curricula, underwriting infrastructure projects, and sponsoring "public benefit" initiatives, they embedded their vision of progress into the very institutions producing the next generation of managers, engineers, and policymakers. The result was a self-reinforcing system: elite institutions produced technocratic professionals, who in turn managed society according to elite-defined goals.

By the 1920s, the efficiency craze had transformed governance, industry, and education into interdependent systems unified by a single assumption: society could be optimized like a machine if handed to the right experts. This belief laid the foundation for the rise of modern technocracy, where authority flows not from public consent but from claims of specialized knowledge. Once engineers became the architects of governance, efficiency became indistinguishable from power - and the systems they built often served elite interests first, cloaked in the promise of scientific neutrality.

In retrospect, the efficiency craze was less about improving society than reorganizing it around the priorities of those who controlled its technologies, resources, and knowledge pipelines. By embedding technocratic authority into education, law, and policy, elites constructed a framework where democracy became increasingly symbolic. The rhetoric of "progress" masked a deeper reality: the more complex the systems became, the easier it was to hide control within them.

Henry Ford transformed industry, labor, and society by perfecting a system that reduced human beings to "process units" - interchangeable components in a mechanized sequence optimized for speed and output. Frederick Winslow Taylor laid the intellectual groundwork with his theories of scientific management, but Ford operationalized them at an unprecedented scale. His moving assembly line, introduced in 1913 at the Highland Park plant in Michigan, did more than revolutionize automobile manufacturing. It rewired human labor itself, redefining the relationship between man and machine, autonomy and efficiency, individuality and control.

Before Ford, manufacturing relied heavily on skilled labor and slower, less standardized processes. Workers often built entire products or managed significant parts of production, drawing on experience and judgment. Ford saw this as wasteful. He envisioned a system where products moved, not workers - where tasks were broken into their smallest possible units and distributed among individuals trained to perform them repetitively with machine-like precision. The assembly line inverted the traditional relationship between humans and tools: workers no longer controlled the process; the process controlled them.

At Highland Park, Ford mounted the automobile chassis on a moving conveyor belt, passing it through fixed workstations where each laborer performed a single, standardized action before the chassis rolled to the next worker. No one built a car; they assembled fragments of one. This segmentation of labor produced unprecedented efficiency. The time required to build a Model T dropped from over twelve hours to roughly ninety minutes. Costs plummeted, profits soared, and Ford's vehicles became affordable to ordinary Americans, reshaping not just industry but society itself.

But this efficiency came at a profound human cost. The moving line dictated the pace of labor, forcing workers to synchronize their bodies with the rhythm of the machine. Tasks were repetitive, monotonous, and physically exhausting, leaving little room for skill or autonomy. Workers became "process units" - bodies measured by their ability to keep pace with mechanical timing. Where Taylor's stopwatch studies optimized individual motions, Ford embedded those optimizations into the system itself, eliminating personal discretion altogether. Labor was no longer negotiated; it was dictated.

Ford understood the alienation his system created and countered it with calculated incentives. In 1914, he introduced the famous "Five Dollar Day" wage, doubling standard pay rates. Heralded as a progressive triumph, the policy was strategic: it reduced turnover, stabilized the workforce, and made Ford's employees potential consumers of the very cars they built. But the gift came with strings. Ford's Sociological Department investigated workers' personal lives, monitoring spending habits, family structure, morality, and even private behavior. To keep their higher wages, workers were expected to conform to Ford's values, effectively surrendering not just their labor but their autonomy.

Ford expanded this philosophy further in 1926, pioneering the five-day, 40-hour workweek. He framed it as an act of benevolence, but it was a calculated maneuver designed to serve his broader economic vision. By shortening the workweek, Ford gave workers more leisure time - time he intended them to spend consuming. Automobiles, home appliances, and other mass-produced goods became symbols of modern prosperity, and Ford understood that sustained profits required cultivating a population conditioned to buy, not just build. The five-day workweek wasn't about liberation; it was about designing a consumer society synchronized with industrial output, embedding dependency on the very systems controlling labor.

Fordism became a global model, influencing governments, corporations, and ideologues alike - including in Nazi Germany. Ford's writings, particularly "The International Jew" (1920–1922), promoted antisemitic conspiracy theories that resonated deeply with Hitler's worldview. In Mein Kampf, Hitler praised Ford by name, calling him an inspiration for industrial nationalism. Ford's photograph reportedly hung in Hitler's Munich office, and in 1938, Ford accepted the Grand Cross of the German Eagle, Nazi Germany's highest civilian honor for foreigners.

Ford Motor Company also maintained industrial ties to Nazi Germany throughout the 1930s. Its German subsidiary, Ford-Werke, supplied trucks, engines, and equipment critical to the Wehrmacht's mobility during the early years of World War II. While Ford claimed ignorance of direct wartime production, corporate records reveal extensive coordination between Dearborn and Cologne well into the late 1930s, driven by Ford's insistence on maintaining profitable operations abroad regardless of political regimes. Ideologically and operationally, Ford's model of standardized, mechanized labor aligned seamlessly with the Nazi vision of total societal mobilization.

The cultural impact of Fordism extended far beyond the factory floor. The assembly line's rhythm dictated life itself. Time became standardized, carved into shifts, schedules, and production quotas, shaping not only workplaces but schools, bureaucracies, and urban planning. Education mirrored factory discipline, conditioning students to adapt to bells, segmented tasks, and hierarchical control. Leisure, too, became commodified, engineered to fit into the narrow intervals carved out by industrial demands. Society reorganized itself around Fordist principles without ever openly debating their adoption.

Beneath Ford's rhetoric of progress and prosperity lay a deeper strategy of control. By coupling higher wages and shorter workweeks with systemic surveillance and behavioral conditioning, he created a compliant workforce while fueling mass consumerism. Ford's workers were taught to produce, paid to consume, and monitored to conform - a closed circuit of dependency that served corporate power first. His methods embedded industrial values into everyday life, conditioning entire populations to align their identities, behaviors, and aspirations with the logic of mechanized efficiency.

Modern algorithmic management systems are Fordism's direct heirs. Where Ford dictated speed with conveyor belts, software now automates scheduling, tracks keystrokes, monitors productivity, and predicts behavior in real time. Amazon warehouses, gig-economy platforms, and office surveillance systems operate as digital assembly lines, reducing workers to data points processed by algorithms indifferent to individuality or context. Ford's vision of continuous, optimized flow persists, now amplified by technology and scaled across global supply chains.

Henry Ford didn't just transform manufacturing; he transformed society. He embedded control into infrastructure, technology, and culture, blurring the lines between labor, consumption, and identity. The assembly line promised empowerment through productivity and prosperity but delivered dependency through design. Ford built cars, yes - but more importantly, he built the framework of a managed society, one where humans were reorganized into units of process, synchronized to systems they neither created nor governed.

Nikola Tesla and Thomas Edison stood at the heart of one of the most consequential battles of the modern age - a war over energy, technology, and the future architecture of society. Their rivalry was framed as a conflict of genius versus genius, innovation versus innovation. But beneath the romantic mythology of two inventors competing for supremacy lay a deeper struggle over who would control the flow of power itself - both electrical and political. The "War of Currents" between Tesla's alternating current (AC) and Edison's direct current (DC) wasn't just a technical debate; it was a turning point where energy became the foundation for monopolies, financial empires, and the consolidation of technocratic control.

Edison represented the emerging industrial establishment. Backed by financiers like J.P. Morgan, Edison promoted a centralized vision of energy: proprietary systems built on direct current (DC) that required expensive infrastructure and limited distribution. Edison's model made sense for urban cores, where dense populations justified localized power stations, but it faltered over long distances - voltage dropped quickly, requiring costly substations every few miles. Edison didn't care; the inefficiency protected profits. Control, not universality, defined his strategy. By owning the infrastructure, patents, and service contracts, Edison Electric could effectively monopolize urban energy markets one city at a time.

Tesla, by contrast, envisioned a radically different future - one built on alternating current (AC), capable of transmitting power over vast distances at minimal loss. Partnering with George Westinghouse, Tesla's AC systems threatened not only Edison's business model but the financial interests of the elites backing him. AC promised scalability, decentralization, and - at least in theory - cheaper, more abundant electricity. Tesla dreamed bigger still, imagining wireless transmission of energy across the globe, bypassing the need for costly grids entirely. His ultimate goal was to make energy freely accessible, undermining the ability of corporations and states to control it.

This clash terrified Edison and his backers, who launched a relentless campaign to discredit Tesla's system. The infamous "War of Currents" escalated into propaganda and spectacle. Edison staged public demonstrations electrocuting animals with AC to portray it as dangerous, even supporting the first use of the electric chair powered by alternating current to associate Tesla's innovation with death. Behind the theatrics, however, Edison and Morgan were fighting for financial survival. Tesla's success would render Edison's patents and infrastructure obsolete, collapsing the value of Morgan's investment in Edison Electric.

The turning point came in 1893, when Tesla and Westinghouse won the contract to power the Chicago World's Fair with AC, dazzling the public and proving its superiority. Two years later, Tesla's design for the Niagara Falls hydroelectric plant delivered commercial power to Buffalo, New York, cementing AC's dominance. Edison's empire was absorbed into General Electric, backed by Morgan, which pivoted reluctantly toward Tesla's system - but not Tesla himself.

Because while Tesla's technology won, Tesla himself lost. Westinghouse, under financial pressure from Morgan's networks, renegotiated Tesla's royalties on AC patents, stripping him of the wealth his inventions should have generated. His dream of wireless global power, embodied in the Wardenclyffe Tower project, collapsed after Morgan - once courted as an investor - withdrew funding. The reason was simple: free energy was unprofitable. Morgan and other financiers understood that controlling energy meant controlling economies, populations, and politics. A system of centralized grids, metered consumption, and perpetual billing would generate wealth and dependency for generations. Tesla's vision of open-access power threatened the foundation of industrial capitalism, and so his innovations were marginalized even as his technology became the standard.

Edison, for his part, played the role of pragmatic industrialist. He may have lost the technical argument, but by aligning himself with Morgan, he secured a legacy within an emerging network of energy monopolies. General Electric, born from Edison's company and Morgan's financing, became one of the most powerful corporations in the world, dominating electrification alongside Westinghouse Electric until consolidation and regulatory frameworks brought them under shared elite control. Tesla, meanwhile, died impoverished and largely forgotten, his patents scattered, his innovations appropriated.

Electrification itself became the lever through which elites consolidated influence over society. Entire populations were reorganized around energy infrastructures they didn't own and couldn't control. Municipalities ceded authority to private utilities, creating centralized grids that dictated where industries flourished, which regions modernized, and who gained access to basic services. Energy companies grew into quasi-governing institutions, determining pricing, rationing, and distribution policies in ways that affected every aspect of modern life. "Public utility commissions" emerged nominally to regulate them but were quickly captured, embedding corporate priorities into governance while maintaining a façade of accountability.

Tesla's defeat marked the suppression of an alternative technological paradigm - one where energy could have been decentralized, abundant, and potentially free. Instead, the industrial model chosen by Edison, Morgan, and their allies ensured that power - in every sense of the word - flowed upward. Centralized grids became instruments of dependency, locking populations into infrastructures controlled by private monopolies that now functioned as essential organs of modern civilization. The framework established during the War of Currents laid the foundation for today's global energy empires, where oil, gas, and electricity remain tightly bound to elite control.

The rivalry also symbolized a broader ideological split between technological liberation and technocratic control. Tesla embodied the dream of science serving humanity, bypassing profit motives to expand individual freedom. Edison represented technology as corporate leverage, entangled with patents, investors, and political influence. Tesla wanted to make energy invisible; Edison, Morgan, and their successors ensured it would be billable, surveilled, and rationed. The victory of AC over DC solved a technical problem, but the ownership of energy - and by extension, the control of modern life - remained firmly in the hands of monopolists.

Today, Tesla's warnings resonate more than ever. His discarded ideas about wireless transmission and decentralized energy anticipated the vulnerabilities of centralized infrastructure: blackouts, resource wars, and corporate capture of public utilities. Meanwhile, the model established by Edison and Morgan evolved into a global architecture of dependency, where electrification became inseparable from governance, economics, and surveillance. The wires Tesla dreamed of eliminating became the conduits of a new form of control, embedding energy monopolies at the heart of the modern technocratic state.

Tesla's vision was buried, but his inventions survived. Edison's system won, but Edison himself was consumed by larger forces - financiers, conglomerates, and an industrial elite building more than products. They built infrastructures of power, locking humanity into grids designed not for freedom but for control. The story of Tesla versus Edison isn't just about technology; it's about who decides how innovation is used - and who benefits from it.

5

Philosophers of Utopia and Control

A uguste Comte's philosophy of positivism laid one of the intellectual foundations for modern technocracy - a worldview in which
science, data, and "expert knowledge" would replace religion, tradition,
and democracy as the organizing principles of society. Writing in the
early to mid-19th century, Comte believed that humanity was entering
its final stage of evolution, moving from theological superstition to
metaphysical abstraction, and finally into what he called the "scientific
stage" - a new era where empirical methods and measurable laws would
govern every aspect of human life. In Comte's vision, science would not
merely describe reality; it would prescribe it, becoming the central authority shaping morality, social organization, and even human identity
itself.

For Comte, positivism was more than a philosophical position; it was a
blueprint for reorganizing civilization. He argued that human progress
followed a predictable trajectory: societies evolved by abandoning mystical explanations and adopting rational, scientific ones. In his framework, politics, economics, religion, and culture should all eventually
subordinate themselves to the "laws" discovered by science. Just as New-
ton had revealed the mathematical principles governing the movement
of planets, Comte believed scientists could discover universal laws governing human behavior, social structures, and historical change. These
laws, once identified, would allow for the engineering of society itself -

not through democratic deliberation, but through the guidance of a new class of scientific elites who understood the underlying mechanisms of collective life.

Comte envisioned a future in which science became a kind of secular theology - what he called the "religion of humanity." He proposed rituals, symbols, and hierarchies modeled after Catholicism but stripped of the supernatural, replacing priests with scientists and philosophers who would act as the moral guides of the population. In this vision, social cohesion would no longer depend on divine commandments but on shared reverence for rationality and collective progress. Citizens would look not to sacred texts but to experts for answers about morality, governance, and the "correct" way to live. Comte's positivism transformed science into a totalizing framework: a belief system where empirical knowledge became synonymous with truth and authority, and deviation from its principles was treated as ignorance or regression.

This ideology resonated powerfully with the industrial and political elites of the 19th century, who faced the challenge of managing rapidly urbanizing, industrializing populations. Comte offered them an intellectual framework that legitimized centralized control by claiming it was not ideological but scientific. If society operated according to discoverable laws, then governing it was not a matter of debate but of technical expertise. This mindset laid the groundwork for the emerging technocratic class: engineers, economists, industrial planners, and social scientists who framed their authority not as political but as objective necessity. The factory system, standardized education, public health initiatives, and urban planning all began to reflect Comtean assumptions that human behavior could be predicted, managed, and optimized like any other system.

Positivism also fed directly into the efficiency craze that swept through elite circles in the late 19th and early 20th centuries. Figures like Frederick Winslow Taylor translated Comte's abstract philosophy into practical tools for managing labor, breaking tasks into measurable units and prescribing the "one best way" to perform them. Auguste Comte provided the ideological foundation; Taylor, Ford, and their successors operationalized it. In this context, the worker became not a citizen or creative agent but a component in a system designed by experts who claimed to know better than those they governed. The promise of scientific progress justified reorganizing human life into optimized routines, from the pace of factory work to the layout of entire cities.

Comte's influence extended into education and cultural institutions as well. Positivism inspired the creation of engineering schools, research universities, and scientific academies designed to produce the technocratic elites of the future. By elevating empirical knowledge above all else, these institutions established hierarchies of expertise that still define modern governance: policy deferred to data, morality subordinated to "facts," and democracy increasingly constrained by claims of "scientific necessity." Comte's dream of science as a secular religion began to materialize quietly, embedded not through sermons but through curricula, bureaucracies, and institutional design.

Yet Comte's vision also carried a darker implication: in a positivist society, dissent becomes irrational by definition. If science reveals the "truth" about human nature and social organization, those who question the resulting systems are framed not as political actors but as obstacles to progress. This dynamic persists today, where challenges to elite narratives about economics, health, or climate are often dismissed as "anti-scientific" rather than debated on their merits. The positivist worldview erodes the space for pluralism, replacing competing visions of society with a single authorized model administered by those deemed most qualified to interpret "the data."

Comte himself believed this technocratic order would bring harmony, but in practice it laid the groundwork for deepening inequalities of power. By granting authority to a narrow class of "experts," positivism created systems where governance became increasingly insulated from popular accountability. The 20th century would see this ideology merge with corporate, financial, and state interests, culminating in a world where unelected elites manage energy grids, financial systems, educational standards, healthcare protocols, and information flows - all justified as scientific necessity rather than political choice.

Comte's dream of science as the "religion of the future" has, in many ways, been realized - but not as he imagined. Instead of a benevolent priesthood of philosophers guiding humanity toward collective well-being, we inherited sprawling technocratic infrastructures serving the priorities of states and corporations. Where Comte saw science as liberation from dogma, elites weaponized it as a new form of dogma - one cloaked in neutrality, administered through algorithms, institutions, and metrics.

The transition from theology to technocracy didn't eliminate faith; it relocated it. Populations are still asked to "believe," but now the object of belief is the authority of experts, the sanctity of data, and the inevitability of "scientific" progress. Comte anticipated the framework; industrialists, financiers, and engineers built it into the machinery of modern life. What began as a philosophical ideal became the operating system of a civilization where science functions less as discovery and more as governance - the new religion of control.

Karl Marx and Friedrich Engels envisioned a world in which history's trajectory would culminate in a centrally planned society - a system where the means of production, resource distribution, and even the direction of technological development would be coordinated under collective authority rather than left to the chaos of market competition. Their collaboration, most famously embodied in The Communist Manifesto (1848) and Das Kapital (1867), offered both a critique of industrial capitalism and a prescription for replacing it. Yet beneath their rhetoric of liberation, their framework laid the ideological groundwork for some of the most powerful centralized systems in modern history, influencing revolutions, nation-states, and eventually the technocratic infrastructures of the 20th and 21st centuries.

Marx and Engels began with a structural diagnosis: capitalism was inherently unstable, exploitative, and self-destructive. In their analysis, the Industrial Revolution had transformed societies into battlegrounds between two dominant classes: the bourgeoisie, who controlled capital and means of production, and the proletariat, who owned nothing but their labor. Machines, factories, and railroads amplified productivity but also concentrated wealth in fewer hands, creating structural inequalities Marx predicted would eventually become intolerable. For him, the evolution of capitalism wasn't a moral failure - it was a scientific inevitability. The logic of industrial capitalism, he argued, contained the seeds of its own collapse: overproduction would lead to crises, competition would destroy smaller enterprises, and workers alienated from their labor would eventually revolt.

The solution, as Marx and Engels saw it, was to abolish private ownership of the means of production and replace it with collective management under a planned system. By centralizing economic decision-making, society could eliminate wasteful competition, stabilize production, and ensure resources served collective needs rather than private profit. This wasn't framed as utopian idealism but as historical determinism: Marx claimed his theory revealed the "scientific laws" of history, predicting that capitalism would inevitably give way to socialism and, eventually, communism. The model was hierarchical, organized, and data-driven long before the word "technocracy" existed - the assumption being that complex industrial economies required expert coordination to function effectively without markets.

In practice, Marx and Engels' vision merged economics with governance. The state, in their framework, would act as the central administrator of society's productive forces, directing resources, labor, and capital according to rational plans designed to maximize collective benefit. Social problems - poverty, unemployment, inequality - would be solved not through debate or negotiation but through systematic design, as though society itself were a machine that could be tuned to optimal performance. In this sense, Marxism contained the seeds of modern technocracy: it imagined a managerial elite capable of mastering data, overseeing distribution, and regulating life at scale, but under the banner of collective ownership rather than private monopolies.

Marx and Engels also envisioned the reshaping of individual identity to fit this centralized framework. In their critique, the alienation of labor under capitalism stripped workers of meaning and agency; in a planned economy, individuals would find fulfillment by contributing to collective progress. But embedded in this ideal was a subtle inversion: personal aspirations, diversity of thought, and local autonomy became subordinate to the needs of the "whole." Freedom was redefined, not as independence from authority, but as alignment with the collective's goals. Dissent, in this framework, became irrational by definition - a challenge not just to policy but to history itself.

The political movements inspired by Marx and Engels operationalized this vision at scale, often with consequences far removed from their theoretical ideals. In the 20th century, revolutions in Russia, China, and Eastern Europe adopted central planning as the backbone of state power. Under Lenin and later Stalin, the Soviet Union constructed a massive bureaucratic apparatus to control agriculture, industry, and energy, turning Marx's abstract framework into concrete policy. Vast datasets were collected, analyzed, and applied to manage production quotas and resource allocation across an empire. Similarly, Mao Zedong's China attempted to reorganize society around planned industrialization, launching sweeping programs like the Great Leap Forward that aimed to rapidly transform agrarian populations into industrial labor forces - often with catastrophic results.

These experiments exposed both the strengths and weaknesses of central planning. On one hand, the state could rapidly mobilize resources to achieve large-scale goals: electrification, infrastructure projects, military buildup, and industrial expansion occurred at unprecedented speeds. On the other hand, concentrating decision-making in a single bureaucratic hierarchy created massive inefficiencies, rigidities, and vulnerabilities. Failures cascaded through entire systems when local knowledge was ignored or suppressed. Famines, resource shortages, and economic stagnation often followed attempts to micromanage production without feedback mechanisms, revealing the limits of imposing top-down control on complex, adaptive societies.

Yet despite these failures, the idea of central planning as a tool of power survived - not because Marxism succeeded, but because its logic of coordination proved irresistible to both socialist and capitalist elites. In the Soviet model, planned economies became a tool for ideological dominance; in the West, corporate monopolists and financial institutions adopted similar centralizing strategies under different names. Whether driven by state bureaucracies or private conglomerates, the underlying principle was the same: manage resources, labor, and populations through data, hierarchy, and expert oversight.

Ironically, Marx and Engels' critique of industrial capitalism helped inspire a system that mirrored its worst tendencies. Where they sought to abolish exploitation, planned economies often reproduced new hierarchies, replacing private capitalists with party bureaucrats and corporate-state hybrids. In both East and West, the end result was a society where control migrated upward into institutions increasingly insulated from public accountability. Central planning became less about liberation and more about administration - a framework where populations were managed, monitored, and optimized according to priorities set far above their influence.

Marx and Engels envisioned a scientific, rational society, but their framework opened the door to the idea that human life could be engineered - reorganized like infrastructure, optimized like supply chains, and managed like industrial processes. This conceptual leap fused with the efficiency craze, positivist ideology, and the emerging technocratic professions of the late 19th and early 20th centuries, accelerating the shift toward governance by experts and systems rather than by democratic consent.

In many ways, we live inside the shadow of their ideas. Centralized control of energy grids, food systems, finance, and information flows is now achieved not by party bureaucracies but by transnational corporations, banks, and algorithmic governance systems - structures Marx could not have imagined but whose logic he predicted. Where Marx dreamed of collective ownership serving the common good, modern technocracy has fused the tools of central planning with the incentives of monopoly capitalism, creating a hybrid model where efficiency and control dominate regardless of ideology.

Marx and Engels provided the blueprint; states, corporations, and elites built the machinery. What began as a revolutionary critique became the intellectual scaffolding for global systems of administration that now govern the rhythms of daily life. Central planning never disappeared - it evolved, digitized, and merged with financial power, embedding itself into infrastructures so vast and seamless that most people no longer notice its presence.

Herbert Spencer became one of the most influential architects of elite ideology in the 19th century, translating Charles Darwin's biological theories into a political and social framework that justified hierarchy, inequality, and centralized control. While Darwin's On the Origin of Species (1859) explored natural selection in the biological realm, it was Spencer who extended these ideas into the human domain, coining the phrase "survival of the fittest." In Spencer's view, society evolved through competition in the same way species did - and those who rose to the top economically, politically, or intellectually were not simply fortunate but naturally superior.

Spencer's philosophy of Social Darwinism gave the ruling elite something they desperately needed during the upheaval of the Industrial Revolution: an intellectual framework to rationalize their power. While Karl Marx and Friedrich Engels condemned capitalism for exploiting labor, Spencer gave industrialists, financiers, and political leaders a moral defense for the widening inequalities of the modern age. If the wealthy and powerful flourished, it was not because of structural manipulation, systemic monopolies, or exploitation - it was because they were evolution's winners. Conversely, poverty, illness, and social instability were framed as evidence of individual failure, weakness, or inherent unfitness.

This worldview dovetailed perfectly with the emerging technocratic class. As industrial production scaled and populations became dependent on centralized systems, elites required an ideology that justified their control. Spencer supplied it. By framing social outcomes as the natural product of evolutionary competition, he helped shift debates about power away from morality and democracy and toward "scientific inevitability." Inequality ceased to be a political problem requiring reform; it became a biological law, and challenging it meant challenging nature itself.

Spencer's ideas influenced everything from economic policy to urban planning. Governments increasingly deferred to "market forces" as though they were as immutable as gravity, justifying deregulation, low taxation for industrialists, and the dismantling of protections for the working class. Corporations, meanwhile, invoked Spencerian logic to resist labor reforms, arguing that interference in "natural competition" would weaken society by protecting the "unfit." Even public health measures and welfare systems were attacked under this ideology, as elites claimed that aiding the poor, disabled, or unemployed would interfere with evolution's "purifying" function.

But Social Darwinism didn't just rationalize inequality; it became a policy weapon. Industrialists like John D. Rockefeller and Andrew Carnegie openly embraced Spencer's ideas, using them to defend monopolies and corporate dominance. Rockefeller famously compared his rise to the "law of nature," declaring: "The growth of a large business is merely the survival of the fittest." Carnegie, despite his philanthropy, shared similar convictions, insisting that wealth concentration in the hands of a few "capable men" ultimately benefited society by directing resources more efficiently than democratic processes ever could. Spencer gave the elite a language to describe their control as service to progress rather than exploitation.

Spencer's influence extended beyond economics into eugenics and population management. By framing social inequality as biologically determined, he paved the way for policies aimed at "improving" the genetic quality of populations - often by restricting the reproduction of those deemed unfit. Beginning in the late 19th century and accelerating into the early 20th, elite-driven eugenics programs emerged in the United States, Britain, and continental Europe, frequently funded by Rockefeller, Carnegie, and Harriman foundations. Laws institutionalized forced sterilizations, restrictive immigration quotas, and racial hierarchies under the guise of scientific necessity, with Spencerian logic embedded at every level of policymaking.

These ideas found their darkest expression in Nazi ideology. German social theorists adapted Spencer's Social Darwinism to justify racial "purification," Lebensraum expansion, and genocide. The Nazis combined Darwinian rhetoric with centralized planning to engineer what they framed as a biologically superior society. Crucially, many of the Nazi regime's policies drew directly from earlier U.S. experiments in sterilization and segregation - programs supported by Spencer-influenced elites in American foundations, universities, and government agencies. In this way, Social Darwinism became one of the intellectual bridges connecting industrial capitalism, technocracy, and authoritarian statecraft.

Spencer also shaped education and the emerging technocratic professions. If society could be understood through "scientific" laws of competition and selection, then "experts" trained to interpret those laws became its natural leaders. Engineering schools, economics departments, and management sciences absorbed Spencerian assumptions, embedding them into curricula that framed efficiency and hierarchy as natural truths rather than political choices. As elites funded these institutions, they perpetuated a self-reinforcing cycle: produce "experts" steeped in Social Darwinist ideology, empower them to administer society, and then cite their "expertise" as proof that elite dominance was both rational and inevitable.

Beneath Spencer's philosophy was a profound redefinition of morality and governance. If evolution rewarded strength, intelligence, and adaptability, then compassion, welfare, and collective responsibility became liabilities. Helping the "weak" slowed progress; resisting elite control meant resisting nature itself. Over time, this narrative normalized mass inequality, conditioning populations to accept corporate monopolies, centralized planning, and growing surveillance infrastructures as the logical price of "civilization." Social Darwinism provided the ideological lubricant for building systems of control - from company towns to compulsory schooling - while cloaking them in the language of science and inevitability.

Spencer himself likely did not foresee the full implications of his work, but his ideas helped create a worldview that merged perfectly with the ambitions of industrial and financial elites. By combining Darwinian metaphors with positivist faith in scientific management, Spencer provided a framework where society could be reorganized like an evolving organism, guided by those at the "top" of the hierarchy. His influence helped set the stage for 20th-century technocracy, where expertise, data, and centralized decision-making replaced democratic consent, always framed as "scientific progress."

We still live with Spencer's legacy. Modern systems of algorithmic governance, predictive policing, performance scoring, and "social credit" operate on an evolved form of the same principle: reduce humans to metrics, rank them, and justify unequal outcomes as natural products of "data." Today's elites may no longer speak in Spencer's language, but his underlying logic - that hierarchy is inevitable and intervention is dangerous - remains embedded in the architecture of control.

H.G. Wells is remembered today as a visionary of science fiction, but beneath the surface of his novels was a deeper and far more radical project: the design of a managed civilization. In works like The Open Conspiracy (1928) and World Brain (1938), Wells laid out a program for reshaping global society through centralized control of knowledge, coordinated elites, and technocratic governance. He believed humanity was on the verge of catastrophic self-destruction - through war, resource exhaustion, and political fragmentation - and argued that survival required a deliberate reorganization of the world under a scientifically guided, coordinated plan. Far from speculative fiction, Wells was mapping a political strategy: a blueprint for a new order where governments, corporations, and technocratic institutions would merge into an openly managed world system.

In The Open Conspiracy, Wells called for nothing less than the dismantling of traditional sovereignty and the replacement of nation-states with a coordinated global authority. He saw existing political structures as obsolete relics incapable of managing the scale of industrial civilization, technological change, and population growth. Nationalism, in his view, was a dangerous anachronism - one that inevitably led to resource competition, militarism, and cycles of war. The solution, he argued, was not revolution but gradual capture: a coalition of scientists, industrialists, educators, and "enlightened elites" who would bypass traditional politics and work in concert to build the foundations of global governance from within existing institutions.

This wasn't meant to be a secret conspiracy in the traditional sense; Wells insisted it should be "open" - normalized, legitimized, and integrated into public life. The Open Conspiracy would operate through universities, international bodies, research foundations, financial systems, and media, aligning them under a shared vision of planetary planning. It would recruit scientists and engineers as the architects of a rational society, replacing political wrangling with "evidence-based" decision-making and coordinated resource management. Democracy, Wells believed, could not survive modernity - too slow, too chaotic, too vulnerable to manipulation - and would inevitably give way to technocratic administration disguised as enlightened governance.

Wells saw knowledge itself as the ultimate lever of control. In World Brain, he proposed a global information network decades before the internet - a centralized "repository of human understanding" that would compile, standardize, and distribute knowledge to the world. Ostensibly, the World Brain would democratize access to information, but in practice it envisioned an elite-managed system where data, education, and public narratives were tightly coordinated to maintain social cohesion. Wells believed that fragmented, competing sources of information - newspapers, local schools, religious traditions - kept humanity divided and irrational. To unify society, knowledge had to be standardized, filtered, and integrated, overseen by experts who would determine what constituted "reliable truth."

Through these writings, Wells positioned science as the new religion and scientists as the new clergy. He imagined a cadre of highly educated, globally connected elites managing everything from economic planning and education to population control and energy distribution. Like Auguste Comte before him, Wells proposed replacing traditional faith with a secular doctrine rooted in empirical rationality - but where Comte dreamed of a symbolic "religion of humanity," Wells provided the operational details. The Open Conspiracy would quietly reorganize institutions around shared objectives while cultivating public belief in their inevitability. Through education, media, and standardized systems of knowledge, populations would internalize the logic of planetary management without perceiving it as coercion.

Wells's ideas weren't abstract thought experiments - they were deeply embedded in the elite networks of his time. He moved comfortably within circles of global planners, financiers, and policymakers. Through the Fabian Society, he collaborated with figures like Sidney and Beatrice Webb, who championed gradual, technocratic socialism administered by experts rather than revolutionaries. Wells engaged with institutions like the League of Nations and academic bodies working on early international law, seeing them as prototypes for the global governance systems he envisioned. His proposals anticipated - and arguably inspired - the rise of 20th-century organizations like the United Nations, UNESCO, and the World Bank, which embody the central pillars of Wells's program: standardized knowledge, centralized planning, and international coordination of elites.

Yet Wells's optimism carried authoritarian undertones. In his model, dissent had no functional place. Competing narratives, cultural identities, and even localized governance were obstacles to be dissolved in the pursuit of planetary efficiency. While he presented his program as a voluntary alignment of enlightened actors, the end state he described resembled a technocratic oligarchy - a system where unelected experts and institutions made decisions for billions under the assumption that rationality justified authority. Critics accused Wells of masking coercion beneath the language of progress, arguing that his Open Conspiracy substituted one ruling class for another - only now legitimized by claims of scientific objectivity.

The influence of Wells's vision persists today, albeit under different labels. The idea of a global knowledge infrastructure manifests in initiatives like the digitization of libraries, standardized educational frameworks, and algorithmic content curation across digital platforms. International "coordination bodies" manage trade, finance, energy, and information flows under frameworks largely inaccessible to public scrutiny. Claims of "following the science" have become political tools wielded by technocratic institutions to dictate policy on issues ranging from climate to health to economics. Wells anticipated this shift: when knowledge is centralized and institutionalized, truth itself becomes managed, and populations governed by it rarely perceive the hidden levers shaping their reality.

Wells's legacy is therefore paradoxical. He championed ideals of universal knowledge and collective progress but framed them within systems inherently controlled by elites. His Open Conspiracy imagined a voluntary coalition of humanity's "best minds," yet the practical mechanisms he outlined enabled the concentration of authority into fewer, more insulated hands. His World Brain promised shared access to information but assumed centralized control over how that information was curated and interpreted. What he conceived as liberation became, in practice, a model for soft power - influence embedded so deeply into education, media, and institutional design that it operates without overt enforcement.

In hindsight, Wells was less a futurist and more an architect of technocracy. His vision of coordinated global elites, standardized knowledge, and planetary planning resonates through contemporary governance structures, from the UN to the IMF to the interwoven networks of corporate, academic, and political power managing the world's resources. Whether one sees this as inevitable evolution or as creeping consolidation, Wells's writings reveal the blueprint: control perception, coordinate elites, and build infrastructures that quietly bind populations into systems they neither designed nor control.

The Fabian Society, founded in London in 1884, became one of the most effective engines of social transformation in modern history, but it worked silently, avoiding confrontation while steadily reshaping society from within. Where Marx and Engels preached revolution, the Fabians perfected a different strategy: gradualist socialism. They believed society could be remade not through barricades and uprisings but through infiltration of existing power structures - policymaking, education, administration, and culture. Their long game was patient and methodical: capture the levers of influence, normalize elite control through "expertise," and redesign society without most people ever realizing it was happening.

Sidney and Beatrice Webb were the intellectual architects of this strategy. They believed data was the ultimate weapon of persuasion. Through exhaustive studies on labor, wages, and economic systems, they produced mountains of research designed to appear neutral and objective, yet always steering policy toward centralized planning and state control. Their reports shaped debates inside Parliament, influenced emerging welfare systems, and provided intellectual cover for a slow transfer of authority from communities to bureaucracies.

In 1895, they founded the London School of Economics, a masterstroke of Fabian strategy. The LSE became the first true academy for technocrats, designed to train a new managerial elite in economics, policy, and administration. Students were taught to see governance as a technical challenge requiring "scientific" solutions rather than democratic negotiation. Over time, LSE graduates would spread across Britain's ministries, colonial administrations, global financial institutions, and international organizations, carrying Fabian ideals into the very infrastructure of governance. The school became a conveyor belt of policymakers, feeding national and global institutions with technocrats who had internalized Fabian methods without necessarily identifying as Fabians.

George Bernard Shaw, another founding Fabian, played a different role. Where the Webbs moved quietly through institutions, Shaw provoked openly. He used his fame and wit to seed controversial ideas into the public conversation: redistribution of wealth, state-directed population control, and the superiority of expert-led governance over mass democracy. His rhetoric often sounded extreme, but this was deliberate. Shaw shifted the Overton window, softening resistance so the Webbs and other Fabians could advance similar proposals more discreetly through committees, reports, and policy frameworks.

Fabianism wasn't limited to economic planning; it extended into population management. Like many elites of the late 19th and early 20th centuries, the Fabians embraced eugenics as part of their vision for a rationally managed society. Sidney and Beatrice Webb supported policies designed to "improve" population quality, and Shaw openly discussed sterilization of those deemed unfit to contribute to the collective good. Through partnerships with institutions like the Eugenics Education Society and with American foundations like Rockefeller, Carnegie, and Harriman, Fabian ideas helped shape laws on immigration, reproductive control, and public health - always under the banner of "scientific progress."

What made the Fabians effective was their patience. They didn't overthrow governments; they rewired them. They understood that ideas become power when they are embedded in institutions - in schools, bureaucracies, professional networks, and media ecosystems. By slowly seeding their worldview into these systems, they ensured it would persist long after the original Fabians had disappeared from public life.

The Fabian Society's real achievement wasn't passing laws or leading protests; it was designing the systems that now pass laws automatically. Their fingerprints are on the growth of centralized welfare states, standardized education, global governance bodies, and the elevation of "experts" above elected representatives. Through careful institutional capture, they built the scaffolding of modern technocracy - a framework where elites manage populations through policy, economics, and information, while presenting these mechanisms as neutral and inevitable.

Unlike Marxists, the Fabians never declared war on the system. They became the system. And by the time the world noticed, it was already living inside the structures they had built.

The founding of the London School of Economics in 1895 was one of the Fabian Society's most strategic moves, a quiet coup disguised as philanthropy and intellectual progress. At first glance, the LSE appeared to be just another university - a place for research, discussion, and higher learning. In reality, it became the first deliberate academy for producing technocrats: a training ground where future policymakers, economists, and administrators would be taught to govern societies from above, armed with data, models, and theories framed as "scientific" truth.

Sidney and Beatrice Webb understood that to reshape a society, it wasn't enough to write manifestos or publish pamphlets; you had to train the people who would run its institutions. The LSE was designed from the outset as a pipeline into power. Its programs specialized in economics, public policy, and social administration - fields that positioned its graduates to control the machinery of government and global finance. Students weren't just educated; they were inculcated with Fabian principles, even when they didn't identify as Fabians. They learned to view governance not as a political struggle between competing values but as a technical challenge requiring "expert solutions" grounded in data and social engineering.

Funding for the LSE came from Henry Hutchinson, a wealthy Fabian sympathizer whose bequest the Webbs used to seed their vision. That vision extended beyond Britain. From the start, the LSE recruited students from across the British Empire and Europe, consciously building an international network of elites who would carry Fabian-influenced methods back to their home countries. Graduates moved seamlessly into positions of influence: central banks, colonial administrations, ministries, and later into emerging international organizations like the League of Nations and, eventually, the United Nations. The result was a self-reinforcing ecosystem: LSE-trained technocrats staffed the very institutions designed to expand centralized governance, embedding the Fabian worldview into their structures and policies.

The school's curriculum reflected its ideological purpose. Economics was taught not as a pluralistic field with competing schools of thought but as a managerial science, with an emphasis on quantification, planning, and top-down coordination. Public policy courses approached society as something to be optimized, broken into components - health, education, welfare, labor - each governed by centralized expertise rather than local autonomy. Students were conditioned to see democracy as cumbersome and inefficient, an outdated system incapable of addressing the complexities of industrial economies and global interdependence. By the time they left the LSE, many graduates had internalized the Fabian view: that rational governance required data-driven technocratic elites managing populations "for their own good."

The success of this model didn't remain confined to Britain. As the 20th century unfolded, the LSE became a global hub for producing architects of centralized governance. Leaders from across Europe, Asia, Africa, and the Americas came through its halls, returning home to influence everything from tax systems and social programs to international trade agreements. Through its graduates, the LSE became one of the primary feeders of personnel into the World Bank, the IMF, UNESCO, and other international bodies - institutions that now dictate policy frameworks for entire nations. This wasn't incidental; it was the realization of the Fabian strategy on a planetary scale: change the people who make the rules, and you change the system itself.

Crucially, the Fabian takeover of the LSE normalized the idea that policy should be based on "scientific expertise" rather than democratic input. By elevating technocrats above elected officials, the school helped reframe governance as an administrative problem solved by experts, rather than a social contract negotiated by citizens. This subtle shift reoriented political power away from public accountability and toward elite-managed systems where authority flows through universities, think tanks, and global institutions rather than parliaments or assemblies.

What makes the LSE so significant is not just what it taught, but who it trained and where they went. Its graduates designed welfare systems in Britain, shaped labor laws in Europe, advised on financial reforms across Asia and Africa, and staffed the growing lattice of international governance. Each graduate carried forward the Fabian model, often unconsciously: a belief in central planning, standardized education, managed economies, and expert-led social policy. Over time, this created a global network of like-minded elites, united less by ideology than by training - but aligned nonetheless in building a world where "scientific governance" overrides local, cultural, and democratic decision-making.

The LSE was never just a school. It was an experiment in manufacturing consent, a quiet factory producing the first generation of administrators for an emerging global technocracy. The Fabian Society didn't need to overthrow governments to gain control; it trained the people who would become the governments. The success of the LSE model spawned imitators worldwide - Harvard's Kennedy School, Sciences Po in Paris, the Hertie School in Berlin - each building on the same formula: produce a managerial class fluent in the language of efficiency and global coordination, and feed them directly into the structures that decide how billions live.

What began as a Fabian project has grown into a network of technocrat academies influencing policy on a scale far beyond anything Sidney and Beatrice Webb could have imagined. But the principle remains the same: train the experts, and you control the systems. The LSE was the prototype - the place where Fabian gradualism became institutionalized, where ideology disguised itself as neutrality, and where the modern administrative elite was born.

PART II - THE BIRTH OF TECHNOCRACY INC. 1920-1945

Organizing the first technocratic movements.

6

Howard Scott and the Energy Economy

In the early 1930s, as the Great Depression gripped the United States and the capitalist order seemed to be unraveling, a radical new vision emerged from the halls of Columbia University - a vision that would attempt to redefine governance, economics, and social control entirely. It was called Technocracy Inc., founded in 1933 by Howard Scott and M. King Hubbert, and it was the first organized movement to propose replacing politics, money, and markets with a system of purely scientific administration.

At its core, Technocracy Inc. argued that the traditional mechanisms of governance - elections, legislation, even capitalism itself - were obsolete in an industrial society powered by science and technology. Parliaments, parties, and political ideologies were seen as inefficient relics incapable of managing the complexity of modern life. Instead, technocrats proposed that society be reorganized along engineering principles. Decisions about energy, production, and distribution would be handled not by elected officials or businessmen, but by scientists, engineers, and data analysts who could rationally manage resources to meet human needs without waste or competition.

The founders of Technocracy Inc. were not fringe figures. Howard Scott, an engineer and charismatic speaker, provided the movement's rhetoric and vision, while M. King Hubbert - later famous for formulating "peak oil theory" - supplied its scientific credibility. Columbia University, under its progressive president Nicholas Murray Butler, briefly served as the headquarters for this audacious project. Backed by intellectuals and industrial researchers, the technocrats imagined designing a completely new continental operating system for North America, abandoning the old economic order altogether.

Their plan was revolutionary: abolish the price-based economy and replace it with an energy-based accounting system. Instead of measuring wealth in dollars, technocrats proposed measuring it in joules or ergs - units of energy consumed and produced. Every citizen would receive a share of society's total energy budget, calculated scientifically based on available resources and technological capacity. Goods and services would no longer have prices determined by markets but would be allocated according to "energy cost" within a centrally managed system. This wasn't socialism in the Marxist sense, nor capitalism as it existed; it was something entirely new - a planned society administered by engineers using real-time data to balance production, consumption, and population.

Technocracy Inc. envisioned the continent divided into functional regions called "Technates," where industries, infrastructure, and populations would be optimized according to energy flows rather than political borders. Rail networks, power grids, and manufacturing systems would be reorganized to maximize efficiency, while "scientific managers" would oversee allocation down to the smallest detail. The human workforce, too, would be managed like a resource: trained, placed, and rotated where needed according to statistical models of productivity and demand. In theory, scarcity would be eliminated, and abundance would be distributed rationally.

For a brief moment, the movement captured public imagination. Amid the chaos of the Depression, when unemployment soared and faith in democratic capitalism faltered, Technocracy Inc. offered a seductive promise: a world without boom-and-bust cycles, political corruption, or corporate monopolies. Columbia University became the nerve center of this vision, hosting lectures, publishing research papers, and attracting thousands of adherents across the country. Technocracy journals and pamphlets spread the idea of a post-monetary society managed by experts, and Howard Scott's charismatic presentations drew large crowds eager for solutions to the economic crisis.

But the movement's radicalism alarmed both government and industry. The idea of replacing money with energy credits, abolishing private ownership of production, and bypassing elected officials triggered backlash from corporate elites and policymakers alike. In 1933, under growing political pressure, Columbia University distanced itself from Scott and dissolved its formal ties to Technocracy Inc. Without the institutional backing of Columbia's prestige, the movement quickly lost momentum. Internal conflicts further fractured its leadership, and by the late 1930s, Technocracy Inc. had faded from mainstream discourse, surviving only as a niche organization.

Yet the ideas didn't die. Technocracy Inc. planted seeds that grew into the foundations of modern technocratic governance. Its vision of replacing monetary economics with energy-based metrics anticipated today's obsession with carbon accounting, ESG frameworks, and algorithmic resource management. Its call for replacing politics with "scientific administration" foreshadowed the rise of unelected regulatory agencies, global coordination bodies, and data-driven policy frameworks. Even its dream of regional "Technates" can be seen echoed in supranational structures like the European Union, where energy markets, manufacturing standards, and population policies are managed centrally by experts far removed from public accountability.

M. King Hubbert's later career provides the clearest proof of technocracy's survival through institutional absorption. After the collapse of Technocracy Inc., Hubbert went on to work at Shell and became a leading figure in energy policy, influencing everything from petroleum economics to government forecasting. The managerial systems envisioned by Technocracy Inc. migrated into government agencies, think tanks, and universities - fragmenting into specialized disciplines like industrial engineering, systems theory, and operations research. In effect, the movement's philosophy was quietly dissolved into existing institutions rather than eliminated.

Technocracy Inc. failed as a mass political movement but succeeded as a paradigm shift. It normalized the idea that experts, not voters, should manage society. The dream of an energy-based economy never materialized directly, but its logic has reemerged in data-driven governance, real-time resource modeling, and automated control systems that now dictate vast areas of modern life. The same Columbia campus where Howard Scott preached the end of politics is today a hub for global policy training, feeding graduates into international agencies and financial institutions - the very technocratic elite Technocracy Inc. once imagined leading openly.

What began in the early 1930s as a bold attempt to reorganize civilization without markets or politics became something more subtle and enduring. While the organization faded, its principles survived by blending into the very infrastructures of governance. In a sense, Technocracy Inc. achieved its goal - not through revolution, but through absorption. The engineers, economists, and systems planners it inspired now operate inside governments, global banks, and transnational organizations, managing populations and resources according to models that would be instantly recognizable to Howard Scott and M. King Hubbert.

The Columbia experiment didn't fail. It succeeded quietly - not by creating a visible technate, but by embedding technocratic logic into the foundations of the modern administrative state.

Howard Scott was the unlikely, charismatic, and deeply polarizing figure at the center of Technocracy Inc. - a man who transformed himself from an obscure engineer into the ideological leader of one of the most radical social experiments of the 20th century. Neither a polished academic nor a political insider, Scott embodied a uniquely American archetype: the renegade visionary convinced he could redesign civilization from the ground up. For a brief moment in the early 1930s, as the Great Depression shattered faith in both capitalism and democracy, Scott's ideas captured the imagination of thousands, challenging the very foundations of governance, economics, and social organization.

Scott's background was unconventional, and his credentials were, at best, self-styled. Born in 1890, he drifted through various engineering jobs without formal recognition from elite institutions. But what he lacked in pedigree, he compensated for with ambition and conviction. Scott viewed industrial civilization as a vast, inefficient machine run by unqualified operators - politicians, financiers, and business leaders - who clung to outdated systems of governance and economics. His radical premise was simple but profound: the modern world had outgrown politics, markets, and ideology. The only way forward was to reorganize society on scientific and engineering principles.

In 1919, Scott co-founded the Technical Alliance, a precursor to Technocracy Inc., gathering a small network of engineers, scientists, and industrial researchers to study energy consumption and production across North America. Their aim was nothing less than to map the entire economic system in technical terms - measuring efficiency, waste, and capacity in joules rather than dollars. Scott believed that energy, not money, was the true basis of value, and that a society's resources could be managed far more effectively by engineers than by bankers or politicians.

By the early 1930s, Scott's ideas coalesced into Technocracy Inc., formally launched in 1933 at Columbia University alongside geophysicist M. King Hubbert. With Columbia briefly serving as its headquarters, the movement gained instant credibility and momentum. Scott's charisma made him its natural spokesperson. He spoke confidently about a future where political parties, legislative debates, and financial markets would be obsolete. In their place would be a continental "technate" - a scientifically managed system where production, distribution, and population flows were optimized according to energy budgets calculated in real time.

Scott envisioned replacing the price system - the foundation of capitalism - with an energy-based accounting system. Every citizen would receive "energy certificates" representing their share of society's productive capacity. These certificates, issued directly by the technate, would replace money entirely, eliminating profit motives, speculation, and what Scott saw as the inefficiencies of market competition. Consumption, production, and population levels would be balanced through continuous data collection and centralized oversight, ensuring neither scarcity nor waste.

For a time, Scott's vision resonated. Amid widespread unemployment, collapsing markets, and failing banks, Technocracy Inc. attracted tens of thousands of members and widespread media attention. Its publications circulated nationally, and Scott's lectures at Columbia drew standing-room crowds. The movement promised something no political party or financial institution could: a clean break from chaos and inequality, managed rationally by experts rather than corrupted politicians or self-serving elites.

But Scott himself became both the movement's driving force and its greatest liability. Charismatic but volatile, he clashed constantly with colleagues and critics alike. He dismissed academics as too timid, politicians as inherently corrupt, and financiers as parasitic. His contempt for established authority made him an appealing figure to frustrated engineers and disillusioned citizens, but it alienated Columbia's leadership and powerful industrial backers. By late 1933, mounting pressure from government officials and business interests forced Columbia to distance itself from Technocracy Inc., stripping the movement of institutional legitimacy almost overnight.

Scott doubled down rather than compromise. He insisted that political institutions were doomed to fail and that his energy-based model was the only viable path forward. But without Columbia's prestige or funding, the movement fractured internally. Scientists like M. King Hubbert drifted into mainstream energy policy roles, while Scott remained committed to building a dedicated technocratic movement, holding rallies, publishing journals, and delivering fiery speeches well into the 1940s. His critics portrayed him as a crank; his supporters saw him as a prophet.

Though Technocracy Inc. eventually faded from public attention, Scott's core ideas survived by seeping quietly into institutional frameworks. Concepts pioneered under his leadership - energy audits, systems analysis, resource accounting, and the idea of measuring economies by technical efficiency rather than price - migrated into government agencies, academic disciplines, and corporate strategy. Even his radical proposal of energy-based "credits" foreshadowed later developments in carbon accounting, ESG compliance frameworks, and data-driven resource management.

Scott himself remained largely outside the mainstream until his death in 1970, never achieving the open technocratic revolution he envisioned. But his impact was indirect and enduring. While Technocracy Inc. collapsed as a mass movement, its logic - the belief that society should be managed by technical experts using real-time data and scientific planning - was absorbed into universities, think tanks, and government institutions. The dream of an openly governed technate was replaced by a quieter reality: a world increasingly run by systems Scott would have recognized as his own, just hidden under the language of progress, sustainability, and efficiency.

Howard Scott's story is one of ambition meeting resistance, of radical vision colliding with entrenched power, but also of ideas too potent to disappear. He failed to seize control, but his framework survived him. Today's automated resource tracking, algorithmic policy models, and centralized infrastructures for managing energy and production all trace intellectual roots back to the technocratic manifesto Scott carried into Columbia's halls in 1933.

Scott wanted to build a new civilization run by engineers. In a way, he got his wish - just not in the open.

M. King Hubbert stood at the crossroads between two eras: the collapse of Technocracy Inc. as a mass movement and the quiet absorption of its ideas into mainstream governance, economics, and energy policy. Where Howard Scott was a volatile visionary, Hubbert was the scientist

- calm, methodical, and credible enough to carry technocratic concepts into institutions that Scott could never penetrate. Trained as a geophysicist, Hubbert became the intellectual backbone of Technocracy Inc., and even after the organization faded from prominence, his theories laid the groundwork for how energy, economics, and governance would intertwine for the rest of the 20th century and beyond.

When Hubbert joined Technocracy Inc. in the early 1930s, he brought with him the analytical rigor Scott lacked. While Scott delivered fiery speeches about ending politics and money, Hubbert built the technical framework to make that vision seem feasible. At Columbia University, where Technocracy Inc. briefly operated, Hubbert helped organize vast studies of North America's energy resources and industrial capacities, mapping the continent as if it were a single integrated machine. He believed that society's real wealth was not money or capital but energy - the capacity to transform resources into goods and services. Dollars, in his view, were abstractions; energy was reality.

From this premise came one of the most radical concepts Technocracy Inc. ever proposed: the replacement of money with an "energy certificate" currency. Hubbert argued that the inefficiencies of the "price system" - profits, speculation, and artificial scarcity - distorted economic reality and caused instability. His solution was to calculate the continent's total energy production capacity, divide it by the population, and issue every citizen an equal allotment of "energy credits" measured in joules or ergs. These credits would expire after a fixed period, preventing hoarding or accumulation, and could only be spent on goods and services whose energy costs were already known and accounted for.

This wasn't socialism as Marx envisioned it, nor capitalism as Wall Street practiced it. It was something more radical: a technate economy where consumption, production, and population were balanced scientifically in real time. Decisions about resource allocation wouldn't flow through markets or parliaments but through engineers, statisticians, and system managers overseeing the energy flows of an entire continent. Hubbert's vision was a closed-loop system: no profit motive, no class hierarchy, no scarcity beyond natural limits, and no economic crises because the system would never "overproduce" or "underdemand." In theory, it was utopian efficiency; in practice, it required replacing political democracy and financial markets with an administrative state run by technical elites.

Technocracy Inc. collapsed publicly in the mid-1930s under mounting political pressure and Howard Scott's abrasive leadership, but Hubbert didn't disappear. He left the movement quietly and went on to a distinguished career in mainstream science, working first at Columbia and later at Shell Oil as a senior geologist. It was here, in 1956, that he unveiled the theory that made him famous: peak oil.

Hubbert's peak oil model predicted that petroleum production in any given region would follow a bell-shaped curve: rapid growth, leveling off, and eventual decline as finite reserves were exhausted. He argued that U.S. oil production would peak around 1970 - a prediction mocked at the time but proven stunningly accurate. By the early 1970s, American oil output plateaued and began to fall, just as Hubbert forecasted. His work reshaped global energy policy, forcing governments and corporations to confront resource limits more seriously.

But peak oil was more than geology. Beneath the technical model lay the same technocratic philosophy Hubbert had developed with Scott decades earlier: energy, not money, was the true basis of economic reality. If energy supplies determined industrial capacity, then managing those supplies - and planning consumption accordingly - became the most critical function of governance. Peak oil forced policymakers to think less like politicians and more like system managers. Behind closed doors, institutions like the Department of Energy, the International Energy Agency, and global financial bodies began integrating Hubbert's logic into their planning frameworks.

Hubbert never returned publicly to the energy-certificate idea, but its influence never disappeared. The notion of pegging economic systems to measurable energy capacity quietly migrated into sustainability metrics, carbon accounting, and resource-based modeling. Today's obsession with tracking energy footprints, greenhouse gas emissions, and "sustainable consumption" echoes Hubbert's early technocratic vision. The idea that populations must align their economic activity with ecological limits - and that experts must manage this alignment - is a direct descendant of the Columbia-era studies he helped design.

Hubbert's legacy lives in another way: the gradual erosion of monetary sovereignty in favor of resource-based governance. While Technocracy Inc.'s dream of abolishing money failed, energy has steadily moved closer to the center of economic and political planning. Institutions now track global energy capacity and consumption with near-constant precision, using these figures to guide industrial policy, taxation, and infrastructure development. Concepts like carbon credits and ESG-compliance frameworks are modern analogues to Hubbert's energy certificates, linking access to goods and services with resource management at a systemic level. What Technocracy Inc. proposed in the 1930s has, in many ways, become the operating logic of 21st-century sustainability regimes - only implemented piecemeal, quietly, and without the revolutionary rhetoric.

Unlike Howard Scott, Hubbert lacked the messianic flair, and that's why his ideas survived. He moved comfortably between corporate, academic, and government spheres, framing technocratic principles not as ideology but as neutral science. In doing so, he helped normalize the concept that society could - and should - be managed through continuous measurement, modeling, and adjustment, overseen by technical experts rather than elected politicians. While the name "Technocracy Inc." faded into obscurity, the systems Hubbert pioneered became embedded inside the very institutions that dismissed Scott as a crank.

Hubbert died in 1989, remembered publicly as the man who foresaw peak oil but privately revered in certain policy and engineering circles as one of the architects of modern resource governance. His proposals for energy-based accounting and scientific management of society never vanished; they were simply absorbed into the sprawling machinery of administrative technocracy. What was once a radical Columbia manifesto now operates invisibly, guiding policies through data dashboards, global energy reports, and climate planning frameworks that few citizens understand but all are governed by.

M. King Hubbert never built the technate he once imagined. Instead, he helped create something subtler and far more enduring: a world where energy, not democracy, dictates policy, and where unelected experts quietly manage the flows of resources, consumption, and, increasingly, behavior itself.

In the 1930s, the founders of Technocracy Inc. proposed one of the most radical ideas in modern economic history: replacing money entirely with a system of "energy quotas" - a precursor to what we would now recognize as programmable currency. At the height of the Great Depression, Howard Scott, M. King Hubbert, and their Columbia University circle argued that the price-based economy had become obsolete. Markets, profits, and speculation, they believed, were artificial constructs that distorted reality and created unnecessary scarcity. For a society running on industrial technology and abundant energy, they argued, money was no longer an effective medium of value or control.

Instead, they envisioned a technate economy where all production, consumption, and resource allocation would be measured, tracked, and distributed according to energy flows. The logic was simple but revolutionary: in a modern industrial civilization, everything - from manufacturing and transportation to food production and labor - ultimately boils down to energy inputs and outputs. Therefore, the only rational way to govern an advanced society was to manage it directly in those terms.

Under this model, dollars, wages, and prices would be abolished. Every citizen within the technate would receive an energy quota: a set number of "energy credits" representing their share of the continent's productive capacity, calculated in joules or ergs. Unlike money, these credits would not accumulate or compound. They would expire after a fixed period, ensuring a constant circulation of resources and preventing wealth hoarding or speculation. Goods and services would carry energy "prices," but these would not fluctuate based on supply and demand. Instead, they would be calculated scientifically based on the exact energy required to produce and deliver them.

In effect, the technate's accounting system would become an automated ledger, constantly balancing inputs and outputs across an entire continental economy. Energy production data, industrial capacity, population numbers, and consumption patterns would all be fed into a central database - a precursor to modern real-time data systems. The goal was absolute equilibrium: every citizen would have access to their share of resources, production would be matched precisely to demand, and waste would be eliminated through constant monitoring and recalibration.

This concept foreshadowed the programmable currencies emerging nearly a century later. Technocracy Inc.'s energy credits had three defining characteristics now mirrored in today's central bank digital currency (CBDC) designs:

1.   Programmability - Credits could be issued with strict usage constraints, limiting how, where, and when they could be spent.

2.   Expiration - Quotas were time-limited, ensuring no long-term accumulation of private wealth or deviation from planned consumption targets.

3.   Total traceability - Every transaction, every resource allocation, every movement of goods and people would be recorded and audited in real time.

At the time, the necessary infrastructure for this system didn't exist. Computing power was primitive, data collection was slow, and energy systems lacked the interconnectedness needed to manage an entire continent as a single coordinated machine. But the principle was in place: replace free-market dynamics with algorithmic governance, using technical data rather than political debate to decide what gets produced, who consumes it, and when.

Hubbert, the movement's chief technical architect, framed the system as neutral science. By removing money and markets, he argued, you also removed inequality, corruption, and political manipulation. But the reality was more complex. In eliminating markets, the technate would also eliminate choice. Citizens would no longer decide what to buy based on personal preference or price signals; their consumption would be optimized according to models designed by engineers and systems planners. Autonomy would be subordinated to efficiency, and participation in the economy would require integration into a vast data-driven apparatus controlling both production and behavior.

Even though Technocracy Inc. collapsed publicly by the late 1930s, its core ideas quietly survived and migrated into modern policy frameworks. The energy-quota model foreshadowed the logic behind carbon accounting, ESG compliance, and resource-based planning - where consumption rights are tethered to ecological limits and managed by centralized authorities. Today's emerging discussions about carbon credits and personal consumption caps echo the technocratic proposal almost directly: allocate energy or resource quotas per person, enforce compliance digitally, and link access to goods and services to your tracked "footprint."

The technological constraints that doomed the 1930s vision have largely disappeared. With the rise of digital identity systems, real-time energy monitoring, and networked payment infrastructures, the architecture for a fully programmable, centrally controlled currency now exists. Central banks worldwide are piloting digital currencies with the capacity to restrict spending, set expiration dates, and enforce behavioral incentives - precisely the kind of automated system envisioned by Scott and Hubbert, but powered by modern computing and global data integration.

In hindsight, Technocracy Inc. was less a failed movement than an early prototype. The energy quotas they imagined have reemerged under new names and in new contexts, embedded within sustainability policies, international climate agreements, and experimental CBDCs. Where Scott and Hubbert dreamed of managing consumption through centralized science, modern systems achieve similar results quietly, hidden beneath layers of "green economics," "resource management," and "digital innovation."

The promise, then as now, is efficiency and fairness. The reality is total oversight: a system where economic participation depends on integration into a programmable, data-driven framework controlling not just what we consume but how, when, and why. Technocracy Inc.'s energy quotas were supposed to liberate humanity from the chaos of markets. In practice, they opened the door to a future where access to resources, mobility, and even personal freedom can be throttled by the algorithms that administer them.

The difference is that in the 1930s, this system was still theoretical. Now, it's becoming operational.

7

The Great Depression and
Corporate Integration

The rise of technocracy in the United States during the early 20th century was inseparable from crisis. The Great Depression shattered faith in both laissez-faire capitalism and political leadership, creating a vacuum that engineers, scientists, and industrial planners rushed to fill. As unemployment soared, banks failed, and markets collapsed, a growing movement of technical experts began to argue that the chaos was not merely economic but systemic - and that the solution was to replace politics with planning.

This was the moment when technocracy stepped out of theory and into strategy. Figures like Howard Scott and M. King Hubbert at Columbia University were already promoting the idea that advanced industrial societies could no longer afford to be governed by elections, parties, or profit motives. To them, politicians were unqualified to manage complex technological systems, and financiers were parasites manipulating scarcity for personal gain. What was needed, they argued, was a planned economy, managed like a giant machine, where production and consumption were calibrated scientifically against available energy and resources.

Technocracy Inc., formally launched in 1933, embodied this new approach. Its founders proposed a complete restructuring of society into a technate - a continental system governed not by political leaders but by engineers and technical managers. They envisioned dismantling the "price system" entirely and replacing it with energy-based accounting. Rather than dollars, wages, and markets, citizens would be issued energy credits pegged to actual resource availability, while production would be optimized according to continental planning models.

These ideas resonated far beyond Columbia's campus. Across industry and government, elites faced an urgent problem: the old system wasn't working. Massive unemployment, industrial overcapacity, and collapsing trade threatened to destabilize the social order, and faith in Washington's ability to manage the crisis was dwindling. Suddenly, the proposals of engineers, economists, and industrial scientists - once fringe concepts - gained traction among influential corporate leaders and policymakers searching for alternatives.

This convergence became most visible during the New Deal era, when corporate boards, government agencies, and academic institutions began merging their efforts in ways previously unthinkable. Federal planning agencies like the National Recovery Administration (NRA), the Tennessee Valley Authority (TVA), and the Public Works Administration (PWA) brought engineers directly into policymaking roles, giving them unprecedented influence over industrial coordination, infrastructure development, and resource allocation. Many of these programs were pitched as temporary responses to emergency conditions but in practice became laboratories for centralized economic management.

Corporate boards, meanwhile, increasingly aligned themselves with this shift. Facing financial collapse, industrial giants like General Electric, U.S. Steel, and Standard Oil began collaborating with federal planners to stabilize production and reorganize markets. Executives sat on government commissions and advisory panels, helping draft the very regulations that governed their industries. The boundary between public and private power blurred as corporate interests and federal planning agencies merged into a single administrative structure.

Universities also played a central role, providing both the intellectual framework and the data needed to justify technocratic reforms. Columbia University, MIT, and Harvard became hubs where engineers, economists, and policymakers designed models for rationalizing entire sectors of the economy. These studies aimed to measure everything - energy flows, production capacities, labor distribution, and resource consumption - with the goal of building systems that could be managed scientifically rather than politically.

Technocracy's rise during this period was not accidental; it was enabled by crisis. When traditional governance fails, populations become receptive to expert rule. Politicians leaned heavily on engineers to rebuild trust and demonstrate competence, framing technical expertise as neutral and objective - above ideology, above partisanship. In reality, this new administrative class was anything but neutral. Engineers and corporate managers shared control over the levers of production, while policymakers deferred to "scientific necessity" to bypass democratic debate. Even as Technocracy Inc. as an organization lost mainstream credibility after its fallout with Columbia in 1933, its ideas survived by being absorbed into the New Deal's expanding bureaucracy and corporate-state partnerships. Planned economies became normalized, not through a formal technocratic revolution but through institutional integration. Engineers moved from designing machines to designing markets. Economists stopped simply studying prices and started creating them. Corporate boards became extensions of federal planning, while government agencies increasingly functioned like managerial boards directing national output.

This period marked a permanent shift in American governance: the slow migration from representative democracy to administrative technocracy. By embedding engineers and corporate elites into policymaking structures, the state effectively outsourced sovereignty to systems designed to optimize efficiency rather than reflect public will. It was never presented as ideology; it was framed as problem-solving. But the outcome was profound: governance itself began functioning like an engineering project, where populations became inputs, outputs, and variables in a controlled model of production and consumption.

The convergence of government, corporate power, and technical expertise during this period set the stage for the technocratic systems we live under today. Energy grids, transportation networks, financial flows, and information systems are now managed as interdependent infrastructures overseen by experts insulated from direct accountability. What began as an emergency response during the Depression became the operating logic of modern governance: crises justify centralization, and centralization never fully recedes.

In the 1930s, engineers argued that planned economies were necessary to stabilize a collapsing system. Today, the same logic has returned - only with far greater tools for control. Digital monitoring, algorithmic planning, and global data integration have made possible what Scott and Hubbert could only theorize: continuous, real-time management of resources, populations, and behavior at continental scale. Where corporate boards once merged with federal planning agencies, we now see public-private governance operating seamlessly through central banks, climate frameworks, and transnational regulatory bodies.

Technocracy didn't seize power through revolution. It entered quietly, during a moment of systemic failure, promising stability and efficiency. And when the crisis passed, the structures remained.

Franklin D. Roosevelt's New Deal was sold to the American public as an emergency rescue mission - a bold intervention to stabilize the economy, restore jobs, and protect ordinary citizens from the devastation of the Great Depression. But beneath the rhetoric of relief and recovery, the New Deal marked the single most significant centralization of power in U.S. history up to that point. It permanently transformed the relationship between government, corporations, and the individual, laying the foundation for an administrative state where technocratic control became the default operating mode.

When Roosevelt took office in 1933, the country was collapsing. One-quarter of the workforce was unemployed. Banks were failing in waves. Agricultural prices had crashed. Confidence in capitalism - and in Washington - was evaporating. Roosevelt's genius wasn't just his ability to craft policy; it was his ability to frame centralization as salvation. He understood that a crisis creates the political permission to reorganize systems rapidly, and he used the shock of the Depression to build a new kind of governance - one where executive agencies, corporate boards, and academic planners worked together to manage the economy at scale. At the heart of this transformation was the National Industrial Recovery Act (NIRA) of 1933, which established the National Recovery Administration (NRA). For the first time, Washington openly partnered with industry leaders to set prices, wages, and production quotas across entire sectors of the economy. In effect, the NRA created industry-wide cartels sanctioned by the federal government, where corporate executives sat alongside bureaucrats to decide how markets would function. The line between public policy and private interest blurred almost completely. Instead of competition driving innovation, industry "codes of fair practice" enforced cooperation under centralized oversight.

To Roosevelt's critics, this was the quiet birth of corporate technocracy. Power flowed upward, away from local communities and state governments, into a dense network of Washington agencies staffed by lawyers, economists, and engineers. Corporations received legal protections in exchange for surrendering some autonomy to federal planners, while labor unions gained government recognition to enforce workplace standards. The result was a managed economy - neither fully capitalist nor socialist, but something new: a partnership between political authority, corporate infrastructure, and technical expertise designed to stabilize society from the top down.

Roosevelt expanded this model across multiple domains. Through the Tennessee Valley Authority (TVA), the federal government took direct control of regional energy production, water management, and infrastructure, constructing dams, power plants, and planned communities to "modernize" entire regions. Agencies like the Public Works Administration (PWA) and the Works Progress Administration (WPA) coordinated massive construction projects, while the Securities and Exchange Commission (SEC) centralized financial regulation under federal authority. Each of these programs built new bureaucracies staffed with specialists - engineers, planners, statisticians, economists - whose decisions increasingly bypassed both Congress and state legislatures.

This wasn't presented as ideology; it was framed as necessity. Roosevelt carefully cultivated the image of technocratic neutrality, describing his programs as evidence-based, pragmatic, and above politics. But in practice, the New Deal embedded a permanent layer of unelected power into the machinery of governance. Decisions once made through markets, town halls, or legislatures were increasingly handled by experts operating within executive agencies. Congress authorized the creation of these structures but rarely dictated their operation, delegating unprecedented discretion to administrative bodies insulated from public accountability.

Universities became key partners in this centralization, supplying the data and personnel needed to design and justify federal planning. Columbia, Harvard, MIT, and the University of Chicago funneled economists and engineers into New Deal agencies, many of them trained in the emerging disciplines of systems analysis and industrial planning. These institutions framed centralized governance as "scientific management," giving Roosevelt intellectual cover to present his policies as rational solutions rather than political consolidation.

Corporate America, initially resistant, adapted quickly. Facing collapse, industrial giants saw cooperation with federal planning agencies as a survival strategy. Boards of directors sent executives to Washington to negotiate directly with regulators and agency heads, embedding corporate influence inside the administrative state from its inception. Through this fusion, corporate priorities became indistinguishable from federal priorities - and both were administered by a rising class of technocrats who treated economic management like an engineering problem.

The Supreme Court eventually struck down parts of the NRA and NIRA in 1935, ruling them unconstitutional. But by then, the structural transformation was complete. Dozens of federal agencies created under the New Deal survived, and the precedent of government-led industrial coordination remained. The administrative state had been born, and it proved highly resilient. Once authority is centralized, it rarely returns to the local level. The "temporary" measures of the 1930s became permanent fixtures of American governance.

This centralization didn't stop with Roosevelt's death in 1945; it expanded. The wartime mobilization of the 1940s deepened the merger between federal authority, corporate boards, and research universities. The Pentagon, Manhattan Project, and Office of Scientific Research and Development accelerated the technocratic model, embedding technical experts and industrialists inside national security planning. By the 1950s, Washington had become the permanent command center of a managed economy, sustained by vast bureaucracies and private-public partnerships that still define governance today.

The New Deal framed centralization as the antidote to chaos, but its deeper legacy was the normalization of technocracy. It embedded federal planning into every domain - finance, agriculture, infrastructure, labor, energy - and conditioned Americans to accept unelected agencies and corporate boards as legitimate decision-makers. Political debates increasingly became procedural theater, while real power shifted into the administrative machinery beneath it.

Roosevelt didn't just rescue the system; he reprogrammed it. The federal government became the coordinating hub of a new model where political authority, corporate resources, and technical expertise converged. The result was a hybrid structure: part state, part corporation, part engineering lab. While it began as an emergency response, it evolved into the operating system of modern governance.

Technocracy did not arrive as a coup; it emerged quietly through the New Deal, legitimized by crisis and cemented by policy. The American people were promised recovery, and they got management. But in the process, they ceded sovereignty to a permanent administrative apparatus whose influence only deepened with each subsequent emergency.

In the early 1930s, at the height of the Great Depression, Columbia University briefly became ground zero for one of the most ambitious experiments in the history of economic thought: the Technocracy Study.

Led by Howard Scott, M. King Hubbert, and a team of engineers, physicists, and industrial planners, this project attempted something no one had ever tried before - to model an entire continental economy not in dollars or markets, but in energy flows, using data, mathematics, and early systems thinking. It was, in many ways, the first attempt at an algorithmic economic model - decades before computing power existed to make such visions fully operational.

The central premise was simple but revolutionary: the real economy isn't financial; it's thermodynamic. Every industrial process, every agricultural output, every human activity can ultimately be measured in terms of energy input and energy output. To Scott and Hubbert, prices were abstractions manipulated by bankers and politicians, whereas energy was a constant, objective reality. If you understood a society's total energy capacity - its hydroelectric plants, coal fields, oil reserves, and industrial efficiency - you could model production and consumption with scientific precision. And if you could model it, you could manage it.

The Columbia team set out to do just that. Between 1931 and 1933, they undertook an unprecedented data-gathering project to map every significant industrial process across North America. They collected figures on power generation, transportation networks, manufacturing capacities, agricultural yields, raw material reserves, labor productivity, and population distribution. The scale was staggering. Hundreds of researchers compiled data from railroads, utility companies, mines, and factories, feeding it into elaborate charts, tables, and cross-referenced calculations - an attempt to quantify the energy metabolism of an entire continent.

Hubbert, a geophysicist, was the project's analytical mind. He developed mathematical models linking energy inputs to industrial outputs, calculating optimal production levels, and projecting resource depletion rates decades ahead. He believed that by understanding the energy budget of North America, engineers could design a balanced system where production matched consumption precisely, waste was minimized, and scarcity was effectively eliminated. In practice, this would mean dismantling the "price system" entirely and replacing it with a resource-based accounting model that allocated goods and services according to scientifically calculated quotas.

What the Columbia team proposed was nothing less than a technate: a continent-wide system managed by scientists and engineers, bypassing politicians and financiers entirely. Economic planning would no longer be based on speculation, profits, or ideology but on real-time measurement of energy flows and material capacities. Citizens would be issued energy "certificates" representing their share of available resources, while industrial output would be calibrated continuously according to demand and energy efficiency. For Scott and Hubbert, the ultimate goal was equilibrium - a self-correcting system where the economy operated like a finely tuned machine, free from boom-and-bust cycles, inflation, and unemployment.

The Columbia Technocracy Study was decades ahead of its time. Though computing power was primitive, the team effectively designed an early form of algorithmic governance. Their massive ledgers and tables foreshadowed what modern economists now do with AI-driven modeling, real-time data analytics, and predictive simulations. They imagined a system where continuous measurement of energy, production, and consumption would feed back into automated controls, dynamically adjusting output and distribution based on resource availability and demand. In concept, it anticipated the logic of smart grids, dynamic pricing algorithms, and central bank digital currencies almost a century before the technology existed to implement them.

But the project faced immediate backlash. The idea of replacing money with energy quotas and sidelining political institutions alarmed both Washington and Wall Street. Corporate interests viewed it as a threat to private ownership and profit, while government officials feared the erosion of political sovereignty. In 1933, under mounting pressure, Columbia University distanced itself from Howard Scott and formally severed ties with Technocracy Inc. The study was shut down before its findings could be fully published.

Despite its abrupt end, the Columbia project left an enduring mark. M. King Hubbert carried its energy-based framework into his later career, where it shaped his famous peak oil theory and influenced federal energy policy for decades. The methods pioneered by the study - resource audits, systems modeling, and energy-based metrics - became foundational tools for governments, corporations, and think tanks managing industrial economies. Today's ESG frameworks, carbon accounting systems, and sustainability indexes are direct descendants of the Columbia experiment, translating environmental and resource data into policy-driven allocation systems.

More importantly, the Technocracy Study anticipated a fundamental shift in governance: the replacement of political decision-making with algorithmic management. Where Scott and Hubbert envisioned engineers crunching numbers by hand, we now have automated systems doing so in real time, shaping markets, consumption, and even individual behavior. From dynamic energy pricing to climate quotas, modern policy increasingly mirrors the Columbia vision: track every input, measure every output, and control the entire system through continuous feedback loops.

What began at Columbia was the first serious attempt to reduce society to code. It was the prototype for today's algorithmic technocracy, where datasets replace debates and engineers - aided by machines - decide how resources are produced, distributed, and consumed. The original experiment failed publicly, but its logic quietly embedded itself into the infrastructures of modern governance. In a sense, the Columbia study succeeded not by building a technate, but by designing the mental framework for one.

The 1930s were a crucible - a decade when economic collapse shattered old systems and created the perfect conditions for elite consolidation on a scale the United States had never seen. The Great Depression wasn't just a financial crisis; it was a systemic breakdown that delegitimized existing institutions and opened the door for new structures of control. As unemployment surged, banks failed, and families lost everything, the vacuum of authority was filled by an emerging alliance between federal agencies, corporate boards, and academic planners. The result was a permanent restructuring of power - one where economic governance shifted away from competitive markets and democratic processes and into the hands of unelected experts and private networks operating above public accountability.

When the stock market collapsed in October 1929, the immediate crisis was chaos - millions unemployed, businesses shuttered, and banks collapsing by the thousands. But for the ruling class, the crash wasn't just disaster; it was an opportunity. With faith in laissez-faire capitalism destroyed, the population became receptive to radical interventions previously unthinkable. Corporate leaders, federal officials, and university-trained economists moved quickly to establish frameworks that would centralize decision-making at the national level. They didn't see the Depression as a temporary disruption - they saw it as a catalyst for redesigning the economic system itself.

The National Industrial Recovery Act (NIRA) of 1933 was the first major turning point. It created the National Recovery Administration (NRA), where corporate executives sat side by side with federal planners to set prices, wages, and production quotas across entire sectors of the economy. For the first time, private business leaders were invited into the federal policymaking apparatus to dictate "fair competition codes" enforced under federal law. In practice, this legalized industry-wide cartels coordinated directly from Washington - ending the pretense of competitive markets in favor of top-down management.

But this wasn't just about stabilizing collapsing industries; it was about creating new networks of influence. Corporate boards gained unprecedented access to federal policy, embedding their priorities into emerging regulatory structures. At the same time, these agencies were staffed heavily by graduates from elite universities like Columbia, Harvard, and MIT - economists and engineers trained in emerging disciplines like operations research and systems planning. These weren't politicians; they were technocrats. Their mandate wasn't to represent voters but to optimize entire sectors of the economy as if they were machines.

The Depression also gave Wall Street new leverage over the state. As smaller banks failed, capital consolidated into the hands of the largest financial institutions, which emerged from the crisis stronger than ever. The Federal Reserve - dominated by banking elites - expanded its influence dramatically, centralizing control of credit and liquidity policy. For the first time, the Fed acted as the national guarantor of economic stability, using its authority to direct money flows in ways that reinforced the power of the largest firms aligned with federal recovery plans.

At the same time, research universities became critical nodes in this consolidation. Columbia University, already hosting Technocracy Inc.'s headquarters in the early 1930s, provided much of the intellectual and technical foundation for energy planning, systems management, and centralized economic modeling. The Columbia Technocracy Study - a massive project mapping energy flows, industrial capacity, and population data - laid the groundwork for what would later become algorithmic economic modeling. These early efforts foreshadowed the integration of data-driven resource management into federal planning, embedding technocratic thinking deep inside the administrative state.

Roosevelt's New Deal acted as the formal mechanism for this centralization, but it was driven by an informal alliance of elites who operated across public and private boundaries. Executives from General Electric, U.S. Steel, and Standard Oil sat on federal commissions that determined their industries' regulatory frameworks. University economists designed models that justified state intervention while securing lucrative federal research contracts for their institutions. Wall Street banks provided the financing, ensuring that capital flows aligned with the emerging federal-corporate agenda. Each sector reinforced the other, and all converged on a single outcome: decision-making migrated upward into smaller and smaller circles of influence.

The Depression didn't just normalize elite consolidation - it institutionalized it. Agencies created in the 1930s didn't disappear when the crisis ended; they became permanent fixtures of governance. The Securities and Exchange Commission (SEC), the Federal Deposit Insurance Corporation (FDIC), and other regulatory bodies created during this era embedded Wall Street-friendly frameworks into law while insulating their decision-making from public influence. Through the New Deal, the federal government became the central hub where corporate and academic elites could coordinate policy without meaningful oversight, establishing the administrative state that still dominates American governance today.

Meanwhile, the public was conditioned to accept this centralization as benevolent. With unemployment high and desperation widespread, federal planning was framed as neutral, scientific, and inevitable - a rescue mission led by experts, not ideology. But beneath the rhetoric of recovery, a quiet revolution had taken place: the mechanisms of power had shifted away from local governments, competitive markets, and legislative debate, and into the hands of interconnected networks of private and public elites.

By the end of the decade, this transformation was complete. The merger of federal authority, corporate infrastructure, and academic expertise had created a new governing architecture - one that bypassed traditional checks and balances in favor of a technocratic model operating through data, regulation, and centralized coordination. The Great Depression did not just trigger temporary reforms; it accelerated the birth of a system where control over money, industry, and policy became structurally integrated.

That system never receded. It evolved quietly, embedding technocratic logic into the very foundations of economic governance. Decisions about energy allocation, industrial policy, and financial stability increasingly flowed through unelected agencies, expert committees, and private-public boards - a consolidation of authority triggered by crisis but made permanent by design.

The 1930s collapse didn't just reshape America's economy. It rewired its power structure, creating the framework for the technocratic order that now manages nearly every critical system - from finance and infrastructure to energy and information. The Great Depression didn't just centralize governance; it normalized elite control, conditioning the public to see concentrated power as both inevitable and necessary.

8

War as the Great Technocratic Accelerator

The Manhattan Project marked the moment when science, technology, and the state fused into a single, coordinated structure of power - a model that reshaped governance forever. It began as an emergency military program to build an atomic bomb before Nazi Germany, but what emerged was far more than a weapons project. It was the first large-scale test of technocratic governance, where government authority, corporate infrastructure, and academic expertise merged seamlessly to solve a singular problem through total mobilization of resources, people, and knowledge. It redefined what "science" meant in the modern state: no longer a field of open inquiry, but a strategic asset weaponized by elites to consolidate control and reshape the global order.

By 1942, Franklin Roosevelt had authorized what became the largest secret project in U.S. history. General Leslie Groves oversaw the military side, but the real driver of the program was its unprecedented network of scientists and engineers drawn from elite universities and research institutes - figures like Robert Oppenheimer, Enrico Fermi, Niels Bohr, and Ernest Lawrence. Columbia University, MIT, the University of Chicago, and the University of California at Berkeley became central nodes in the network. These institutions were transformed almost overnight into extensions of the federal government, producing designs, theories, and prototypes under direct state supervision.

More than 130,000 people were employed across over 30 sites, including the sprawling research hubs at Los Alamos, Oak Ridge, and Hanford. Entire cities were constructed in secrecy, controlled by the U.S. Army, yet staffed by private contractors and university-trained experts. Every layer of the project blurred traditional boundaries: the military coordinated with corporate boards from DuPont, Union Carbide, and Westinghouse, while scientists working under academic titles operated inside a command structure where decisions ultimately flowed from Washington.

The Manhattan Project represented total centralization of knowledge. Information was compartmentalized under strict clearance protocols, creating a hierarchical system where even senior scientists were denied access to the full scope of the program. Surveillance and censorship were built into daily operations, transforming scientific discovery into a controlled process managed through need-to-know clearance and military oversight. For the first time, research at the highest levels was no longer an open exchange but a state-directed enterprise, where discoveries were national assets rather than contributions to humanity.

This consolidation extended beyond secrecy. The Manhattan Project institutionalized a model where science became an arm of state power. Government funding, channeled through agencies like the Office of Scientific Research and Development (OSRD), dwarfed traditional university budgets, binding research agendas to federal priorities. Once tied to this system, scientists became dependent on state contracts, shaping not only their work but also the political alignments of entire institutions. From this point forward, the idea of "independent research" became a myth.

At the corporate level, the project forged a new relationship between private enterprise and federal authority. DuPont ran the Hanford plutonium plant. Union Carbide operated Oak Ridge's uranium enrichment facilities. Westinghouse built specialized reactors. These companies did not just provide materials; they built the infrastructure of a new kind of economy, one where private firms executed projects planned, financed, and controlled by the state. In return, they secured preferential access to patents, funding, and postwar defense contracts, setting the precedent for the military-industrial complex that would dominate the rest of the 20th century.

The success of the project fundamentally altered geopolitical power structures. With the detonation of the first bomb at the Trinity test in July 1945, the United States possessed not just a weapon but a new governing principle: science as leverage. Control over advanced knowledge became synonymous with control over the global order. Washington rapidly reorganized its research infrastructure to secure this advantage, leading to the creation of the Atomic Energy Commission in 1946 and the embedding of nuclear research deep inside the machinery of the national security state.

The Manhattan Project also redefined the role of universities. Institutions like Columbia, MIT, and Berkeley became permanent arms of federal research agendas. Laboratories built for the project transitioned into centers for classified work on nuclear weapons, energy systems, and advanced technologies. Research became professionalized and militarized, aligning intellectual inquiry with state objectives. Academic freedom was replaced by controlled funding streams tied directly to federal priorities, ensuring that breakthroughs in physics, chemistry, and engineering would serve strategic goals rather than independent exploration.

The project's legacy was twofold. On the surface, it marked a triumph of coordination - proof that massive, multidisciplinary problems could be solved through centralized planning and technical expertise. Beneath the surface, it set in motion a permanent realignment of power: science, once imagined as independent, was now inseparable from the state, corporate infrastructure, and military command. Knowledge itself became a weapon, managed and controlled by a small elite under the justification of national security.

The Manhattan Project created the architecture for what followed: the Pentagon system, DARPA, the National Laboratories, and vast classified research networks that still shape global politics today. It normalized secrecy, militarized discovery, and cemented the idea that scientific progress equals strategic dominance. This model didn't end with nuclear weapons - it expanded into computing, aerospace, genetics, and artificial intelligence, building a permanent technocratic infrastructure where research is guided less by curiosity than by the imperatives of control.

Science, after 1945, stopped being neutral. It became statecraft.

The founding of the RAND Corporation in 1948 marked a turning point in the history of technocratic governance. If the Manhattan Project represented the fusion of science, industry, and state power, RAND was the next phase - where knowledge itself became a weaponized system. RAND transformed research from open inquiry into predictive modeling, creating tools to forecast, simulate, and engineer future events before they happened. It wasn't simply a think tank; it was the first institutionalized brain of the U.S. administrative state, built to translate data into strategy, uncertainty into probability, and possibility into control.

RAND's origins lay directly in the structures created during World War II. After the Manhattan Project and other classified programs proved the effectiveness of centralized scientific planning, the U.S. military wanted a permanent institution to formalize the partnership between government, private industry, and academia. General Henry "Hap" Arnold, head of the U.S. Army Air Forces, spearheaded the idea. He envisioned a research organization that would combine engineering, mathematics, psychology, economics, and systems theory to solve problems beyond the capacity of traditional bureaucracies or political debates.

Initially launched as Project RAND within Douglas Aircraft in 1946, the initiative quickly outgrew its corporate incubator. By 1948, it was spun off as an independent, nonprofit research institution: the RAND Corporation, headquartered in Santa Monica, California. Its mandate was deceptively simple - provide "objective" analysis for national security and long-term policy planning - but its influence extended far beyond defense. RAND pioneered an entire new discipline: systems analysis, the art of converting human behavior, logistics, and global events into data-driven models capable of predicting outcomes and optimizing decisions.

At the core of RAND's approach was the idea that uncertainty could be tamed. Through game theory, simulation, and statistical modeling, RAND researchers sought to map every variable in complex geopolitical and economic systems. The premise was simple but transformative: if you could quantify reality accurately enough, you could predict it, and if you could predict it, you could control it. This logic created the first algorithmic frameworks for global management - a direct extension of the technocratic vision incubated at Columbia during the 1930s and refined in the Manhattan Project's command structures.

RAND's early projects focused on nuclear strategy. Figures like John von Neumann, one of the architects of game theory, worked with RAND to design models of mutually assured destruction (MAD), deterrence, and escalation dynamics. RAND quantified the unthinkable: how many bombs, dropped where, would achieve "acceptable" losses? Which response strategies minimized casualties or maximized geopolitical leverage? Every human, city, and life became a variable in a mathematical function optimized for state objectives.

But RAND's ambitions didn't stop at war. By the 1950s and 1960s, RAND researchers were applying their models to economics, urban planning, education, health care, and communications. They were early pioneers of predictive economic modeling, building computational frameworks to simulate national productivity, consumer behavior, and labor markets decades into the future. In education, RAND proposed optimizing learning systems through psychometric analysis and early computer-based assessment. In infrastructure, it developed algorithms to design transportation systems and resource allocation models for cities. The ultimate goal was always the same: convert uncertainty into measurable inputs, optimize outcomes, and manage society through data-driven planning.

RAND also played a critical role in the birth of the digital age. Its Cold

War research on communications security directly influenced the creation of ARPANET, the precursor to the modern internet, as part of its work on decentralized information systems capable of surviving nuclear attack. By embedding control mechanisms into emerging technologies, RAND helped lay the foundations for networked governance, where information flows could be monitored, redirected, and weaponized at scale.

What made RAND different from traditional think tanks was its integration into the deepest levels of the U.S. state. Its reports weren't speculative white papers; they shaped policy directly. The Department of Defense, CIA, NSA, and later NASA treated RAND analyses as operational blueprints. RAND alumni populated the highest ranks of government, corporate leadership, and international agencies, creating a revolving door between its research desks and the levers of power. Its findings influenced nuclear posture, space exploration, economic planning, and counterinsurgency strategies from Vietnam to Afghanistan.

Crucially, RAND normalized the idea that models could replace politics. If a sufficiently advanced algorithm could forecast likely outcomes, then "rational" policy became whatever the model prescribed. Decisions previously subject to public debate - resource distribution, security priorities, even cultural policy - were reframed as technical problems best handled by experts. This mindset accelerated the migration of authority away from legislatures and toward specialized administrative systems insulated from democratic oversight.

By the late 20th century, RAND's influence had become global. International organizations like the World Bank, IMF, and OECD adopted its modeling frameworks to guide economic policy across dozens of countries. RAND-trained economists and systems analysts exported these methods worldwide, embedding predictive algorithms into everything from development strategies to trade negotiations. The institution's techniques - energy forecasting, environmental simulations, and behavioral analytics - became the operating logic of governance at the highest levels.

RAND was, in many ways, the Manhattan Project's intellectual successor. Where the bomb centralized physical power, RAND centralized informational power. It turned data into leverage, probabilities into policies, and algorithms into governance. By shifting the focus from solving present problems to engineering future ones, it built the foundations for today's algorithmic state - a system where predictive analytics, AI-driven modeling, and automated decision-making increasingly bypass politics altogether.

What began as a Cold War necessity evolved into the infrastructure of permanent technocracy. RAND proved that with enough data, control could be extended beyond weapons and borders into economies, behaviors, and even thought itself. It marked the moment when modeling became strategy, and strategy became governance.

The Second World War didn't just redraw borders; it rewired power itself. As the global conflict escalated, the U.S. and U.K. invested heavily in technologies designed to process information at speeds human intelligence could not match. Code-breaking, early computing, and primitive artificial intelligence emerged together in this crucible, giving rise to an entirely new kind of control: the ability to predict, simulate, and direct outcomes by managing flows of data. While radar and nuclear weapons defined the battlefield, information systems defined the future.

It began with the code-breaking war. At Bletchley Park in the U.K., a team led by Alan Turing developed techniques to decrypt Germany's Enigma and Lorenz ciphers. To break codes fast enough to keep up with changing encryption patterns, Turing and his colleagues built the Bombe and later Colossus, the world's first programmable electronic digital computers. These machines could process vast amounts of cipher traffic automatically, reducing computations that once took days into minutes. By 1943, Colossus was operational, scanning intercepted signals and finding decryption keys through brute-force search - a primitive but groundbreaking form of algorithmic problem-solving.

In the U.S., similar efforts unfolded at the Naval Computing Machine Laboratory and the Signal Intelligence Service, where teams built electromechanical computers to tackle Japanese codes and logistics modeling. At Harvard, physicist Howard Aiken collaborated with IBM to produce the Harvard Mark I, an early programmable computer designed for ballistic calculations. By the war's end, these systems were processing data at speeds never before imagined, integrating computing power directly into military planning and weapons design.

This explosion of computational capability had cascading effects. It created the intellectual and technical foundation for primitive artificial intelligence - not AI in the modern sense, but automated logic systems designed to mimic elements of human reasoning. Turing's 1944 memorandum, later expanded into his 1950 paper Computing Machinery and Intelligence, laid out the core principles of machine-based cognition: symbolic manipulation, feedback loops, and adaptive problem-solving. Wartime successes demonstrated that computation could replace intuition in specific, well-bounded tasks. If a machine could predict an enemy's next move by analyzing historical signals, it could also forecast other complex behaviors - economic flows, logistics bottlenecks, even population movements.

Simultaneously, the U.S. military was experimenting with operations research, applying statistical models and early computers to optimize supply chains, troop deployments, and resource allocation. This integration of computation into decision-making represented a profound shift: the battlefield - and increasingly the economy itself - became a data environment to be modeled, simulated, and controlled. The seeds of predictive governance were being planted in real time.

These breakthroughs converged most visibly in the Manhattan Project. The design of nuclear weapons required solving unprecedented mathematical problems under extreme time pressure. Los Alamos relied on IBM punch-card machines and newly developed numerical methods to model neutron diffusion, energy release, and chain reactions. For the first time, industrial-scale computation became inseparable from scientific discovery - the physics of the bomb was inseparable from the machines built to simulate it.

By 1945, the digital state had been born, even if the term didn't yet exist. Code-breaking programs fed into real-time intelligence systems. Early computers automated tasks once considered the exclusive domain of experts. Predictive algorithms became central to war strategy, from submarine hunting in the Atlantic to strategic bombing campaigns over Europe and Japan.

After the war, these tools didn't disappear - they expanded. Research networks like the RAND Corporation, founded in 1948, absorbed wartime computing expertise into projects on nuclear strategy, logistics modeling, and eventually civilian policy. Bletchley veterans carried their methods into the design of early commercial computers, while Turing and others pushed the boundaries of machine intelligence into peacetime research. In the U.S., the federal government consolidated computing projects into national laboratories and emerging agencies like the Office of Naval Research, ensuring that advances remained tightly coupled to state priorities.

These systems also laid the groundwork for what would become surveillance infrastructure. The same cryptographic breakthroughs used to break Axis codes were repurposed after the war for monitoring Soviet communications. Massive data-collection programs began during this period, combining human intelligence with machine processing to track, classify, and analyze signals at unprecedented scale. The Cold War would accelerate this exponentially, but the framework - linking computation, prediction, and control - was already in place by the late 1940s.

Perhaps the most profound shift was philosophical: information itself became a strategic weapon. The ability to process data faster than adversaries, model possible futures, and automate decision-making reshaped the meaning of power. States, corporations, and research institutions began competing not just over territory or resources but over control of information flows and the machines capable of interpreting them. Computation moved from being a supporting tool to a governing principle.

By the time ENIAC, the first fully electronic general-purpose computer, came online in 1945, the trajectory was set. What began as code-breaking and ballistics modeling during wartime had unlocked a new paradigm: systems could be governed by simulation. Decisions no longer needed to be reactive; they could be predictive, even preemptive. Every variable - from energy production to population growth - could, in theory, be tracked, modeled, and optimized through machines.

The modern technocratic state was born in these labs, encoded into early algorithms and primitive logic systems. It didn't arrive through politics or ideology but through computation itself, quietly embedding control mechanisms into the infrastructures of science, security, and industry. Code-breaking had evolved into predictive modeling, and predictive modeling into algorithmic governance.

The tools were primitive, but the principle was clear: whoever mastered information would master the future.

PART III - SYSTEMS OF CONTROL (1945–1970)

The Cold War, cybernetics, and global governance.

9

RAND, DARPA, and the AI Seed

Norbert Wiener's work in the 1940s and 1950s marked a decisive turning point in the history of technocracy, where science stopped being confined to machines and began extending its reach directly into human behavior. Widely regarded as the "father of cybernetics," Wiener developed a framework that transformed how elites, governments, and corporations conceived of control: societies, like machines, could be measured, modeled, and regulated through continuous feedback loops. His theories provided the intellectual foundation for modern surveillance systems, predictive algorithms, and automated governance - embedding the logic of self-regulating control into the very architecture of the modern administrative state.

Wiener, a mathematician and former MIT prodigy, rose to prominence during World War II working on predictive aiming systems for anti-aircraft guns. These weapons had to fire where enemy planes would be, not where they were, requiring calculations that anticipated motion several seconds into the future. Wiener's solution was revolutionary: design systems that learn from their own errors in real time, constantly correcting course based on incoming data. This was the birth of feedback-driven prediction - machines capable not just of responding to commands but of anticipating and adjusting to changing conditions autonomously.

In 1948, Wiener published Cybernetics: Or Control and Communication in the Animal and the Machine, a book that became an intellectual bombshell. Cybernetics proposed that every complex system - machines, ecosystems, economies, even entire societies - operates on the

same underlying principles: information flows, feedback loops, and regulation. Behavior, whether mechanical or biological, could be reduced
to data processed through mathematical models. Inputs generated outputs; outputs informed new inputs. Apply this logic at scale, and the
boundaries between technology, biology, and society blur.

For military planners, corporate strategists, and government agencies,
Wiener's framework was electrifying. If societies behaved like systems,
they could be steered like systems. Once you could track the flows of
information and energy within a population - communications, consumption, movement, sentiment - you could design interventions to
maintain stability or drive desired outcomes. In effect, Wiener handed
elites a scientific model of predictive social control, and within a few
years, his ideas were embedded deep inside Cold War planning.

Cybernetics shaped the rise of operations research, systems analysis, and
control theory at institutions like MIT, RAND Corporation, and Bell
Labs. RAND, already developing predictive models for nuclear strategy, absorbed Wiener's methods into its simulations of human decision-
making, treating entire societies as adaptive machines. The same logic
used to stabilize anti-aircraft fire was applied to stabilizing economies,
populations, and global alliances. Models could now simulate not just
military outcomes but social dynamics, predicting labor unrest, political
movements, and even cultural shifts decades in advance.

Wiener also influenced the early development of artificial intelligence.
His theories suggested that machines could be designed to process information the same way human nervous systems do - responding dynamically to feedback, optimizing performance, and even learning patterns
of behavior. By the early 1950s, MIT researchers were experimenting
with primitive "learning machines," applying Wiener's mathematics to
build computers capable of adaptive decision-making. These were the
conceptual ancestors of the algorithms that now govern predictive
policing, credit scoring, consumer targeting, and social media curation.
But cybernetics wasn't just about modeling; it was about intervention.
Once you define a society as a system, you define its problems - eco-

nomic instability, dissent, scarcity - as failures of regulation. Fixing them becomes a matter of adjusting inputs: change incentives, restrict flows, alter communication patterns. By the mid-1950s, cybernetic principles underpinned early efforts in psychological operations, propaganda, and population management. The CIA's MK-Ultra program, Pentagon behavioral research, and RAND's "human factors" studies all drew on Wiener's insights, translating them into mechanisms for shaping attitudes and behaviors at scale.

This merging of computational prediction and social steering became a new form of soft power. Instead of openly coercing populations, cybernetic systems sought to influence them subtly through constant, invisible corrections - nudging decisions, shaping perception, and preempting instability before it emerged. Wiener had imagined cybernetics as a tool for human flourishing, but its most powerful applications quickly gravitated toward surveillance, manipulation, and control.

By the 1960s, Wiener's ideas had migrated into corporate management, advertising, and consumer analytics. Businesses began tracking purchasing habits, response times, and brand loyalty with the same mathematical frameworks used for targeting aircraft. In effect, cybernetics laid the foundation for what we now call behavioral prediction markets, where every human choice becomes data to be measured, anticipated, and monetized.

The real power of Wiener's work was not in the machines themselves but in the worldview it created. Cybernetics reframed society as an engineered system, one where humans, technologies, and environments are interdependent nodes in a vast, self-regulating network. That logic - monitor everything, predict everything, adjust everything - now permeates governance, finance, policing, and communication infrastructures worldwide.

You can see Wiener's fingerprints everywhere today:

• Predictive policing algorithms mapping crime probabilities before incidents occur.

• Social media recommendation engines shaping collective perception through feedback loops.

• Climate and economic models forecasting decades into the future to justify regulatory policies.

• Central bank digital currencies (CBDCs) and carbon credit systems tied to real-time consumption tracking.

Norbert Wiener didn't set out to build a control system, but his mathematics became the skeleton key for one. By reducing complexity to patterns of information, he created a framework where governance could become predictive - a permanent shift from reacting to events to anticipating and managing them algorithmically. In doing so, he handed the administrative state, military planners, and corporate elites the tools to engineer society itself.

What began as anti-aircraft calculations became the foundation of the algorithmic state. Today, Wiener's cybernetic principles underpin the systems that monitor our communications, score our behaviors, and shape our choices - often invisibly, always in real time. He gave us the mathematics of prediction, and in doing so, he gave technocracy its nervous system.

The RAND Corporation became the laboratory where the cybernetic vision of Norbert Wiener - the idea that society could be treated as an interconnected system governed through data, feedback, and prediction - was operationalized at scale. If Wiener provided the theory, RAND built the machinery. Founded in 1948 as a spin-off of Douglas Aircraft, RAND transformed from a Cold War think tank into the nerve center of systems theory, war gaming, and large-scale simulation. What began as a military research hub evolved into a model for algorithmic governance itself, where decision-making would increasingly be driven not by debate or democratic consent, but by the outputs of models, simulations, and predictive frameworks.

In the early years, RAND's mandate was clear: create frameworks for managing nuclear strategy in an unstable, multipolar world. The stakes were existential - avoiding total destruction while maintaining U.S. dominance in an arms race measured in megatons and minutes. To solve problems of this scale, RAND pioneered systems analysis: the science of breaking down complex environments into measurable components, quantifying every possible interaction, and modeling outcomes across millions of scenarios.

RAND researchers like John von Neumann, Herman Kahn, and Albert Wohlstetter applied mathematical tools to simulate nuclear exchanges, geopolitical crises, and resource allocation challenges. They developed game theory models to predict Soviet behavior, calculate optimal deterrence strategies, and identify thresholds of escalation. War was no longer viewed as chaos but as an equation - a rational environment where probabilities, payoffs, and expected outcomes could be quantified and optimized.

This approach gave birth to war gaming, a RAND innovation that merged systems theory with live simulation. Military officers, policymakers, and analysts would role-play adversaries within modeled environments, testing scenarios ranging from limited skirmishes to full-scale nuclear exchange. These exercises became embedded into U.S. defense strategy, institutionalizing simulation as a planning tool not just for conflict but for policy itself. If a model could predict an adversary's likely move, it could also predict economic responses, political unrest, or technological adaptation.

From this foundation, RAND expanded its scope far beyond nuclear planning. By the 1950s and 1960s, it was conducting research on urban planning, transportation networks, education policy, and economic forecasting - applying the same frameworks used for modeling thermonuclear war to entire societies. Cities were treated like machines, populations like datasets, and governance became an optimization problem. RAND developed computational models to simulate energy flows, resource scarcity, and labor migration decades before modern ESG frameworks and climate modeling inherited the same logic.

Crucially, RAND pioneered the idea of closed-loop governance, where data about society continuously feeds into models, the models generate "optimal" decisions, and those decisions are implemented through policy - generating new data to refine the system further. This approach, directly descended from Wiener's cybernetics, laid the foundation for modern algorithmic control systems.

RAND also drove the evolution of computing itself. Its requirements for large-scale modeling pushed hardware and software design forward, accelerating advances in memory storage, parallel processing, and programming languages. The RAND-developed SAGE system (Semi-Automatic Ground Environment), built for continental air defense, became the first massive, networked, real-time data system - linking radar, command centers, and computational nodes across the U.S. in a single predictive platform. SAGE became the prototype for later systems ranging from air traffic control to digital financial networks and eventually the early internet.

By the late 1960s, RAND's work had begun to bleed into predictive social modeling. Its researchers developed simulations for everything from counterinsurgency operations in Vietnam to urban unrest in American cities, using inputs like economic inequality, demographic pressures, and propaganda saturation to forecast potential flashpoints. These models informed both domestic and foreign policy, operationalizing the idea that behavior - at the scale of individuals, communities, and nations - could be anticipated, managed, and influenced before crises emerged.

At its peak, RAND functioned less like a research institute and more like the central nervous system of technocratic governance. Its alumni occupied senior roles across the Department of Defense, CIA, NASA, the World Bank, and Fortune 500 companies, creating a revolving-door network where RAND's frameworks became institutional policy. Whether planning nuclear deterrence, optimizing resource distribution, or managing cities, RAND's influence extended into nearly every domain where uncertainty had to be reduced and control asserted.

Perhaps RAND's most lasting contribution wasn't any specific model but the worldview it institutionalized: that simulation is governance. If a model predicts an outcome, it implicitly defines the "rational" policy response. Over time, this blurred the boundary between analysis and authority. Policy stopped being a matter of ideology or democratic debate; it became a technical optimization problem. Governments, militaries, and corporations increasingly outsourced decision-making to RAND-style simulations, reinforcing the authority of unelected experts and computational systems.

Today, RAND's legacy echoes everywhere. The war-gaming techniques it pioneered inform Pentagon strategy and NATO planning. Its systems analysis frameworks underpin global climate models, pandemic response simulations, and financial risk assessments. Its predictive social modeling survives in algorithmic policing, behavioral targeting, and real-time population surveillance. In many ways, RAND bridged the gap between Norbert Wiener's early cybernetics and the algorithmic state now emerging - a world where feedback-driven control is automated, and simulations increasingly govern reality itself.

RAND didn't just study the future; it built the tools to control it.

The founding of the Defense Advanced Research Projects Agency (DARPA) in 1958 marked a pivotal acceleration in the convergence of science, state power, and corporate infrastructure. If RAND represented the intellectual brain of Cold War technocracy, DARPA became its engineering arm - the operational pipeline where breakthroughs in computing, communications, weapons systems, and surveillance moved from theory into deployable tools of control. It institutionalized an innovation model where the U.S. federal government acted not just as a regulator or funder but as the central architect of technological development, coordinating universities, private industry, and the military into a single, tightly integrated network.

DARPA's creation was a direct response to Sputnik, the Soviet satellite launched in October 1957 that shocked Washington into fearing technological inferiority. President Eisenhower, under intense political pressure, ordered the reorganization of U.S. science policy and defense strategy. Within months, Congress authorized the creation of the Advanced Research Projects Agency (renamed DARPA in 1972) under the Department of Defense. Its mandate was deceptively simple: "to prevent technological surprise" - to ensure that the United States would never again be outpaced in science and innovation by an adversary.

But DARPA's deeper function went beyond defense preparedness. From its inception, it served as a permanent innovation engine for the U.S. military-industrial complex. It acted as a bridge between cutting-edge academic research, private corporate capabilities, and federal strategic priorities, ensuring that emerging technologies flowed seamlessly into national security infrastructure. Over the decades, DARPA became a pipeline - from idea to prototype to operational deployment - compressing timelines and bypassing bureaucratic inertia to deliver technological dominance.

One of DARPA's earliest breakthroughs came in computing and networking. Building on early RAND and MIT research, DARPA funded the development of ARPANET in 1969 - the first decentralized packet-switching network, designed to ensure communication resilience in the event of nuclear war. ARPANET became the direct precursor to the modern internet, embedding DARPA's fingerprints into the infrastructure of global information exchange. Alongside networking, DARPA supported innovations in time-sharing, interactive computing, and early artificial intelligence research at MIT, Stanford, Carnegie Mellon, and other elite universities. These projects laid the foundation for nearly every element of modern digital life, from distributed systems to machine learning.

DARPA also drove major advances in surveillance, reconnaissance, and control systems. In the 1960s, it oversaw Project Corona, developing the first U.S. spy satellites capable of capturing photographic intelligence from orbit. Later, it invested heavily in sensor networks, satellite-based geolocation (leading to GPS), and real-time battlefield data integration. These projects represented the evolution of cybernetic control envisioned by Norbert Wiener: linking sensors, computational models, and decision systems into closed feedback loops, where commanders - and increasingly, algorithms - could monitor, predict, and direct events at planetary scale.

Unlike conventional research institutions, DARPA's power lay in its integration model. It deliberately bypassed traditional academic silos and bureaucratic hurdles, channeling billions of dollars directly into handpicked research labs, corporate R&D divisions, and classified military facilities. It funded projects at IBM, Xerox PARC, Bell Labs, and Lockheed Skunk Works while simultaneously underwriting graduate programs at elite universities. This created a permanent public-private innovation cartel, where intellectual property and technological breakthroughs developed under federal funding flowed seamlessly into both military operations and private markets.

By the 1970s and 1980s, DARPA became a central driver of autonomous systems and AI research, funding robotics, natural language processing, and machine vision long before these fields were commercially viable. It spearheaded projects like Shakey the Robot at SRI International, the first mobile machine capable of reasoning about its environment, and financed early neural network experiments decades before deep learning entered mainstream consciousness. It also supported cognitive modeling programs designed to simulate decision-making and predict adversarial behavior, extending RAND's war-gaming frameworks into algorithmic control over human systems.

The agency's influence extended well beyond defense into civilian technologies. DARPA-backed innovations include microprocessors, graphical user interfaces, voice recognition, virtual reality, and early self-driving vehicle prototypes. GPS, originally conceived as a military navigation system, became foundational for global logistics and consumer technologies. ARPANET evolved into the internet backbone, transforming commerce, communication, and surveillance in ways DARPA's architects anticipated - and deliberately structured to maintain federal leverage over information networks.

By centralizing funding and coordination, DARPA institutionalized a closed innovation pipeline:

1.   Define strategic objectives at the federal level - often tied to perceived existential threats.

2. Fund cross-disciplinary research at elite universities, corporations, and defense labs.

3. Integrate breakthroughs into defense systems first, ensuring military dominance.

4. Spin off technologies into commercial markets under frameworks favoring government influence.

This model blurred the distinction between public and private innovation, creating a seamless interface between military needs, corporate profit, and academic prestige. DARPA didn't just fund research; it built the ecosystem that still governs technological development today.

By embedding itself at the core of both defense and civilian innovation, DARPA helped create what President Eisenhower would later describe in his 1961 farewell address as the military-industrial complex - an interdependent network of government, corporations, and universities driving technological advancement under centralized strategic priorities. Crucially, this structure removed many of the mechanisms of public accountability. DARPA's projects operated under secrecy, protected by national security exemptions, while their outputs shaped markets, communication infrastructures, and surveillance capabilities worldwide.

Today, DARPA's influence is everywhere. Its early investments underpin cloud computing, GPS logistics, drone warfare, AI-driven analytics, and global sensor networks. It has become the prototype for modern transnational innovation frameworks - replicated in agencies like Europe's ESA, China's 863 Program, and private-sector-military hybrids like Google's Project Maven. Through DARPA, technological progress became institutionalized as a strategic weapon, placing its development squarely in the hands of interlocking elites managing the flow of innovation from laboratory to battlefield to consumer device.

DARPA didn't just prevent technological surprise; it designed the infrastructure of control. It created a permanent, adaptive pipeline where innovations in computation, surveillance, and automation pass seamlessly from concept to implementation, consolidating power within the nexus of the military, academia, and industry. In many ways, DARPA became the command hub of a technocratic future - one where innovation itself is governed.

The ARPANET project, launched by DARPA in 1969, began as a technical experiment in communications resilience during the Cold War - but it became something much larger. While framed publicly as a tool to connect researchers and universities, ARPANET was designed from the outset to solve a strategic problem: how to build a distributed communications network that could survive nuclear attack, route around damage, and maintain operational command in a fractured environment. In creating the first functional digital packet-switched network, DARPA inadvertently - or perhaps deliberately - laid the foundation for the modern internet. Yet embedded within its architecture was something more enduring: the framework for global mass surveillance, an infrastructure where every node, every packet, and every connection could eventually be tracked, analyzed, and controlled.

The origins of ARPANET trace directly to DARPA's mission after Sputnik: ensure that U.S. communications, intelligence, and command systems could withstand existential threats. During the early 1960s, RAND researchers like Paul Baran developed the concept of packet switching - breaking data into discrete, addressable units and routing them across multiple redundant paths rather than relying on centralized exchanges. The logic was simple: a nuclear strike could destroy specific nodes, but the network would survive as long as enough paths remained intact. This was resilience by decentralization - but it also implied visibility by design. Each packet carried routing and addressing metadata, making it traceable, loggable, and reconstructable if intercepted.

DARPA formalized the project under its Information Processing Techniques Office (IPTO) in 1966, led by J.C.R. Licklider, a visionary computer scientist who imagined "man-computer symbiosis" long before it was possible. Licklider saw ARPANET not just as an engineering challenge but as the creation of a command-and-control nervous system, where humans and machines would interact seamlessly to manage increasingly complex systems. Under his leadership, DARPA funded elite universities like UCLA, Stanford, UC Santa Barbara, and the University of Utah to build the network's first nodes.

The breakthrough came on October 29, 1969, when UCLA and Stanford successfully sent the first ARPANET message: "LOGIN" (though the system crashed after "LO"). Within months, the network expanded to four nodes, and by 1971 it had grown into a multi-site grid linking research labs, military facilities, and private contractors. While officially described as an academic collaboration, ARPANET's early participants were tightly integrated into defense research ecosystems, with much of the initial funding tied directly to classified projects.

From a technical perspective, ARPANET pioneered multiple concepts that define the internet today:

- Packet switching for efficient, redundant data routing.
- Decentralized architecture designed to maintain functionality under attack.
- Protocol layering, eventually leading to TCP/IP (finalized in 1974), which standardized communication across incompatible systems.

These breakthroughs were transformative - but they also created structural visibility. In a packet-switched network, every communication contains metadata: source, destination, routing paths, timestamps, and size. This made ARPANET inherently auditable, enabling near-total logging of user activity, file transfers, and system connections. While privacy wasn't yet a mainstream concern, DARPA's architects understood from the beginning that control over packet routing implied control over information flows.

By the mid-1970s, ARPANET was handling classified traffic alongside academic research. Integration with military networks like MILNET deepened this convergence, creating a dual-use system where civilian communications coexisted with defense coordination. Simultaneously, DARPA and the NSA began funding research into network monitoring, packet sniffing, and encryption standards - ensuring that while the network appeared decentralized, command structures retained centralized oversight.

Even ARPANET's openness served strategic aims. By connecting civilian researchers to military-backed infrastructure, DARPA accelerated innovation while embedding defense priorities directly into emerging computing cultures. Protocols like TCP/IP, designed under DARPA contracts, became the foundation of the global internet, standardizing not just data exchange but also data visibility. Once TCP/IP became dominant in the 1980s, it created a uniform technical environment where surveillance could scale globally - every connection, anywhere, would eventually traverse systems that originated in DARPA-funded architectures.

As ARPANET transitioned into the broader NSFNET and, later, the commercial internet, the same institutions that designed its backbone retained privileged influence over its evolution. DARPA alumni and contractors staffed advisory boards, set technical standards, and shaped security frameworks that aligned with U.S. strategic interests. By the time the Cold War ended, ARPANET's descendants had become the world's communication infrastructure - but one born inside the military-industrial-technocratic complex.

This history also explains why the internet became the perfect substrate for mass surveillance. ARPANET's packet-based architecture meant every digital interaction was quantifiable. Each request, transfer, or session generated discrete, machine-readable traces. Once storage, processing, and algorithmic analysis caught up decades later, those traces became raw material for real-time monitoring and predictive modeling at planetary scale. Projects like the NSA's ECHELON network in the 1980s, and later PRISM under the Five Eyes alliance, exploited exactly this structural visibility - leveraging DARPA's original architecture to index global communications flows automatically.

In effect, ARPANET wasn't just the proto-internet; it was the prototype for integrated digital governance. By designing a network to survive nuclear war, DARPA created an infrastructure where connectivity and traceability were inseparable. Every user, every machine, and every piece of data became a potential node in an intelligence system capable of reconstructing behaviors, relationships, and intentions.

Today's networked surveillance systems - from real-time geolocation tracking to algorithmic content filtering - operate on principles embedded into ARPANET's DNA. Its architects weren't designing Facebook or Google, but they created the rules of the game: an internet optimized for resilience, standardization, and central oversight disguised beneath decentralized topology.

The illusion was always freedom; the reality was always control.

The first experiments in predictive policing didn't begin with modern AI or big data - their roots stretch back to the 1950s and 1960s, when RAND Corporation researchers, FBI analysts, and DARPA-funded behavioral scientists began exploring how crime, social unrest, and individual behavior could be predicted and managed using statistical models, early computing, and feedback-driven control systems. These early projects weren't framed as "surveillance" at the time; they were presented as rational, scientific approaches to stabilize society. In reality, they were the first attempts to transform entire populations into data environments - measurable, forecastable, and ultimately controllable.

The initial impetus came from two converging fears during the Cold War: rising urban crime rates and widespread anxiety about social instability. RAND, fresh from developing nuclear war simulations and systems theory models, applied the same frameworks to domestic policing. If war games could predict Soviet nuclear responses, why couldn't similar simulations model "high-risk" neighborhoods, forecast protest movements, or even anticipate specific criminal activity? By reframing social dynamics as engineering problems, RAND gave police departments and federal agencies a new toolkit: treat populations like systems, identify variables, and intervene before events occur.

One of the earliest formal programs began in 1967 with the President's Commission on Law Enforcement and Administration of Justice under Lyndon Johnson. Tasked with modernizing policing, the commission funneled funding from the newly formed Law Enforcement Assistance Administration (LEAA) - a federal agency established to integrate com-

puters, statistical analysis, and behavioral modeling into law enforcement operations nationwide. RAND was contracted to lead several
studies, using data from Los Angeles, Chicago, and Washington, D.C.
RAND's Criminal Justice Program pioneered what we would now recognize as predictive crime mapping. Its analysts built some of the earliest algorithmic models correlating historical incident data with
geospatial patterns, demographics, and socioeconomic indicators. They
proposed allocating patrols, resources, and surveillance based on areas of
predicted "high-risk activity" rather than reactive calls for service. This
was framed as efficiency, but it fundamentally redefined policing: prevention became preemption, embedding constant monitoring into the
structure of law enforcement.

At the same time, RAND researchers partnered with the Los Angeles
Police Department (LAPD) and the FBI to pilot computer-assisted decision systems. Early mainframe models ingested arrest records, call logs,
and neighborhood statistics to produce "crime probability scores" for
geographic zones. This work laid the foundation for later systems like
CompStat in the 1990s and modern AI-driven platforms like PredPol
- but unlike those, RAND's early models operated in an environment
largely unregulated and unexamined, allowing federal agencies to test
intrusive monitoring techniques long before public debate emerged.

Meanwhile, DARPA-funded behavioral studies were integrated into
these policing experiments. Cybernetic principles pioneered by Norbert
Wiener were applied to population-level modeling: view urban neighborhoods as dynamic systems governed by flows of people, money, and
information. By identifying "feedback loops" - such as unemployment,
migration, or policing intensity - early models attempted to predict social unrest before it materialized. The FBI's COINTELPRO program,
while primarily focused on political dissidents, drew on similar techniques, combining data analysis with real-time informant reports to
preemptively disrupt civil rights groups, anti-war movements, and labor
organizations.

By the late 1960s, IBM 360 mainframes and other DARPA-funded computing systems enabled increasingly sophisticated simulations. RAND developed a prototype known as the Urban Simulation Project, which modeled entire city ecosystems: crime rates, infrastructure, population growth, and protest likelihood. These simulations were used to test different "interventions" - increasing patrol density, deploying social workers, altering zoning laws - and forecast their effects years into the future. Behind the scenes, this meant that policies were being tested algorithmically before being implemented in reality, turning cities into experimental data environments.

Crucially, these early predictive policing programs also became entangled with the rise of federal surveillance infrastructures. The same packet-switching research that produced ARPANET was being leveraged for centralized criminal databases, linking local departments with federal systems for near-instantaneous data sharing. By 1970, the FBI's National Crime Information Center (NCIC) was online, aggregating arrest records, fingerprints, and incident reports from across the country. Combined with RAND's predictive models, NCIC provided the first real-time feedback loop between local police activity and federal monitoring - a precursor to the integrated surveillance state we know today.

These early experiments faced little public scrutiny but shaped decades of policing. By treating crime as a systems problem, RAND and its partners bypassed traditional political debates about causes and solutions. Instead, they embedded technocratic assumptions directly into law enforcement:

- Crime is predictable if enough data is collected.
- Social behavior can be modeled like traffic flows or supply chains.
- Prevention justifies preemptive intervention.
- Surveillance is necessary for "efficiency."

By the 1980s, these ideas had become institutionalized. RAND-trained analysts and LEAA-funded projects evolved into nationwide crime data systems, eventually merging with predictive modeling in urban planning, counterinsurgency, and intelligence operations. The logic first tested in inner-city neighborhoods became central to counterterrorism frameworks after 9/11 and later informed modern platforms like Palantir, which integrates multi-agency data to forecast threats before they occur.

Looking back, these early predictive policing experiments were less about solving crime than about prototyping algorithmic control over populations. They shifted the role of police from responding to events to managing probabilities, embedding statistical risk assessments into policy decisions and resource allocation. The tools were crude, but the philosophy was revolutionary: measure everything, model everything, and intervene before the system destabilizes.

Today's predictive policing platforms - AI-driven, GPS-integrated, and linked to biometric databases - operate on the same cybernetic logic RAND introduced in the 1960s. The difference is scale. Where early experiments tracked a few thousand data points across a handful of cities, modern systems ingest billions of signals in real time, feeding decisions not just about crime but about creditworthiness, mobility, and citizenship itself.

The path from RAND's pilot studies to today's algorithmic policing is direct. What began as a Cold War experiment in predicting dissent became the backbone of a governance model where populations are continuously monitored, modeled, and managed - often invisibly, always preemptively.

10

Global Governance Gets
Organized

When the United Nations Educational, Scientific and Cultural Organization (UNESCO) was founded in 1945, its stated mission was simple and idealistic: promote peace by fostering global cooperation in education, science, and culture. But beneath this humanitarian veneer, UNESCO became one of the most effective tools of cultural engineering in modern history. From its earliest days, the organization was dominated by a technocratic worldview shaped by elite planners, philanthropic foundations, and intelligence-linked networks. Its real power was not in funding schools or preserving art but in reshaping the minds, values, and narratives of entire populations - using education, media, and standardized knowledge systems to align global society under a unified framework of governance.

The roots of UNESCO's philosophy can be traced to the postwar technocratic vision of figures like Julian Huxley, its first director-general (1946–1948). Huxley, an evolutionary biologist, Fabian socialist, and eugenics advocate, was explicit about UNESCO's purpose: to manage humanity's "psychological evolution" and create a global scientific culture. In his 1946 manifesto, UNESCO: Its Purpose and Its Philosophy, Huxley argued that national traditions, religious structures, and independent cultural frameworks were obstacles to "world unity." Education, he insisted, should be used to reprogram human values, harmonizing populations around shared narratives of progress, science, and planetary interdependence.

Huxley viewed UNESCO as a laboratory for planned social transformation. Drawing heavily on cybernetics, behavioral psychology, and early anthropological studies, he envisioned global education systems designed to standardize "desirable attitudes" while discouraging "outdated" cultural identities. This wasn't conspiracy - Huxley stated it openly. To achieve peace, he argued, UNESCO needed to "guide the evolution of humanity" by shaping collective consciousness, which meant using schools, media, and cultural institutions as instruments of behavioral conditioning.

From the outset, UNESCO was deeply entangled with Western elite networks. The Rockefeller Foundation, Carnegie Endowment, and Ford Foundation funded its early programs, shaping priorities that aligned closely with their interests in global governance and technocratic planning. U.S. State Department officials and British Fabian intellectuals saw UNESCO as a soft-power tool, capable of influencing populations without overt coercion. Where NATO managed military security, UNESCO would manage cognitive security: aligning how people understood history, identity, and morality.

One of UNESCO's most powerful mechanisms was the standardization of education. Through its global frameworks, UNESCO designed model curricula, teacher training programs, and literacy campaigns that emphasized "universal values" and "scientific rationalism" over local traditions. While pitched as neutral, these programs effectively embedded a specific worldview - one that prioritized technological progress, economic integration, and institutional trust. National school systems became vectors for a coordinated cultural shift, dissolving independent epistemologies in favor of a shared technocratic narrative.

UNESCO also acted as a gatekeeper of knowledge and information flows. In the 1950s and 1960s, it began publishing technical guidelines for mass media development, funding state broadcasting systems, and training journalists in "responsible communication." By the 1970s, it launched initiatives to influence content in textbooks, museums, and public education materials, ensuring alignment between historical narratives, scientific framing, and geopolitical objectives. Entire generations grew up consuming information structured to reinforce UNESCO's preferred worldview: global interdependence, scientific authority, and centralized solutions to shared problems.

Cultural engineering also extended to identity and social norms. UNESCO funded anthropological research aimed at reshaping concepts of race, ethnicity, and belonging, framing them within scientific universalism. After World War II, it commissioned the famous 1950 Statement on Race, drafted by a panel of social scientists, which explicitly rejected biological definitions of race and reframed human identity around collective social integration. While this positioned UNESCO as a progressive force against racism, it also centralized authority over how identities were defined, categorized, and discussed globally.

UNESCO's influence deepened during the Cold War, where it became a battleground for narrative control. While publicly neutral, UNESCO's leadership consistently aligned with Western strategies to counter Soviet influence, embedding soft propaganda in educational programs and cultural initiatives. It produced documentaries, curated museums, and coordinated with Western media to normalize certain political ideals while marginalizing dissenting worldviews. Information, increasingly, was treated as a strategic resource - not unlike energy or finance - to be distributed, filtered, and managed at scale.

By the 1980s and 1990s, UNESCO shifted its focus toward global information infrastructure, anticipating the rise of the internet and digital communications. Through programs like the Memory of the World Project and Information for All, UNESCO positioned itself as a central authority in digitizing archives, managing knowledge repositories, and setting international standards for information access. Framed as open and democratic, these projects quietly concentrated control over which knowledge was prioritized, preserved, and circulated. In effect, UNESCO became the editor-in-chief of global memory.

Today, UNESCO's fingerprints are everywhere - in standardized testing frameworks, museum exhibits, open-data policies, and international cultural campaigns. Its influence over national education systems is rarely visible but deeply embedded: teachers, curricula, and textbooks across the globe increasingly reflect priorities set by transnational bodies, not local communities. Through partnerships with the World Bank, OECD, and World Economic Forum, UNESCO continues to promote policies that align education with "sustainability goals," "digital literacy," and "global citizenship" - phrases that mask centralized cultural management beneath progressive branding.

UNESCO's legacy is not about building schools or preserving heritage. It is about reprogramming collective perception. By shaping what children learn, what cultures celebrate, and what information circulates, UNESCO functions as one of the most powerful levers of soft power ever created. Through education and culture, it engineers consensus, dissolving competing narratives into a managed system of thought aligned with elite-defined "global priorities."

This was Julian Huxley's vision from the beginning: a coordinated global framework where institutions guide not only what people know, but how they think. In many ways, UNESCO succeeded. It created a world where information is standardized, history is curated, and cultural identity is increasingly subsumed into a technocratic paradigm - all under the banner of peace and progress.

The classroom became the control room.

The World Health Organization (WHO), founded in 1948 as a specialized agency of the United Nations, was framed as a neutral, humanitarian institution dedicated to eradicating disease and improving global health. But from its inception, the WHO has functioned as much more than a medical organization. Behind its stated mission lies its real power: leveraging public health as a political control mechanism. Through health mandates, emergency declarations, and the ability to shape global policy, the WHO became a key instrument for consolidating authority, steering economies, and influencing the behavior of entire populations under the banner of "science" and "safety."

The WHO's founding came at a time when the postwar international order was being engineered around technocratic governance. Like UNESCO, the International Monetary Fund, and the World Bank, the WHO was designed to bypass the messy variability of national sovereignty by creating a central authority over global health policy. Its early frameworks were heavily shaped by the Rockefeller Foundation, which had spent decades funding medical schools, vaccine programs, and public health initiatives worldwide. This influence wasn't incidental - the Rockefeller networks saw health not simply as a humanitarian project but as a mechanism for standardizing populations, controlling resources, and embedding elite-driven priorities into sovereign nations.

From the beginning, the WHO's authority rested on its ability to define crises. By setting international health standards and controlling the declaration of "Public Health Emergencies of International Concern" (PHEIC), it established itself as a gatekeeper with enormous geopolitical leverage. When the WHO declares an emergency, it unlocks extraordinary powers: governments redirect budgets, suspend liberties, and enforce compliance measures aligned with WHO recommendations. Even in the 1950s and 1960s, early vaccination campaigns and quarantine protocols revealed the WHO's capacity to dictate domestic policy under the justification of preventing "pandemics."

Over the following decades, the WHO built a global infrastructure for data collection and surveillance. Through partnerships with national ministries of health, universities, and pharmaceutical firms, it assembled vast epidemiological databases, tracking disease outbreaks, birth rates, and mortality statistics across hundreds of countries. While presented as neutral science, this integration established a centralized nervous system for monitoring population health - a feedback loop between WHO analysts, national governments, and corporate stakeholders. This gave the WHO extraordinary influence over which threats mattered, which treatments were prioritized, and which solutions became mandatory.

By the 1970s, the WHO had shifted from purely medical interventions to political health management. It coordinated massive global vaccine campaigns for smallpox eradication, polio, and measles, deploying its frameworks directly through schools, workplaces, and entire city infrastructures. These campaigns did more than manage disease; they normalized top-down mandates, conditioning populations to equate compliance with safety. At the same time, WHO-backed initiatives began shaping national health laws, embedding WHO standards into regulatory regimes worldwide. Sovereign governments increasingly deferred to WHO recommendations on food safety, pharmaceuticals, and pandemic preparedness - a process accelerated by financial dependencies created through World Bank and IMF-linked funding.

During the late 20th century, the WHO became deeply entangled with private power structures. As global health expenditures surged, pharmaceutical conglomerates, philanthropic foundations, and multinational NGOs became central players in shaping WHO priorities. Entities like the Bill & Melinda Gates Foundation, which now contributes more to the WHO budget than most nation-states, gained outsized influence over which diseases are targeted, which technologies are developed, and how public health narratives are framed. By aligning global health policy with corporate innovation pipelines, the WHO helped consolidate medical monopolies under the banner of humanitarianism.

The real shift, however, came in the 21st century. Following the 2005 revision of the International Health Regulations (IHR), the WHO gained unprecedented legal authority to override national policies during declared emergencies. Under these frameworks, WHO directives can compel countries to adopt specific responses - lockdowns, travel restrictions, digital tracing, mandatory vaccination, or the deployment of experimental treatments - regardless of local political processes. For the first time, global health governance became a de facto mechanism for suspending sovereignty in the name of collective security.

The COVID-19 pandemic made this dynamic visible to the public. Through its PHEIC declaration in early 2020, the WHO coordinated a synchronized global response: border closures, mass quarantines, economic shutdowns, and unprecedented restrictions on personal freedoms. While national governments executed policies, the frameworks, data models, and behavioral guidelines originated largely within WHO-aligned expert groups and private-public partnerships. Even more significant was the WHO's influence over information itself. By labeling certain narratives as "misinformation," partnering with social media platforms, and coordinating messaging with governments, the WHO became an arbiter not just of health policy but of permissible speech.

At the same time, the WHO's pandemic response accelerated the deployment of digital infrastructure linked to public health. Vaccine passports, QR-based mobility systems, and centralized digital ID frameworks were piloted under WHO-aligned initiatives, tying access to education, travel, and commerce directly to compliance with health mandates. These systems, developed in collaboration with tech giants, financial institutions, and NGOs, represent the fusion of biopolitics and digital governance - where your health status becomes a gatekeeper to participation in society.

In this light, the WHO functions less as a medical organization and more as a policy engine for technocratic control:

• It sets global standards that filter into domestic law.
• It defines emergencies to trigger exceptional powers.
• It coordinates information narratives with governments and corporations.
• It integrates digital technologies to enforce behavioral compliance.
• It aligns pharmaceutical and biotech priorities with global funding flows.

These dynamics make the WHO one of the most strategically significant institutions in the modern technocratic architecture. Its power doesn't stem from force but from framing: whoever defines the health crisis defines the political response. And by centralizing definitions, the WHO indirectly governs access - to resources, mobility, and rights - in ways that transcend national sovereignty.

Health, under this model, becomes a pretext for governance. Public health emergencies enable sweeping measures that would be politically impossible under normal circumstances. Through behavioral mandates and digital tracking infrastructures, the WHO acts as a soft but pervasive instrument of control, subtly reorganizing society around centralized authority while presenting itself as a neutral, benevolent actor.

The implications are profound. By merging health, technology, and governance into a single operational framework, the WHO has helped normalize algorithmic oversight of human life itself. In doing so, it transformed medicine from a practice of care into a lever of compliance - one capable of steering economies, shaping culture, and conditioning populations to accept increasingly integrated systems of control.

The doctor's office became the control room.

The International Monetary Fund (IMF) and the World Bank, both founded in 1944 at the Bretton Woods Conference, were introduced as instruments to stabilize global finance and promote reconstruction after World War II. But their real function quickly evolved beyond economic recovery. Together, they became the central nervous system of financial technocracy - institutions designed not simply to manage money but to engineer the political and economic behavior of entire nations. Under the banner of "stability" and "development," they built a global architecture where debt, credit, and monetary policy became tools for structural control, enabling unelected financial elites to dictate the economic direction of sovereign states.

Bretton Woods was the inflection point. As the war wound down, the U.S. and its allies sought to replace the chaos of interwar monetary competition with a system that centralized financial authority. The IMF was created to manage exchange rates, provide emergency loans, and stabilize currencies, while the World Bank focused on funding infrastructure and "development" projects in war-torn and emerging economies. Publicly, these institutions were framed as neutral, cooperative, and humanitarian. Privately, they were designed to lock in U.S. dominance within a dollar-backed system where credit, liquidity, and reconstruction financing would flow through mechanisms controlled by Western elites.

From the outset, the IMF and World Bank functioned as gatekeepers of capital. Nations seeking financial support were required to adopt policies designed in Washington, often drafted by technocrats trained at Harvard, MIT, and the University of Chicago. The language of "conditionality" - reforms mandated in exchange for loans - became the lever through which these institutions reshaped domestic economies. Entire sectors were privatized, subsidies removed, and labor protections dismantled under the doctrine of "efficiency." What began as crisis relief evolved into economic restructuring, embedding neoliberal principles into the policy frameworks of dozens of sovereign states.

During the 1970s and 1980s, this control deepened with the rise of the Washington Consensus - a package of standardized economic reforms promoted by the IMF, World Bank, and U.S. Treasury. Nations facing debt crises were told they must liberalize trade, deregulate industries, cut social spending, and open domestic markets to foreign capital. Failure to comply meant exclusion from global credit systems. Through this model, the IMF and World Bank effectively became enforcers of globalization, ensuring that national policies aligned with the priorities of multinational corporations, Western banks, and strategic U.S. interests. One of the most consequential tools deployed was structural adjustment programs (SAPs). These programs imposed sweeping policy changes in exchange for access to financing. In practice, SAPs dismantled domestic industries, eroded food sovereignty, and transferred public assets into private hands, often to foreign investors. For countries in Africa, Latin America, and Southeast Asia, this meant trading national autonomy for debt-driven dependency. Once trapped in this cycle, states became permanently reliant on IMF and World Bank support, forfeiting meaningful control over fiscal policy, resource management, and even social priorities.

The World Bank played a complementary role, financing massive infrastructure and development projects - dams, power plants, highways, and resource extraction - under the banner of "modernization." But these projects often served global corporate supply chains rather than local communities. Contracts flowed to multinational engineering firms and resource conglomerates, while recipient nations absorbed the debt. When projects failed to deliver promised growth, the same countries returned to the IMF for "rescue loans," deepening the spiral of dependency.

Throughout this period, the Rockefeller Foundation, the Council on Foreign Relations, and other elite networks exerted significant influence over IMF and World Bank policy. Key executives and economists moved interchangeably between these institutions, Wall Street firms, and U.S. federal agencies, creating a revolving-door ecosystem where public authority merged with private financial interests. The IMF and World Bank became less accountable to member nations and more aligned with the imperatives of global capital, cementing an elite technocratic consensus that prioritized stability and growth metrics over sovereignty and democracy.

By the 1990s, the integration of IMF and World Bank frameworks into global governance accelerated. Through partnerships with the World Trade Organization (WTO), OECD, and later UN agencies, these institutions helped design policies regulating everything from carbon markets and digital finance to intellectual property and energy use. Under the pretext of "global coordination," financial technocracy extended into nearly every domain of public life. A country's compliance with IMF-driven "reforms" increasingly determined not just its credit rating but its participation in international trade, investment flows, and strategic alliances.

In the 21st century, their power consolidated further through digital financial infrastructures. IMF research teams and World Bank task forces began championing central bank digital currencies (CBDCs), programmable payment systems, and biometric-linked financial identities as solutions to "financial inclusion." Framed as tools for empowerment, these systems concentrate transactional visibility and control at unprecedented scale, enabling real-time monitoring of spending patterns and capital flows. In practice, this allows supranational institutions to track compliance, enforce sanctions, and influence consumer behavior without direct political intervention.

Crisis became the accelerant. Each global shock - from the 1997 Asian financial crash to the 2008 global recession to the COVID-19 pandemic - expanded the IMF and World Bank's reach. Emergency lending programs came bundled with deeper conditionalities, tighter integration of data systems, and greater harmonization of fiscal policies across nations. The same pattern repeated: destabilization produced dependency, dependency enabled centralization, and centralization entrenched technocratic governance on a global scale.

Through this process, the IMF and World Bank evolved from lenders of last resort into architects of compliance. Their leverage over debt, credit, and international capital flows gives them de facto veto power over national policy. By setting "best practices" in everything from tax regimes to energy transitions, they define the acceptable boundaries of sovereignty in the 21st century. Their technical language - efficiency, sustainability, modernization - masks the reality: a coordinated system of economic management where decision-making increasingly bypasses legislatures, local communities, and democratic consent.

At their core, the IMF and World Bank are not simply financial institutions. They are instruments of technocracy:

- Debt as leverage - enforcing policy alignment through financing dependencies.
- Conditionality as control - reshaping domestic laws to fit global priorities.
- Standardization as strategy - embedding uniform economic frameworks worldwide.
- Digital integration - linking compliance to programmable currencies and identity systems.
- Crisis as catalyst - using instability to expand central authority.

What began at Bretton Woods as a promise of reconstruction and cooperation became, over decades, the foundation for a managed global economy. Sovereignty is now conditional on adherence to frameworks designed by unelected technocrats, executed through institutions that present themselves as neutral but operate in alignment with elite financial interests.

The IMF and World Bank don't just manage economies; they engineer them. Through metrics, models, and mandates, they turned debt into a tool of governance and finance into a mechanism of global behavioral control. Nations no longer compete on their own terms; they compete within an architecture designed to standardize them - economically, legally, and digitally - for integration into a single, networked system.

In short, Bretton Woods didn't just create two financial institutions. It built the operating system of financial technocracy, one still running in the background of nearly every national decision today.

The Club of Rome, founded in 1968 by Italian industrialist Aurelio Peccei and Scottish scientist Alexander King, became one of the most influential elite policy networks of the late 20th century. While its stated mission was to foster dialogue on global challenges, its actual impact was far more profound: it introduced a technocratic framework for governing populations, economies, and natural resources under the guise of "planetary stewardship." Through publications like The Limits to Growth (1972), the Club pioneered a population control narrative - framing humanity itself as a threat to planetary stability and proposing centralized, algorithm-driven management of human behavior and resource use.

The timing of the Club's creation was no accident. By the late 1960s, rapid industrialization, postwar population growth, and geopolitical tensions had generated deep anxieties among Western elites about the sustainability of economic expansion - and, more importantly, about the stability of their control over global systems. Backed by influential figures like David Rockefeller and organizations like the OECD, the Club of Rome was conceived as a global think tank where political leaders, corporate executives, scientists, and economists could align around "solutions" that transcended national sovereignty.

In 1972, the Club commissioned a team at MIT, led by systems analyst Dennis Meadows and supported by Jay Forrester's world modeling group, to produce a groundbreaking report: The Limits to Growth. Using the cutting-edge techniques of the time - systems theory, cybernetics, and early computer simulations - the report modeled the interaction of five variables on a planetary scale: population, industrial output, pollution, food production, and natural resources. The findings were stark: continued economic and population growth, if unchecked, would lead to environmental collapse within decades.

The report's message was revolutionary - and polarizing. It shifted global policy discourse from development to degrowth, reframing humanity's relationship with the planet as one of inherent conflict. Instead of expanding prosperity indefinitely, the report implied that growth itself was unsustainable and would need to be tightly managed through coordinated interventions in population, consumption, and production. The recommendations were deliberately vague, but their underlying logic was clear: the survival of civilization required centralized control over resources, technology, and demographics.

At the heart of The Limits to Growth was an early form of algorithmic governance. The MIT team used a modeling platform called World3, one of the first large-scale computer simulations of global systems, to test thousands of scenarios under different policy conditions. In this worldview, the planet became a single dynamic system, human beings were inputs and outputs, and political decisions became variables to optimize through simulation. This was a direct extension of the technocratic ideas developed at RAND, DARPA, and MIT's own systems labs: govern the future by modeling it first.

But the Club of Rome's influence went beyond academic modeling. Its members - a network of politicians, executives, and thought leaders - used The Limits to Growth to justify a wide range of global initiatives aimed at managing population size and resource consumption. During the 1970s, elite foundations and Western governments began integrating population control into development policy, funding programs that linked foreign aid to reproductive health targets and family planning quotas. The Club provided the intellectual framework, while organizations like the World Bank, Rockefeller Foundation, and later the Bill & Melinda Gates Foundation operationalized it through on-the-ground interventions.

The Club also shaped the climate change narrative decades before it entered mainstream consciousness. In its 1991 report, The First Global Revolution, the Club declared:

"In searching for a common enemy to unite us, we came up with the idea that pollution, the threat of global warming, water shortages, famine and the like would fit the bill... The real enemy, then, is humanity itself."

This framing was deliberate. By constructing a planetary crisis around human activity, the Club created a rationale for transnational governance. Solutions to climate change, resource depletion, and "overpopulation" would require unprecedented cooperation - but in practice, this meant concentrating authority in unelected institutions, private foundations, and global regulatory frameworks like those championed later by the UN, IMF, and World Economic Forum.

Throughout the 1970s and 1980s, the Club cultivated relationships with power centers across governments, academia, and industry. It worked closely with the OECD, World Bank, UNESCO, and later the UN Framework Convention on Climate Change (UNFCCC) to integrate its systems-based approach into global policy. Environmental limits became a policy justification for deindustrialization, resource rationing, and the redesign of national economies around sustainability metrics - policies often presented as grassroots but coordinated at elite levels.

Population control remained central to the Club's philosophy. It endorsed policies to reduce fertility rates in the Global South, often tied to IMF and World Bank lending conditions. Programs introduced in countries like India, Bangladesh, and Kenya incentivized sterilization, contraceptive adoption, and "family size regulation" under the guise of modernization and environmental protection. While marketed as empowerment, these initiatives frequently served as mechanisms of resource gatekeeping, ensuring that economic development remained subordinate to global population targets set by Western planners.

In many ways, The Limits to Growth normalized a technocratic ideology that persists today:

• Humanity is a problem to be managed, not a source of solutions.

• Global crises require centralized responses administered by experts, not local autonomy.

• Computer models and simulations are treated as objective authorities, even when based on highly selective assumptions.

• Policy is increasingly preemptive, designed to intervene before potential crises occur.

The Club's legacy is everywhere in modern governance. Its frameworks underpin climate treaties, "net zero" carbon policies, biodiversity credits, and the United Nations' Sustainable Development Goals (SDGs). Through its influence over academia and media, the Club helped embed a worldview in which ecological limits justify political limits - where control over energy, food, and population is no longer debated democratically but managed algorithmically through global institutions.

What began as a small gathering of technocratic elites became a cornerstone of planetary governance. By linking human activity directly to planetary instability, the Club of Rome gave policymakers, corporations, and NGOs a shared narrative to justify deeper integration of economic, technological, and environmental management. Under the language of "saving the planet," the levers of control shifted upward, away from nation-states and into transnational networks aligned around a single model of "sustainability."

The Club did not just publish The Limits to Growth. It established the limits of sovereignty.

Maurice Strong was not just a businessman or a bureaucrat; he was one of the key architects of environmental technocracy - the man who helped transform "saving the planet" from an activist slogan into a global governance framework. Across the second half of the 20th century, Strong operated at the nexus of the United Nations, elite financial networks, corporate boardrooms, and private philanthropic foundations. His genius lay in reframing ecological concerns into a planetary emergency that could only be solved through centralized authority, integrated policy, and technocratic control. Where others saw environmentalism as a social movement, Strong saw it as the lever for reorganizing power on a global scale.

Born in Manitoba, Canada, in 1929, Strong began his career in the oil and energy sector, working for Dome Petroleum before joining the Rockefeller network through the CalTex group and eventually serving as the president of Petro-Canada. These connections proved critical. By the late 1960s, Strong had become a trusted operator within elite circles, including the Rockefellers, the Club of Rome, and international banking institutions. His access to capital, corporate leaders, and political power made him a bridge between public policy and private influence.

In 1970, the United Nations appointed Strong to organize the 1972 Stockholm Conference on the Human Environment - the first major UN summit on global environmental issues. Strong used Stockholm to fuse the environmental concerns of scientists, activists, and developing nations into a single, unifying narrative: planetary survival depended on coordinated, top-down management of humanity's impact on the biosphere. This was the origin point of what later became the environmental governance movement - a system where energy use, industrial output, and population growth would be managed as interconnected variables within a single global framework.

Stockholm marked the beginning of Strong's rise as the strategist of "planetary management." Drawing heavily on the Club of Rome's Limits to Growth report (released the same year), he positioned resource scarcity, industrial pollution, and population growth as interconnected threats requiring transnational solutions. To operationalize this vision, Strong became the founding executive director of the United Nations Environment Programme (UNEP), which he built into a central hub for environmental policymaking. Under Strong's leadership, UNEP didn't just study ecological issues - it coordinated with the IMF, World Bank, and OECD to embed environmental priorities directly into international finance and development strategies.

Strong's philosophy was explicit: environmental challenges were inseparable from economic control. In his 1972 book, Only One Earth, co-authored with Barbara Ward, Strong argued that humanity had entered an era where traditional political sovereignty must give way to global governance mechanisms capable of managing energy consumption, population trends, and resource allocation. National governments could no longer be trusted to balance competing priorities; planetary-scale modeling and centralized decision-making were, in his view, the only way forward.

In 1992, Strong reached the height of his influence as Secretary-General of the UN Conference on Environment and Development (UNCED) in Rio de Janeiro, known as the Earth Summit. The Rio Summit produced Agenda 21, the non-binding but globally adopted framework for "sustainable development." While presented as a voluntary plan, Agenda 21 became the blueprint for environmental technocracy:

•   Integrate environmental, economic, and social policy into a single global planning system.

•   Establish centralized reporting frameworks to monitor compliance by nations.

•   Link resource usage, land development, and industrial production to sustainability metrics.

•   Align education, culture, and public messaging with standardized sustainability narratives.

The Rio Summit also paved the way for the creation of the United Nations Framework Convention on Climate Change (UNFCCC), institutionalizing the notion that climate change represented a planetary emergency requiring continuous transnational governance. This framework enabled subsequent agreements like the Kyoto Protocol (1997) and the Paris Accord (2015), each expanding centralized oversight over national energy policy, industrial activity, and environmental regulation.

Strong was also instrumental in integrating private-sector power into environmental governance. Through his relationships with the World Economic Forum and corporate leaders from energy, finance, and tech sectors, he built the public-private partnership model that now dominates global policymaking. Multinational corporations were repositioned not as polluters but as stakeholders in managing planetary systems, giving them preferential access to emerging green markets and regulatory influence over "sustainable" technologies.

At the philosophical level, Strong's vision was aligned closely with population control narratives promoted by the Club of Rome and early Rockefeller-funded initiatives. He repeatedly argued that rapid population growth, especially in the developing world, threatened planetary stability. Through UNEP, World Bank programs, and UN development initiatives, he supported integrating family planning and fertility reduction into sustainability frameworks. These policies were often tied to aid conditions, merging environmental imperatives with soft demographic engineering.

Critics accused Strong of using environmental crises to advance a technocratic global order - one where unelected international bodies, corporate coalitions, and NGOs would wield unprecedented influence over energy, agriculture, land use, and even education. And they weren't wrong. The system he helped design deliberately bypassed national legislatures, embedding frameworks like Agenda 21 and the SDGs into trade agreements, corporate governance standards, and financial compliance systems. By aligning the IMF, World Bank, and transnational corporations with UNEP's sustainability agenda, Strong created a global regulatory regime without democratic accountability.

Strong's fingerprints are on nearly every major environmental policy framework of the last 50 years:

- Stockholm 1972 - launched the planetary management narrative.
- UNEP - institutionalized global environmental governance.
- Rio 1992 - produced Agenda 21 and the UNFCCC.

- World Economic Forum - fostered corporate integration into sustainability systems.
- Kyoto Protocol & Paris Accord - advanced long-term frameworks for carbon regulation.

Today, the architecture Strong helped build forms the backbone of the UN Sustainable Development Goals (SDGs) and the climate finance economy. Through carbon markets, ESG scoring systems, and green infrastructure funds, environmental policy now directly influences capital allocation, creating a feedback loop where private investment flows toward projects compliant with global sustainability metrics. Under this model, control over energy, resources, and population dynamics flows upward into transnational institutions that answer not to voters but to elite networks coordinating strategy behind closed doors.

Maurice Strong didn't just advocate environmentalism; he weaponized it. By transforming ecological concern into a planetary-scale emergency narrative, he enabled the creation of a governance model where data-driven management of humanity's relationship with nature became the organizing principle of political and economic power. In doing so, he helped establish the blueprint for environmental technocracy: a system where climate models set policy, sustainability metrics dictate investment, and individual behavior is reshaped by mandates linked to global frameworks.

What Julian Huxley envisioned for UNESCO - reprogramming human values - Maurice Strong operationalized through environmental governance.

The green movement became the control system.

11

Kissinger, Brzezinski, and the Technetronic Era

Henry Kissinger understood something few others in 20th-century geopolitics fully grasped: power in the modern age is not simply exercised through armies, treaties, or economies - it's exercised through information, modeling, and the ability to predict and shape outcomes before they happen. Kissinger's entire career, from his Harvard years to his tenure as National Security Advisor and Secretary of State, reflects a deep commitment to realpolitik - power divorced from ideology, focused on the manipulation of systems, perception, and timing. But beneath the public diplomacy and back-channel negotiations, Kissinger quietly helped pioneer a predictive-simulation framework for statecraft, merging geopolitical strategy with emerging tools in systems theory, game theory, and behavioral modeling developed at RAND and Harvard.

Kissinger's worldview was shaped by his early studies at Harvard under William Yandell Elliott and his close association with the Harvard International Seminar - a program funded covertly by the CIA through the Congress for Cultural Freedom. From the beginning, Kissinger operated at the intersection of academia, intelligence, and elite policymaking networks. His 1957 book Nuclear Weapons and Foreign Policy, written while at Harvard, established his reputation as an advocate for limited nuclear war strategies, but it also revealed his deeper philosophy: decision-makers must move beyond ideology and "moral absolutes" to treat geopolitics as a dynamic system driven by competing variables and feedback loops.

By the early 1960s, Kissinger was working closely with the RAND Corporation, which had become the intellectual engine of predictive modeling in U.S. defense policy. RAND's game-theoretic frameworks, pioneered by figures like John von Neumann, Herman Kahn, and Albert Wohlstetter, sought to simulate Soviet decision-making and U.S. responses under varying scenarios of escalation. Kissinger integrated these tools into his own strategic doctrine, viewing international relations as a constantly shifting equation rather than a fixed contest between ideology or morality.

This synthesis became most visible when Kissinger entered government under Richard Nixon in 1969. As National Security Advisor and later Secretary of State, Kissinger leveraged RAND-style war-gaming simulations to shape responses to crises from Vietnam to the Middle East. These exercises didn't merely model outcomes; they tested psychological levers, probing how adversaries might react to misinformation, back-channel diplomacy, or limited shows of force. By manipulating perceptions as much as facts on the ground, Kissinger perfected a model of predictive influence operations, where shaping an opponent's expectations became as important as moving troops or signing treaties.

One of the most striking examples was Operation Linebacker II in 1972, the so-called "Christmas Bombings" of Hanoi. While publicly portrayed as a military escalation, internal planning documents reveal that Kissinger viewed the operation primarily as a behavioral experiment: testing how calibrated destruction, combined with private negotiations, would alter North Vietnam's decision-making calculus. RAND's predictive models simulated Hanoi's likely responses under varying thresholds of violence, enabling Kissinger to time concessions and ultimatums with maximum psychological effect.

Kissinger also applied these frameworks to global economic policy, particularly during the 1970s energy crises. The 1973 Yom Kippur War and subsequent OPEC oil embargo triggered seismic shifts in global markets, and Kissinger used emerging econometric models to simulate scenarios involving production cuts, currency flows, and geopolitical alignments. Working closely with the Treasury Department, the Council on Foreign Relations, and the Trilateral Commission - founded by David Rockefeller in 1973, where Kissinger was a key participant - he helped redesign international financial policy around predictable interdependence. The aim was not to eliminate conflict but to engineer a system where no major player could act outside modeled constraints without destabilizing their own position.

This technocratic bent became explicit in National Security Study Memorandum 200 (NSSM 200), commissioned by Kissinger in 1974. The report, classified until the 1990s, framed population growth in the Global South as a national security threat to U.S. access to resources. It recommended integrating population control into foreign aid and development programs, coordinating with the UN, IMF, and World Bank. While presented as humanitarian policy, NSSM 200 operationalized demographic modeling as a strategic tool - forecasting fertility trends, migration patterns, and food security decades in advance to preemptively influence regional stability.

Kissinger's secretive diplomacy also mirrored cybernetic principles emerging from Norbert Wiener and RAND: treat global events as interconnected nodes in a complex feedback system. His shuttle diplomacy during the 1973 Arab-Israeli conflict, for instance, wasn't just about brokering peace - it was about stabilizing flows: energy, alliances, arms, and influence. Each concession, treaty, and military shipment was calibrated through iterative simulations, modeling both immediate and downstream effects on U.S. power.

Perhaps Kissinger's most enduring contribution was to normalize the use of predictive simulation as a governing principle. Under his influence, the National Security Council became less a political advisory body and more a real-time strategic laboratory, integrating data streams from intelligence agencies, financial institutions, and military planners. RAND-style decision trees, scenario modeling, and dynamic forecasting became embedded into statecraft itself, accelerating the transition from reactive policymaking to preemptive governance.

By the late 1970s, Kissinger had constructed a geopolitical operating system grounded in three pillars:

• Systems thinking - treat global events as interdependent, modelable processes rather than isolated crises.

• Predictive simulation - use war games, economic models, and behavioral analytics to anticipate adversaries' moves before they act.

• Perception management - engineer expectations through diplomacy, selective information, and calibrated displays of power.

These principles have since become the backbone of U.S. and transnational strategy. NATO war-gaming exercises, IMF debt negotiations, climate security planning, counterterrorism models - all borrow from the predictive frameworks Kissinger helped operationalize. His influence reaches beyond Washington: the World Economic Forum, Trilateral Commission, and Bilderberg Group - all networks Kissinger helped shape - continue to coordinate elite consensus using tools grounded in systems simulation.

Kissinger didn't simply practice realpolitik; he upgraded it. By merging Cold War statecraft with RAND's algorithmic modeling and MIT's systems theory, he pioneered a style of governance where policy emerges from simulation rather than debate. In his worldview, chaos can be managed, crises can be staged, and adversaries can be herded - if you control enough of the inputs, you can anticipate and shape the outputs.

The Kissingerian framework lives on today in predictive policing, financial stress-testing, pandemic modeling, and even climate "risk" dashboards. The logic is the same: if the models say a future is probable, governance assumes the authority to act preemptively - whether the modeled threat materializes or not. Kissinger helped normalize this epistemology: simulation becomes justification, prediction becomes policy. He didn't just master the game. He rewrote its rules.

Zbigniew Brzezinski, National Security Advisor to President Jimmy Carter and one of the most influential geopolitical strategists of the 20th century, was more than a Cold War tactician. Through his 1970 book Between Two Ages: America's Role in the Technetronic Era, Brzezinski articulated a blueprint for global governance - a vision of centralized control, transnational institutions, and the merging of technology, surveillance, and behavioral engineering into a new operating system for power. Where Henry Kissinger refined predictive statecraft inside the machinery of U.S. diplomacy, Brzezinski went further, laying out the ideological and technological framework for a post-national world order.

Brzezinski's worldview was shaped by his personal history as a Polish-born scholar who fled Soviet totalitarianism, giving him a lifelong obsession with managing superpower rivalry. After earning his Ph.D. at Harvard, he rose rapidly through elite policy networks: teaching at Harvard and Columbia, joining the Council on Foreign Relations, advising the Rockefeller Brothers Fund, and ultimately co-founding the Trilateral Commission in 1973 with David Rockefeller. These circles positioned Brzezinski at the intersection of academia, banking, and geopolitical strategy - where he became a leading advocate for transnational integration as the only way to manage emerging systemic crises.

In Between Two Ages, Brzezinski argued that the 20th century marked the transition from the Industrial Era to the Technetronic Era - a new phase of civilization driven by computerization, automation, and global interconnectivity. This transformation, he believed, required a corresponding transformation of governance. Nation-states, rooted in territorial sovereignty and slow-moving democratic processes, were ill-equipped to manage planetary-scale challenges like energy scarcity, financial instability, population growth, and environmental degradation. The solution, according to Brzezinski, was to build transnational institutions capable of integrating policy across borders and using technological tools to manage societies in real time.

Brzezinski's writing was remarkably candid about the technocratic shift he envisioned. He described a coming world where elites would leverage "the latest scientific techniques" to monitor, predict, and influence human behavior at scale:

"The technetronic era involves the gradual appearance of a more controlled society... dominated by an elite, unrestrained by traditional values. This elite would use modern technology for political purposes, obtaining continuous surveillance over every citizen and maintaining up-to-date files containing even the most personal information about them."

This was not speculative science fiction - Brzezinski was describing projects already underway. Drawing from RAND research, MIT cybernetics labs, and early computer networking experiments like ARPANET, he anticipated a world where digital infrastructures would underpin governance itself. The fusion of surveillance, real-time data collection, and algorithmic decision-making would allow leaders to manage populations not reactively but preemptively, shaping behavior through subtle nudges, economic incentives, and cultural programming.

Between Two Ages also framed the United States' role in this transformation. Brzezinski saw America as the necessary architect of this new order but not its permanent hegemon. Instead, U.S. power would be leveraged to create supranational frameworks - integrating NATO, the IMF, World Bank, and emerging organizations like the G7 into a networked governance model. Sovereignty would remain nominal, but real decision-making would migrate upward into expert-driven, technocratic bodies insulated from electoral politics.

Brzezinski's ideas became operational when he co-founded the Trilateral Commission with David Rockefeller in 1973. Bringing together political leaders, corporate executives, bankers, and academics from North America, Europe, and Japan, the Commission sought to synchronize policy among the advanced industrial nations. Its reports emphasized "interdependence" - a euphemism for embedding nations into shared regulatory regimes, standardized financial systems, and common energy and resource policies. Brzezinski believed this elite coordination was necessary to prevent "chaotic nationalism" from destabilizing the emerging global order.

During his tenure as Carter's National Security Advisor (1977–1981), Brzezinski applied these principles directly to U.S. foreign policy. He expanded the use of real-time intelligence and predictive modeling within the National Security Council, integrating satellite reconnaissance, economic forecasting, and behavioral analysis into decision-making. He oversaw the formalization of the National Security Directive system, which streamlined executive control over foreign and defense policy, bypassing many traditional checks and balances in Congress. Under Brzezinski, the NSC became a technocratic command center, leveraging simulations and multi-variable risk models to anticipate Soviet actions, energy disruptions, and regional conflicts before they escalated.

Brzezinski was also central in framing population control and resource management as security issues. Like Kissinger's NSSM 200, he viewed demographic trends - particularly in the Global South - as destabilizing variables in global simulations. Through collaborations with the World Bank, IMF, and UNESCO, Brzezinski advocated integrating fertility reduction, agricultural planning, and energy rationing into broader development programs. These weren't pitched as coercive policies but as technical solutions to avoid planetary catastrophe, embedding behavioral engineering within the language of sustainability and humanitarianism.

Crucially, Brzezinski anticipated the rise of algorithmic governance decades before it became explicit policy. He predicted that digital communication networks, financial clearing systems, and global databases would converge into a unified infrastructure for real-time population management: economic transactions, health records, political affiliations, and even personal attitudes would be quantifiable, trackable, and influenceable through centralized systems. While his language was cautious, his meaning was clear - information itself would become the substrate of power.

This vision now underpins much of what we see in today's governance frameworks:

- The IMF and World Bank standardizing fiscal policy through programmable debt structures.

• The UN Sustainable Development Goals (SDGs) embedding global benchmarks into national laws.

• The integration of digital ID systems, biometric passports, and centralized payment rails into mobility and financial networks.

• Global climate governance frameworks aligning energy consumption, carbon markets, and behavioral metrics under transnational coordination.

Brzezinski also understood the importance of manufacturing consensus. Beyond raw data collection, he emphasized the need for managing culture, information flows, and perception to sustain legitimacy. Through partnerships with media, academia, and NGOs, he advocated aligning narratives with long-term strategic objectives. In this sense, his approach foreshadowed today's information control regimes, where search engines, social platforms, and algorithmic curation shape public opinion inside closed feedback loops optimized for political stability.

By the time he published Between Two Ages, Brzezinski had already mapped the contours of the technetronic state - a world where technology, surveillance, and centralized governance merge into a seamless system of behavioral prediction and management. Unlike traditional empires, this new order wouldn't require overt domination; it would operate invisibly through standards, algorithms, and dependencies.

Brzezinski's influence is still everywhere. The Trilateral Commission, World Economic Forum, UN frameworks, and climate governance agendas all bear his fingerprints. The modern push for digital currencies, carbon markets, and centralized data infrastructures follows precisely the trajectory he outlined: a transition from sovereign nation-states toward an integrated, model-driven system of global governance.

Where Kissinger perfected the art of manipulating geopolitical variables, Brzezinski designed the architecture for managing them. He envisioned a world where governments become subsystems within a planetary operating model, coordinated not through ideology or democratic debate but through real-time data, predictive simulation, and elite consensus.

This wasn't conspiracy. It was the plan - written openly, implemented methodically, and now embedded in the frameworks that define the 21st century.

The map to global governance was drawn in Between Two Ages.

he 20th century began with tanks, trenches, and territorial conquest, but by the second half of the century, the mechanisms of power had fundamentally shifted. Modern empires learned that they no longer needed to occupy land with armies to control it. Direct military domination gave way to economic leverage, psychological manipulation, and algorithmic influence - a quieter, more insidious form of warfare conducted through finance, information, and perception. The world moved from bombs and borders to models and minds, where domination was achieved not by destroying cities but by shaping behavior, controlling narratives, and engineering dependencies.

This transformation accelerated after World War II, when two lessons became clear to global elites. First, industrial-scale conflict had reached technological limits: nuclear weapons made direct great-power war potentially suicidal. Second, maintaining influence over vast populations and resources required methods less visible and more sustainable than armies stationed on foreign soil. The result was a strategic pivot - a shift from hard power to soft power, from kinetic force to control over economies, information systems, and psychological states.

The Bretton Woods Conference in 1944 symbolized the beginning of this transition. Instead of dividing the postwar world through military occupations alone, Western elites created financial governance systems - the IMF, World Bank, and eventually the dollar-based global reserve system - that allowed them to control economic behavior indirectly. Debt became a weapon as effective as artillery. By conditioning access to capital on compliance with structural reforms, these institutions reshaped national economies without firing a shot. Developing nations seeking reconstruction or modernization were trapped in cycles of conditionality, privatization, and dependency - a process often described as "development" but functioning in practice as economic conquest.

Simultaneously, the Cold War turned psychological warfare into a central strategic tool. Recognizing that populations could be managed through perception rather than force, U.S. and Soviet agencies invested heavily in information operations, propaganda systems, and cultural programming. The CIA funded magazines, films, and academic conferences to promote Western liberal ideals, while the Soviet Union flooded media with counter-narratives about capitalist exploitation. The battlefield moved into minds and classrooms, where controlling how people thought became more powerful than controlling where they lived.

By the 1960s and 1970s, advances in behavioral science and cybernetics expanded the arsenal of psychological tools. Research funded by DARPA, RAND, and the Rockefeller networks revealed that societies could be modeled like dynamic systems - with inputs (information, incentives, fear), outputs (behavior, compliance, unrest), and feedback loops for continuous adjustment. Military think tanks, intelligence agencies, and advertising conglomerates converged around a shared goal: engineer predictable responses at scale. This approach birthed "hearts and minds" campaigns in Vietnam, predictive policing programs in U.S. cities, and large-scale perception management experiments - all precursors to today's algorithmic targeting and social media manipulation.

The emergence of global broadcast media amplified this shift. By the 1980s, television, radio, and satellite news created a shared perceptual environment where narratives could be shaped instantly and globally. Events like the fall of the Berlin Wall, Desert Storm, and later 9/11 demonstrated that images and emotional triggers could achieve strategic outcomes faster than armies could mobilize. Wars no longer required occupation; they required consensus manufacturing, where populations consented to policies, sanctions, and even invasions because the information environment was carefully engineered to justify them.

At the same time, economic warfare evolved beyond simple trade policy into financial weaponization. With the creation of globalized markets, multinational banking networks, and transnational supply chains, states could now destabilize adversaries by manipulating currencies, choking off credit, or redirecting investment flows. Sanctions became precision tools for shaping behavior, from Iran to Venezuela to Russia. The introduction of petrodollar recycling in the 1970s tied global energy markets directly to U.S. monetary dominance, transforming resource flows into strategic levers. Nations that resisted integration into this financial order found themselves isolated, indebted, or destabilized.

By the turn of the millennium, the digital revolution merged economic and psychological warfare into a single infrastructure of control. Surveillance systems, data analytics, and real-time feedback loops - pioneered by DARPA, RAND, and the NSA - made it possible to monitor not just borders or bank accounts, but minds, preferences, and social behaviors at planetary scale. Platforms like Google, Facebook, and Twitter were integrated into a broader network of algorithmic governance, where information feeds were weaponized to polarize, pacify, or mobilize populations as needed. Influence operations no longer required state-run propaganda departments; private corporations became the proxy battlefield commanders, working in lockstep with intelligence agencies and supranational institutions.

This shift also reframed the very concept of sovereignty. Traditional military occupations were costly and politically unsustainable; economic entanglements and perception management were cheaper and harder to resist. Programs like the UN's Sustainable Development Goals (SDGs), ESG scoring frameworks, and WHO-aligned digital ID initiatives now operate as non-military levers of compliance, standardizing laws, energy policies, and financial systems across nations without deploying a single soldier. What was once enforced by armies is now achieved by dependency and data.

Modern warfare, in this sense, is increasingly invisible. It operates through:

- Economic subjugation: debt leverage, sanctions, currency manipulation, and financial dependencies.

• Cognitive manipulation: managing perception through algorithmic feeds, "fact-checking," and emotional priming.

• Behavioral nudging: using predictive analytics to subtly guide decisions, from consumer purchases to political allegiance.

• Crisis exploitation: framing pandemics, climate events, and economic shocks as justifications for emergency powers and centralization.

• Digital integration: linking identity, finance, and mobility to networked infrastructures controlled by transnational institutions.

Military force has not disappeared - but it now serves as the final step, deployed only when economic coercion or psychological influence fails. Even kinetic conflicts today are mediated through information dominance: drone strikes are justified via "narrative battlespaces," and entire populations are corralled into ideological positions through preemptive narrative control long before the first shot is fired.

This transformation reflects a broader philosophical shift in governance itself: from ruling bodies to managing systems. Population movements, economic flows, environmental impacts, and political attitudes are now treated as dynamic variables inside predictive models, continuously adjusted through policy, media, and markets. Wars are no longer declared; they are modeled, simulated, and optimized.

In this new paradigm, conquest happens quietly. Borders remain, flags still wave, and parliaments convene - but sovereignty is hollowed out. Control flows through debt agreements, trade dependencies, media ecosystems, and behavioral data. Armies are secondary. Algorithms are primary.

It is the invisible battlefield of the 21st century: a seamless integration of economic, psychological, and technological power designed not to destroy populations, but to manage them.

The Vietnam War became RAND Corporation's most ambitious laboratory - not just for military strategy but for testing predictive modeling, population control, and managed conflict on a massive scale. While publicly framed as a fight to contain communism, RAND's role in Vietnam reveals a deeper transformation in how war was conceived and waged: not as a contest to win outright, but as a system to measure, simulate, and optimize.

From the early 1960s onward, RAND embedded analysts directly into South Vietnam under Pentagon contracts. Their mission was ostensibly to study insurgency and counterinsurgency, but in practice, they were building feedback loops between real-time battlefield data, computer simulations, and Washington policy decisions. RAND treated Vietnam as a living system. Every variable - troop movements, village loyalties, food supply, propaganda saturation - was quantified, mapped, and fed into primitive computational models designed to forecast outcomes and recommend interventions weeks or even months ahead of events.

One of RAND's most ambitious undertakings was the "Hamlet Evaluation System," designed to score thousands of villages across South Vietnam based on population size, economic productivity, political allegiance, and vulnerability to Viet Cong influence. These scores were intended to predict which hamlets were most at risk of "flipping" and which could be secured through aid, targeted propaganda, or military presence. Behind the rhetoric of "hearts and minds," RAND was operationalizing algorithmic control of populations decades before predictive policing became policy.

Behavior itself became a weapon. RAND analysts, drawing on psychology, anthropology, and cybernetics, studied how fear, deprivation, incentives, and messaging could alter compliance and allegiance. Food distribution, targeted radio broadcasts, and infrastructure projects weren't just humanitarian efforts - they were inputs in a model designed to steer attitudes systematically. Even strategic bombing was analyzed less for physical destruction than for psychological shock. RAND simulations tested how calibrated levels of violence would break morale, fragment loyalties, or force negotiation. Vietnam became an early proving ground for behavioral warfare, where the primary battlefield was perception, not terrain.

By the mid-1960s, RAND's internal memos revealed a striking shift:

the goal was no longer necessarily to "win" the war in the traditional sense. Instead, Vietnam was increasingly treated as a managed conflict, one calibrated to drain adversaries' resources, test counterinsurgency strategies, and refine predictive models for future theaters. Escalation and de-escalation decisions were often driven less by ground conditions and more by RAND's simulations, which ran thousands of scenarios projecting likely Vietnamese, Soviet, and Chinese responses under varying pressures. War became less about battlefield victory and more about systems optimization.

This approach informed some of the most controversial U.S. strategies in Vietnam. RAND's research directly influenced the CIA-backed Phoenix Program, designed to dismantle the Viet Cong's political infrastructure through targeted "neutralizations." By combining village-level data, informant networks, and RAND's risk-scoring models, Phoenix identified suspected insurgents and sympathizers based on probabilistic assessments. Tens of thousands of people were detained, interrogated, or killed as a result of these methods. It was one of the earliest instances of predictive analytics driving real-world lethal decisions - the direct ancestor of today's algorithmic profiling in counterterrorism and domestic policing alike.

Despite U.S. withdrawal in 1975, RAND's Vietnam experiments succeeded in reshaping how modern conflicts are fought. The lessons learned were rapidly integrated into future doctrines. Counterinsurgency strategies in Iraq and Afghanistan drew heavily on Vietnam-era frameworks, combining social data, population scoring, and behavioral targeting. Psychological influence operations - once tested on hamlets - became global in scale, amplified by social media algorithms decades later. Surveillance infrastructures pioneered during Vietnam evolved into today's integrated systems, linking signals intelligence, economic modeling, and real-time sentiment analysis to manage populations at scale.

Vietnam demonstrated that conflicts didn't have to be "won" to serve strategic objectives. They could be engineered, prolonged, and managed. RAND's simulations and population models created a template for perpetual interventionism: conflicts remain unstable enough to justify continuous oversight yet controlled enough to avoid systemic collapse. It was a subtle but profound pivot from decisive conquest to maintenance of controlled instability, where the war's value lies not in its resolution but in the data it produces and the leverage it creates.

This was the turning point where war became information. RAND fused systems theory, behavioral science, and computational modeling into a single operational framework. Villages became datasets. Loyalties became variables. People became risk scores. Vietnam wasn't just a battleground; it was the prototype for algorithmic governance. The techniques tested there now underpin predictive policing in U.S. cities, counterterrorism frameworks abroad, and the information architectures used to influence global perception today.

RAND didn't simply study the Vietnam War; it programmed its logic. What began as a counterinsurgency experiment became the foundation for a model of power that transcends battlefields entirely - one where populations are monitored, modeled, and managed continuously, and where simulation dictates strategy more than reality itself.

PART IV - THE CORPORATE COUP (1970–2000)

D avos, deregulation, and Silicon Valley's birth.

12

Klaus Schwab and the Birth of Davos

The World Economic Forum (WEF), founded in 1971 by German economist Klaus Schwab, is often portrayed today as an open platform where global leaders gather to "shape a better future." But from its inception, the WEF was never a neutral meeting ground. It was conceived as an elite coordination hub, created and financed by some of the most powerful financial, political, and corporate networks of the late 20th century. Behind the public image of multilateral dialogue and economic cooperation, the WEF's founding reflects a deliberate strategy: to synchronize global policy agendas, integrate corporate and political power, and centralize influence within a small circle of unelected actors. Schwab established the organization under the name the European Management Forum, with the first meeting held in Davos, Switzerland, in January 1971. Ostensibly, the purpose was to bring together European business leaders to discuss modern management techniques and competitiveness in a rapidly changing global economy. But Schwab's vision was never confined to corporate best practices; from the start, he aimed to build a networked infrastructure of influence where business, government, academia, and media could align behind long-term objectives - bypassing traditional democratic processes.

The official origin story highlights Schwab's education at Harvard's Kennedy School of Government, where he studied under Henry Kissinger. This connection was pivotal. Kissinger's mentorship shaped

Schwab's geopolitical worldview and gave him access to American corporate networks, while also embedding him within elite policy circles tied to the Council on Foreign Relations and the newly founded Trilateral Commission. Schwab's proximity to Kissinger connected him to David Rockefeller's network, which at the time was actively constructing frameworks for transnational governance that would merge political decision-making with corporate power.

Behind the scenes, hidden sponsors helped incubate the forum. Funding and institutional support flowed quietly from the European Commission, NATO-aligned think tanks, and major U.S. foundations tied to Rockefeller and Carnegie interests. The CIA-linked Congress for Cultural Freedom - active in shaping intellectual networks across Europe - also intersected with early WEF participants, seeding ideological alignment around free markets, technological modernization, and "global interdependence." In Europe, the Club of Rome, founded just three years earlier in 1968, had begun advocating for systems-based management of resources and population growth. Schwab invited several of its key members to Davos, embedding their narratives of sustainability and limits-to-growth into the WEF's DNA from the very first meeting.

Schwab's Harvard connections also introduced him to the emerging U.S. tech-industrial elite. Companies like IBM, General Electric, and ITT were early backers of Schwab's vision, providing sponsorships and leveraging the WEF as a platform to integrate Europe into American-led economic frameworks. Meanwhile, German industrial giants like Siemens, Volkswagen, and ThyssenKrupp provided European corporate legitimacy and resources. From the beginning, the WEF's funding structure mirrored its agenda: public messaging about collaboration cloaked a deeper alignment of Western finance, defense, and technology sectors under a shared vision of integrated governance.

By the mid-1970s, the WEF's scope expanded rapidly. What began as a regional business forum became a global policy laboratory, drawing not just CEOs but heads of state, central bankers, intelligence advisors, and media barons. Schwab intentionally blurred the boundaries be-tween public and private authority, cultivating what he later called the "multi-stakeholder model" - a governance framework where corpora-tions, NGOs, and supranational bodies share equal or greater power than elected governments in setting global priorities.

This model had quiet but powerful patrons. The Trilateral Commis-sion, co-founded by David Rockefeller and Zbigniew Brzezinski in 1973, strongly overlapped with WEF participants, supplying ideological framing for "interdependence" and shared sovereignty. Meanwhile, funding from Rockefeller-affiliated foundations provided continuity between initiatives launched at Davos and programs coordinated through the World Bank, IMF, and later the United Nations. NATO and the OECD discreetly provided policy experts and strategic research, ensuring WEF discussions aligned with broader Western defense and economic objectives.

The WEF's early conferences reveal just how deeply these interests were embedded. Among its first guests were members of the Club of Rome, architects of The Limits to Growth, which framed humanity itself as a destabilizing variable requiring centralized management of energy, re-sources, and population. Schwab seized on this narrative, integrating environmental governance into the WEF's long-term agenda decades before "climate policy" entered mainstream discourse. These ideas would eventually evolve into the forum's later promotion of Agenda 21, the Sustainable Development Goals, and the framing of global crises as justification for coordinated interventions by technocratic institutions.

By the 1980s, the WEF had become a trusted interface for elite syn-chronization. Heads of state like Helmut Schmidt, Pierre Trudeau, and Jimmy Carter attended Davos alongside central bank governors and Fortune 100 executives, shaping frameworks for trade liberalization, deregulation, and cross-border integration. Technology firms used the WEF to position themselves as central actors in the coming digital in-frastructure revolution, while financial institutions leveraged Davos to influence emerging global regulatory standards.

From the start, the WEF was never simply a business conference. It was conceived as an alignment hub - a place where narratives, policies, and corporate strategies could be harmonized above the level of national debate. Behind Schwab's public persona as a facilitator, the forum operated as a shadow policy network, incubating frameworks that would later be adopted wholesale by the UN, IMF, and G20. Its founding sponsors and intellectual architects ensured that Davos was designed not to empower democratic participation but to centralize influence within an interlocking web of financial, political, and corporate elites.

The language of cooperation and progress masked a deeper project: building an integrated technocratic governance model, where supranational institutions, corporations, and NGOs would set the rules of global order. Over decades, this "multi-stakeholder" vision has steadily advanced, embedding WEF-driven policies into climate regulation, ESG standards, digital infrastructure, and even public health coordination - all without requiring formal consent from national electorates.

The WEF's founding in 1971 marked the quiet creation of an elite coordination platform designed to accelerate this transformation. Schwab's Harvard mentorship under Kissinger, Rockefeller-linked sponsorships, and integration with Club of Rome systems theory ensured that Davos would become the interface layer between private wealth, public authority, and emerging technological systems. Its power has always been less about overt declarations and more about controlling what gets discussed, what gets funded, and what becomes inevitable.

From the very beginning, the WEF positioned itself as neutral. In reality, it was built as a steering mechanism for a world where economic, technological, and political power are consolidated into transnational networks - coordinated, invisible, and insulated from democratic accountability.

Klaus Schwab's concept of "stakeholder capitalism" sounds innocuous - even progressive - on the surface. First introduced in his 1971 book Modern Enterprise Management in Mechanical Engineering and later expanded through the World Economic Forum (WEF), the idea reframes corporations not as entities serving only shareholders but as institutions accountable to "all stakeholders": employees, communities, governments, NGOs, and even the environment.

But behind the rhetoric of inclusivity and responsibility lies a profound shift in the architecture of governance. Stakeholder capitalism was designed not to democratize decision-making but to elevate CEOs and corporate boards into the role of unelected policymakers, consolidating power within transnational networks insulated from national legislatures, public consent, and traditional accountability structures.

Schwab unveiled his vision during the founding years of the WEF, just as neoliberal globalization was accelerating. By the early 1970s, financial elites, central bankers, and policymakers were grappling with systemic volatility: the collapse of the Bretton Woods system, oil shocks, rising inflation, and political unrest. Schwab, influenced heavily by Henry Kissinger's realpolitik and the emerging Club of Rome systems theory, positioned stakeholder capitalism as a framework to stabilize global governance without relying on messy democratic processes.

At its core, stakeholder capitalism proposes that corporations are no longer just market actors; they become governing institutions. Instead of answering exclusively to investors, multinational companies are encouraged to "balance the interests" of governments, NGOs, and citizens - yet they are never elected, never subjected to transparent oversight, and never held to the same standards of public accountability as legislatures. Schwab envisioned CEOs as strategic coordinators of societal priorities, integrating economic, environmental, and social objectives into their business decisions in alignment with global frameworks rather than national policy.

The WEF operationalized this ideology through its "multi-stakeholder governance" model, which Schwab promoted as a more "inclusive" alternative to traditional democratic processes. In practice, this meant creating private-public governance structures where CEOs, central bankers, NGOs, and supranational agencies like the UN and IMF could collaborate on policy agendas directly - bypassing parliaments, voters, and even sovereign governments. Schwab framed this as an evolution beyond outdated nation-state politics: "The sovereign state," he wrote, "has become too small for the big problems of life and too big for the small ones."

This philosophy became institutionalized through WEF initiatives launched at Davos. Working groups on climate policy, digital infrastructure, pandemic preparedness, and financial integration brought together executives from companies like Microsoft, BlackRock, Pfizer, Google, Shell, and JPMorgan alongside UN officials, IMF economists, and government ministers. These "multi-stakeholder task forces" drafted policy frameworks that would later inform international treaties, ESG compliance standards, and cross-border regulatory regimes. National legislatures were largely sidelined, presented with pre-engineered policies marketed as global "consensus."

Stakeholder capitalism gained momentum in the late 1990s and 2000s, particularly as the WEF aligned itself with the United Nations Sustainable Development Goals (SDGs) and Agenda 21 frameworks. Schwab positioned CEOs as the essential drivers of sustainability, innovation, and "inclusive capitalism." Under this model, the private sector would no longer simply react to regulation; it would define it. Global corporations began setting their own environmental and social targets, leveraging frameworks built in Davos to shape laws in their favor - from carbon markets and energy policy to data governance and digital identity systems.

Crucially, stakeholder capitalism integrates with financial technocracy. Through ESG (Environmental, Social, and Governance) scoring systems - heavily promoted by WEF and BlackRock - access to capital is increasingly tied to corporate alignment with global sustainability and governance goals. These metrics are created and enforced by private consultancies, rating agencies, and transnational organizations, granting unelected actors enormous influence over which companies succeed, which industries survive, and which national policies receive investment.

The 2020 launch of the Great Reset initiative made stakeholder capitalism explicit. Schwab argued that the COVID-19 pandemic represented a "narrow window of opportunity" to "reshape the global economy" and "revamp all aspects of our societies and economies." WEF documents outlined sweeping transformations in energy, labor, supply chains, and digital governance - coordinated not by parliaments or voters but by networks of CEOs, central bankers, and technocrats. The pandemic became a catalyst for normalizing corporate-led governance, using emergency narratives to accelerate integration of private actors into decision-making at every level.

Under stakeholder capitalism, power migrates upward into a networked oligarchy:

• Corporations set policy targets through multi-stakeholder task forces.

• Supranational agencies like the UN, IMF, and WHO embed these frameworks into "global priorities."

• Financial institutions enforce compliance through ESG scoring and capital flows.

• National governments implement policies drafted elsewhere, often under pressure from investment and trade dependencies.

This arrangement creates the appearance of inclusivity - more "voices at the table" - but in reality, it concentrates authority among a small circle of actors with no direct accountability to the populations they govern. Unlike democratic systems, where policies are debated openly and representatives can be voted out, stakeholder capitalism operates through elite consensus, closed-door negotiations, and financial incentives.

In Schwab's vision, the CEO becomes a kind of meta-policymaker, sitting above elected governments, collaborating directly with global institutions, and shaping society through control over capital, infrastructure, and technological ecosystems. Citizens are reframed not as voters but as "stakeholders" - participants without power in a system where decisions are pre-negotiated by corporate, financial, and supranational elites.

This ideology now dominates nearly every sphere of global policy. Climate agreements, digital governance frameworks, pandemic response strategies, and energy transition plans are all coordinated through WEF-style multi-stakeholder partnerships. Through these mechanisms, corporations influence - and often write - the rules under which they operate, effectively positioning themselves above the state while appearing to act in the public interest.

Stakeholder capitalism was never about redistributing power downward. It was about pulling governance upward - from parliaments to boardrooms, from voters to unelected networks, from messy democratic negotiation to centralized, algorithm-driven consensus. Schwab's Davos model reframes sovereignty as a liability and positions technocratic coordination as the inevitable future.

What emerges is not democracy, nor free-market capitalism in its classical sense, but a hybrid system where policy and profit converge under the stewardship of a transnational managerial class. In this model, CEOs are no longer just market actors; they are de facto architects of society, wielding authority without electoral mandates, insulated from the accountability mechanisms that define representative governance.

Stakeholder capitalism, in effect, was the opening gambit for the WEF's long game: a governance model where corporate power and global institutions fuse into a seamless, unelected policymaking apparatus - one where the levers of change are controlled by those who own the infrastructure, set the metrics, and manage the data flows that define modern life.

The façade is inclusivity. The reality is control.

Elite grooming networks are the quiet engines behind modern governance. They operate in the shadows, shaping who rises to positions of power, what narratives dominate global discourse, and which policies become "inevitable" long before the public ever hears about them. These systems don't function like secret cabals in smoke-filled rooms. They're far more sophisticated - interconnected pipelines of education, funding, mentorship, and access designed to manufacture influence and ideological conformity at scale.

This model stretches back over a century. The early example was the Rhodes Scholarship, established in 1902 by British imperialist Cecil Rhodes. Its explicit goal was to identify talented young leaders across the English-speaking world, bring them into elite academic environments like Oxford, and inculcate them with a vision of global integration aligned with British geopolitical priorities. It wasn't just about education; it was about network seeding. Alumni returned to their countries carrying the same frameworks, forging bonds that transcended national interests and aligned future power blocs under shared values and objectives.

By the mid-20th century, this template had expanded dramatically. Institutions like Harvard, Yale, Cambridge, and the London School of Economics became central nodes in cultivating a managerial class built for transnational governance. Backed by foundations like Rockefeller, Carnegie, and Ford, these universities evolved into incubators for technocratic thinking, where emerging leaders were trained to view national sovereignty as an obstacle and interdependence as inevitable. Their graduates - presidents, central bankers, CEOs, NGO directors - emerged already aligned with the priorities of global elites long before they ever held office.

The grooming extended beyond academia into tightly controlled policy networks. The Council on Foreign Relations (CFR) in the U.S., Chatham House in the U.K., and the Trilateral Commission - cofounded by David Rockefeller and Zbigniew Brzezinski in 1973 - all served as staging grounds where corporate executives, academics, diplomats, and military strategists coordinated long-term agendas behind closed doors. These weren't forums for open debate; they were alignment machines. Attendees entered with national perspectives but left with consensus on financial integration, deregulation, security priorities, and global governance frameworks.

Alongside these policy hubs emerged influence manufacturing ecosystems. Private think tanks, philanthropic foundations, and NGOs became conduits for embedding elite agendas into government and culture without appearing coercive. Organizations like the Brookings Institution, Carnegie Endowment, and Rockefeller Foundation funded research that conveniently aligned with preferred narratives, from economic liberalization to population control. White papers produced in these circles flowed downstream into legislation, media talking points, and educational curricula, creating the appearance of "grassroots consensus" when in reality the narrative was engineered upstream by unelected actors.

In the 1970s, the rise of the World Economic Forum (WEF) transformed this architecture into a more direct operating system for global power. Klaus Schwab's "multi-stakeholder" model positioned corporations alongside governments, NGOs, and supranational bodies as equal partners in policymaking. Over time, this evolved into an inversion of democratic norms: policies were often designed in Davos first, then presented to legislatures as fait accompli. The WEF's Young Global Leaders (YGL) program, launched in 2004, made this process explicit. Through YGL, hundreds of carefully selected politicians, tech entrepreneurs, central bankers, and media figures were trained to operate inside Davos-aligned frameworks.

The results are everywhere. YGL alumni now occupy positions as heads of state, ministers of health, central bank governors, and corporate CEOs. Figures like Emmanuel Macron, Mark Zuckerberg, Jacinda Ardern, and numerous European and African leaders passed through WEF grooming programs that emphasize sustainability narratives, digital governance frameworks, and corporate-public partnerships. When these leaders later implement policies aligned with WEF priorities - ESG compliance, carbon markets, vaccine passports, central bank digital currencies - it is framed as organic political consensus, not the result of upstream ideological engineering.

Media plays a critical role in this ecosystem. Elite fellowships funded by institutions like the Reuters Institute, Open Society Foundations, and the Poynter Institute cultivate editors, journalists, and influencers who carry approved narratives into mass communication. From climate policy to pandemic response to financial integration, these curated pipelines ensure message alignment across networks without requiring overt censorship. Influence is laundered through "independent" voices who are part of the same circles writing the scripts.

This is how policy now moves:

• Grooming networks select and elevate the next generation of leaders before they enter the public eye.

• Think tanks and NGOs engineer narratives aligned with transnational priorities.

• Media and academic ecosystems amplify and normalize those narratives under the guise of independent expertise.

• Legislatures, operating downstream, are presented with frameworks that already enjoy "global consensus."

The result is a managed spectrum of ideas where dissent rarely reaches the mainstream because the boundaries of debate are drawn long before it begins. Whether it's energy policy, public health, or digital infrastructure, the apparent diversity of voices masks a deeper monoculture of thought cultivated by the same institutions funding, training, and promoting those voices.

This isn't conspiracy; it's infrastructure. Over decades, elites built overlapping pipelines of education, funding, access, and media amplification designed to shape not only who leads but how they think and what they believe is possible. Influence is manufactured, not debated. Consent is engineered, not earned.

Democracy becomes choreography. Leaders appear to compete on stage, but their scripts are written by the same upstream networks, trained in the same institutions, aligned with the same "inevitable" frameworks for global governance. The audience is invited to cheer, protest, or debate within the confines of narratives that were pre-selected long before ballots are cast.

This is the quiet efficiency of elite grooming. It doesn't seize power; it curates it. It doesn't silence dissent; it renders it irrelevant. The result is a seamless machinery of influence that produces leaders, policies, and narratives that appear independent yet move in lockstep - synchronized not by conspiracy but by design.

13

The Financial Overlords

D avid Rockefeller was more than a banker; he was one of the principal architects of modern transnational governance. As chairman of Chase Manhattan Bank and heir to the Rockefeller legacy, his influence spanned finance, energy, media, philanthropy, and geopolitics. But his most enduring creation came in 1973 with the founding of the Trilateral Commission - a network designed to synchronize economic, political, and technological strategies across the U.S., Europe, and Japan during a period of profound global transformation. Far from being a simple policy discussion forum, the Commission served as an alignment engine, manufacturing consensus among elites and bypassing traditional democratic processes to advance a model of technocratic integration.

Rockefeller established the Trilateral Commission alongside Zbigniew Brzezinski, then a rising geopolitical theorist and author of Between Two Ages: America's Role in the Technetronic Era. Brzezinski's book framed the 1970s as a pivotal transition between the industrial age and the technetronic era - an emerging phase where technological systems, data networks, and economic interdependence would redefine sovereignty and power. Rockefeller, with his vast networks across banking, corporate boards, and international philanthropy, recognized the opportunity to operationalize Brzezinski's vision. Together, they launched the Commission to integrate three major industrial blocs - North America, Western Europe, and Japan - into a single coordinated framework. The timing was strategic. The early 1970s marked a period of deep systemic stress: the collapse of the Bretton Woods monetary system, the 1973 oil shock, rising stagflation, and political upheaval. These crises created an opening for elites to redefine the architecture of governance, arguing that national governments were incapable of solving "global problems" in isolation. The Commission's solution was to bring together corporate CEOs, central bankers, academic theorists, media executives, and political leaders into one network - one where policies could be pre-aligned behind closed doors before being implemented publicly. From the start, the Trilateral Commission was not a think tank in the traditional sense. Its members weren't debating ideology; they were engineering consensus. The goal was to harmonize trade policy, fiscal strategies, resource management, and regulatory standards across the three regions. Rockefeller leveraged his influence at Chase Manhattan and within the Council on Foreign Relations (CFR) to recruit participants with reach inside governments and corporations alike. By concentrating decision-makers in a single closed-loop network, the Commission ensured that the same frameworks flowed seamlessly through media narratives, legislative priorities, and corporate strategies across continents.

A central focus of the Commission's early work was the integration of global financial systems. With the U.S. dollar newly decoupled from gold in 1971, Rockefeller and his peers sought to stabilize global liquidity and capital flows while cementing dollar dominance. Reports authored by Commission task forces laid the groundwork for the liberalization of international capital markets, setting the stage for financial globalization. Policies promoting deregulation, free capital mobility, and resource interdependence - drafted within Commission meetings - were later implemented through institutions like the IMF, World Bank, and OECD, embedding Rockefeller's priorities within the infrastructure of global finance.

But the Commission's ambitions extended beyond economics. Brzezinski, serving as its first director, pushed for frameworks of shared sovereignty in areas such as energy, defense, and technology. Member discussions addressed topics like coordinated oil stockpiling, joint military basing, and integrated energy planning, arguing that no single nation could independently secure its future. These conversations directly influenced U.S. foreign policy during Brzezinski's later role as National Security Advisor under President Jimmy Carter (a Trilateral Commission member himself), particularly regarding Middle East strategies, arms control agreements, and the normalization of relations with China.

Critics at the time accused the Commission of undermining democracy - and with reason. Its reports routinely emphasized the "crisis of governability" within Western democracies, suggesting that populations were becoming too politically active and that decision-making needed to shift toward "responsible elites" insulated from public pressures. A 1975 Commission report, co-authored by Harvard political scientist Samuel Huntington, openly argued that excessive public participation created instability and inefficiency, proposing instead a model where unelected technocrats, corporate stakeholders, and global institutions would set priorities beyond electoral cycles. This philosophy became a blueprint for post-democratic governance: the appearance of democratic choice remained, but real decisions increasingly migrated to elite-managed networks operating above national politics.

The Commission also seeded media influence as a tool of alignment. Prominent editors, publishers, and media executives were invited as members, ensuring that the Commission's frameworks could be disseminated as "objective consensus" rather than debated ideology. Major newspapers, television networks, and wire services subtly reinforced policy narratives crafted inside the Commission, creating the perception of spontaneous agreement across regions while concealing the role of coordinated messaging.

By the 1980s, the Trilateral Commission had become deeply integrated with other elite networks, including the World Economic Forum, Bilderberg Group, and Club of Rome. Its frameworks around energy policy, environmental regulation, and technological governance heavily influenced Agenda 21 and later the Sustainable Development Goals (SDGs). Many of the same members participated in multiple organizations simultaneously, cross-pollinating narratives that framed climate change, digital integration, and population management as global challenges requiring centralized solutions.

Rockefeller's genius was in institutionalizing alignment. Through the Commission, he created a self-reinforcing architecture where corporations, governments, supranational bodies, NGOs, and media outlets shared not just information but objectives. Once a framework was established - whether liberalizing trade, standardizing ESG compliance, or embedding carbon markets - it cascaded downward into law, finance, education, and public discourse through a tightly controlled network of influencers.

This model was not democratic. It was technocratic governance designed to bypass democratic friction. Decisions were hashed out behind closed doors by a small circle of individuals who controlled capital, technology, policy, and narrative simultaneously. National sovereignty became increasingly symbolic as domestic policies were shaped upstream by trilateral task forces, then filtered into public-facing legislation under the veneer of independent consensus.

The Trilateral Commission still exists today, but its early decades reveal its deeper purpose: not as a discussion club but as a coordination hub for global integration, one that merged Rockefeller's financial empire with Brzezinski's vision of the technetronic era. The system it helped design now operates seamlessly: WEF initiatives, IMF frameworks, ESG scoring systems, and UN SDGs all trace their origins back to the alignment strategies incubated within these closed networks.

David Rockefeller understood that lasting power doesn't come from commanding governments directly - it comes from shaping the architecture within which governments operate. Through the Trilateral Commission, he built that architecture: a transnational ecosystem where financial flows, technological standards, and policy agendas are synchronized across borders, managed by elites, and presented to the public as inevitabilities rather than choices.

It was the beginning of a post-democratic world order, planned decades before most people realized the shift had already happened.

The story of GATT to WTO is the story of how national sovereignty was quietly surrendered in the name of "free trade" and "economic efficiency." What began in 1947 as the General Agreement on Tariffs and Trade (GATT) - a temporary framework to reduce tariffs and encourage postwar recovery - evolved, step by step, into the World Trade Organization (WTO) by 1995: a supranational enforcement body with the power to override domestic laws, rewrite regulations, and dictate policy priorities inside sovereign states. Behind the language of globalization, the transformation was deliberate, coordinated, and methodical - embedding global economic integration into binding legal frameworks while placing unelected technocrats above democratically elected governments.

After World War II, Western elites recognized the need to stabilize global markets and expand U.S.-led influence. At the Bretton Woods Conference in 1944, the IMF and World Bank were established to manage monetary policy and reconstruction, but an ambitious third institution - an International Trade Organization (ITO) - failed to gain approval in the U.S. Senate. In its place, a stopgap measure was introduced: the General Agreement on Tariffs and Trade. Framed as a voluntary pact among 23 countries, GATT's initial purpose was simple: lower tariffs and encourage economic cooperation. But from the start, it contained the seeds of deeper integration.

Under GATT, trade negotiations occurred in multi-year "rounds," each producing agreements that gradually reduced trade barriers. What seemed like incremental liberalization was, in reality, policy harmonization by stealth. Tariff reductions were paired with "non-tariff" reforms: rules around subsidies, intellectual property, labor standards, and product safety were slowly standardized across borders. Over time, this eroded each country's ability to set its own regulatory priorities, replacing national control with frameworks drafted in closed negotiating sessions dominated by corporate lobbyists, international banks, and U.S.-European trade blocs.

The turning point came with the Uruguay Round (1986–1994), the largest and most consequential negotiation under GATT. This round created the World Trade Organization, a permanent institution with far greater authority than its predecessor. Unlike GATT, which operated on consensus, the WTO was given binding legal power: it could hear disputes between nations and enforce rulings through trade sanctions. For the first time in modern history, an unelected body gained the authority to invalidate domestic laws if they conflicted with "free trade" rules. National policies on environmental protection, labor rights, food safety, and even internet regulation could now be challenged by foreign governments or multinational corporations - and overturned if found "trade restrictive."

The WTO didn't just manage trade; it restructured governance itself. By expanding its mandate to cover services, intellectual property, agriculture, and investment flows, the WTO became the de facto global regulatory authority. Agreements like the General Agreement on Trade in Services (GATS) and the Trade-Related Aspects of Intellectual Property Rights (TRIPS) forced countries to adopt uniform standards drafted largely by corporate representatives from the U.S., Europe, and Japan. Developing nations, desperate for market access, often ceded control over critical sectors - pharmaceuticals, energy grids, and telecommunications - in exchange for WTO membership, locking themselves into systems they could no longer independently regulate.

Behind the WTO's creation was a coalition of powerful interests. The Council on Foreign Relations, Trilateral Commission, and World Economic Forum coordinated strategies to promote globalization as inevitable, framing sovereignty as an outdated obstacle. David Rockefeller's networks within Chase Manhattan, the IMF, and the World Bank facilitated funding and ideological alignment, while multinational corporations lobbied aggressively to ensure their industries dominated the drafting of agreements. Institutions like Harvard's

Kennedy School, OECD policy groups, and private think tanks supplied the intellectual cover, producing studies that painted trade liberalization as the only rational path forward while minimizing the costs to local industries, jobs, and autonomy.

The WTO also embedded an enforcement mechanism that operates outside democratic control. Disputes are adjudicated by panels of unelected trade experts whose rulings are binding on member states, regardless of domestic laws or court decisions. Countries that refuse compliance face retaliatory sanctions, effectively giving the WTO power to coerce policy changes without firing a shot. In this way, national parliaments are rendered subordinate to global trade law - laws written, reviewed, and enforced by actors unaccountable to the populations affected by them.

For corporations, the WTO became a shield and a weapon. Under its framework, companies gained the right to sue governments indirectly through investor-state dispute settlement (ISDS) mechanisms, claiming that domestic regulations - environmental protections, food labeling, labor laws - amounted to "barriers to trade." Cases exploded in the late 1990s and 2000s, with corporations successfully challenging sovereign policies and extracting billions in damages, reinforcing the subordination of public interest to private capital.

The consequences have been profound:

• Regulatory convergence eroded the ability of nations to set independent labor, environmental, and digital policies.

• Privatization pressures forced developing nations to sell off infrastructure and natural resources under the banner of market efficiency.

• Investor dominance shifted policymaking priorities toward protecting capital flows over protecting citizens.

• Economic vulnerability deepened, as domestic industries were dismantled by global competition without equivalent protections or sovereignty over supply chains.

The WTO's framework dovetails with broader technocratic agendas advanced by the IMF, World Bank, and WEF. By linking trade compliance to access to credit, energy markets, and technological infrastructure, these institutions collectively built a global economic operating system where national policies are subsumed under supranational "best practices." Through its partnerships with the UN Sustainable Development Goals (SDGs), ESG scoring systems, and emerging digital trade frameworks, the WTO is now central to coordinating policies around climate, data, and finance - areas far beyond its original mandate.

The shift from GATT to WTO represents a deliberate, decades-long transfer of sovereignty upward:

- Trade negotiations moved from public parliaments to private committees.
- Laws migrated from national legislatures to unelected tribunals.
- Economic priorities shifted from citizen welfare to corporate integration.
- Governance itself became transnational by design, insulated from local accountability.

The public was sold globalization as prosperity, efficiency, and opportunity. In practice, it produced dependency, homogenization, and the hollowing out of democratic authority. Today, when nations attempt to regulate data flows, control food systems, or restrict foreign investment, WTO compliance frameworks frequently override their decisions. Local autonomy has been traded for participation in a system where the rules are written elsewhere and enforced from above.

GATT was the gateway. The WTO became the gatekeeper. And sovereignty, once assumed to be the foundation of democracy, was quietly rewritten as a conditional privilege within a globalized framework managed by technocrats, financiers, and multinational corporate interests.

The Bank for International Settlements (BIS) is often called "the central bank of central banks," but that description understates its true role. Founded in 1930 and headquartered in Basel, Switzerland, the BIS operates as a sovereign-exempt institution - shielded from taxation, oversight, and accountability - yet wields extraordinary influence over the global financial system. Behind the scenes, the BIS has become the hidden architect of monetary policy coordination, quietly aligning the world's central banks under common frameworks designed by unelected technocrats, insulated from democratic control.

Unlike the IMF or World Bank, the BIS avoids public attention. It was created initially to manage German reparations after World War I but quickly evolved into a policy coordination hub for elite bankers and finance ministers from the U.S., U.K., France, Germany, and Japan. Its founding charter granted it diplomatic immunity: BIS officials are beyond prosecution, its communications cannot be seized, and its archives are inaccessible to most governments. From this protected perch, the BIS became a private club where monetary authorities discuss, design, and synchronize policies far from public scrutiny or parliamentary debate.

During World War II, the BIS maintained operations despite deep geopolitical divides, facilitating covert financial flows between Axis and Allied powers alike. After the war, its role expanded dramatically. As the Bretton Woods system took shape, the BIS became the informal nerve center for managing currency exchange rates, capital flows, and cross-border settlements among the world's most powerful economies. This informal role formalized over time, transforming the BIS into a permanent institution of supranational monetary governance.

By the 1970s, following the U.S. abandonment of the gold standard and the collapse of Bretton Woods, global markets entered an era of volatility. Rising inflation, energy shocks, and currency crises created demand for a centralized forum to manage systemic risk. The BIS seized the opportunity, establishing the Basel Committee on Banking Supervision in 1974. This committee - composed of representatives from the G10 central banks - designed global regulatory frameworks to standardize banking rules, capital requirements, and liquidity ratios. These frameworks, known collectively as the Basel Accords, effectively overrode national regulatory sovereignty: central banks and domestic regulators implemented BIS standards automatically to maintain access to global credit markets.

This was the quiet genius of the BIS: it doesn't legislate; it coordinates compliance through dependency. Nations that reject BIS frameworks risk exclusion from global payment systems, foreign investment, and interbank liquidity - making adherence functionally mandatory. Through its committees, the BIS has standardized everything from bank capital reserves to systemic risk modeling, stress-testing protocols, and cross-border derivatives reporting. What appears voluntary on paper becomes binding in practice through financial interdependence.

Today, the BIS hosts an ecosystem of policy laboratories developing tools that shape not just banking but monetary sovereignty itself. Its Financial Stability Board (FSB), established after the 2008 crisis, drafts global frameworks on systemic risk and digital asset regulation, while its Innovation Hub develops infrastructure for Central Bank Digital Currencies (CBDCs) - programmable money systems poised to redefine the relationship between individuals, banks, and governments.

CBDCs represent the culmination of the BIS's long-term vision: real-time, centralized oversight of every transaction on Earth. Working closely with the IMF, World Bank, and WEF, the BIS is piloting interoperability standards to integrate digital currencies across borders into a unified settlement infrastructure. Once operational, this system would allow central banks to monitor, approve, or restrict financial activity instantaneously, embedding behavioral compliance directly into the monetary architecture itself.

Behind these technological developments lies an ideological agenda: the BIS promotes "financial stability" as its guiding principle, but stability here means centralized control. Policy papers from the BIS repeatedly emphasize the need for coordinated responses to global risks - inflation, climate change, cyberattacks, pandemics - implying that local autonomy must yield to supranational management. This isn't hypothetical; BIS guidelines already influence national interest rates, bond issuance, and fiscal priorities, dictating how governments borrow, spend, and regulate.

The BIS operates through three mechanisms that make its influence profound yet invisible:

Consensus Manufacturing

Through closed meetings like the bimonthly "Basel gatherings," central bank governors from the world's major economies meet privately to align policies on interest rates, liquidity provision, and regulatory responses. These agreements are rarely publicized but cascade into synchronized global shifts that appear "spontaneous."

Framework Standardization

The Basel Accords, liquidity guidelines, and CBDC interoperability standards give the BIS de facto legislative power without passing a single law. Because global banks require cross-border access, countries comply automatically or risk systemic exclusion.

Crisis Leverage

Financial crises - from the 1970s oil shocks to the 2008 collapse to pandemic-driven disruptions - are used to expand BIS authority. Each crisis justifies deeper integration and tighter surveillance under the banner of "global stability."

In effect, the BIS sits above central banks, yet below the visibility of public awareness. Its leadership - unelected, largely unknown, and shielded from oversight - directs the rules that govern money supply, credit flows, and now, potentially, digital identity-linked currencies. National governments and parliaments debate fiscal budgets, but the architecture of monetary power is increasingly dictated from Basel, coordinated with IMF lending strategies, WTO trade rules, and WEF-driven ESG frameworks.

This alignment is not accidental. The BIS works hand-in-glove with other supranational institutions to harmonize governance across domains once considered sovereign:

• The IMF enforces debt conditionalities tied to BIS frameworks.

• The WTO aligns trade compliance with BIS-sanctioned capital flows.

• The WEF integrates BIS-driven financial tools into ESG and sustainability metrics.

- The UN SDGs embed BIS standards into development and infrastructure financing.

Central banks, once symbols of national independence, are now operational nodes inside a coordinated monetary network. Through the BIS, unelected technocrats have designed a system where financial sovereignty exists in theory but not in practice.

The BIS avoids headlines by design, operating as a shadow command center for the integration of monetary policy, banking standards, and, increasingly, programmable currency systems. It does not campaign, legislate, or vote. It simply sets the defaults - and in a global financial system, the defaults become destiny.

This isn't conspiracy; it's architecture. Over decades, the BIS has positioned itself at the top of the monetary pyramid, building the frameworks within which all other actors must operate. In doing so, it has quietly transformed money itself into a tool of governance - one where transactions, identity, and behavior are increasingly integrated into a single, centralized control grid.

The BIS doesn't manage central banks. It manages the system they operate within. And as that system shifts toward digital currencies, algorithmic oversight, and programmable capital, the BIS is poised to become the invisible governor of the global economy - unelected, untouchable, and indispensable.

The 1980s Latin American debt crisis was not just an economic catastrophe - it was a controlled demolition. Behind the headlines of default, hyperinflation, and social unrest, the Bank for International Settlements (BIS) played a quiet but decisive role in managing the collapse, restructuring entire national economies, and embedding Latin America into a permanent architecture of financial dependency. What appeared to be a sovereign debt crisis was, in practice, a leverage operation - one where the BIS acted as the hidden coordinator between Wall Street banks, the IMF, and Western governments to ensure that control over monetary policy, resource flows, and fiscal priorities shifted away from local parliaments and toward supranational institutions.

By the late 1970s, Latin America had become awash in cheap credit. U.S. commercial banks - Chase Manhattan, Citibank, Bank of America, and others - aggressively pushed dollar-denominated loans to developing countries, encouraged by the Federal Reserve's low interest rates and assurances from U.S. Treasury officials that sovereign lending was effectively "risk-free." Countries like Mexico, Brazil, Argentina, and Chile borrowed heavily to fund infrastructure, industrial development, and social programs, accumulating hundreds of billions in external debt.

Then came the trap. In 1979, Federal Reserve Chairman Paul Volcker initiated his "shock therapy" - hiking U.S. interest rates from around 10% to over 20% to fight domestic inflation. This sudden tightening of global liquidity caused the cost of servicing Latin America's dollar-denominated debt to explode overnight. At the same time, the U.S. dollar strengthened dramatically, compounding repayment burdens and triggering cascading defaults across the region.

This is where the BIS stepped in - quietly, but decisively. Acting as the coordination hub for the G10 central banks, the BIS organized emergency lending packages to keep Latin American governments solvent enough to service interest payments owed to U.S. and European commercial banks. These packages weren't bailouts for nations; they were backdoor rescues for Western lenders. By pooling funds from the Federal Reserve, the Bank of England, the Bundesbank, and others, the BIS ensured that private banks avoided catastrophic losses while pushing the real costs of the crisis onto Latin American populations.

The BIS's central role was threefold:

1. Crisis Containment for Western Banks

BIS emergency "bridging loans" provided liquidity to debtor nations - but on the condition that funds were used primarily to repay foreign creditors rather than sustain domestic programs or protect citizens. The BIS acted as a firewall, ensuring Wall Street's exposure was contained and preventing defaults from cascading into U.S. and European banking systems.

2. Enforcement Arm of IMF Conditionality

While the BIS coordinated central bank liquidity, the International Monetary Fund (IMF) became the enforcer. Countries seeking BIS-backed support were compelled to accept IMF "structural adjustment programs" (SAPs) - austerity measures designed to prioritize debt repayment above all else. These programs dismantled subsidies, slashed public spending, privatized state-owned industries, and liberalized trade - policies drafted not by elected officials but by technocrats in Washington, Basel, and New York.

3. Embedding Dependency Through Basel Standards

Even as the crisis unfolded, the BIS began laying the groundwork for the Basel I Accords (1988), which standardized global capital requirements. These rules forced Latin American central banks to restructure their domestic financial systems around BIS-approved frameworks to regain access to global credit markets. Nations that failed to comply faced exclusion from interbank settlements, foreign investment, and international trade financing - effectively locking them out of the global economy.

The results were devastating on the ground. Across the 1980s, Latin America endured what economists later called the "lost decade." GDP contracted, unemployment soared, and public services collapsed under IMF-imposed austerity. Hyperinflation ravaged Argentina, Bolivia, and Brazil, while debt burdens paradoxically grew larger despite repeated "rescue" packages. By the end of the decade, Latin America had paid back more in interest than it had originally borrowed, yet total external debt had doubled.

This was by design. The crisis allowed the BIS and its allied institutions to restructure entire economies around export dependency, financial liberalization, and external oversight:

• Privatization Mandates - State-owned assets in energy, telecommunications, and mining were sold off at fire-sale prices, often to foreign corporations linked to BIS-member banks.

• Trade Liberalization - Domestic industries were exposed to global competition overnight, eroding local production capacity and deepening reliance on foreign imports.

•   Monetary Policy Subordination - Central banks across the region were pressured to adopt BIS-aligned frameworks, reducing their ability to manage inflation, set independent interest rates, or control capital flows.

•   Permanent IMF Surveillance - Even after "recovery," debtor nations remained under IMF monitoring and periodic policy reviews, effectively outsourcing economic sovereignty indefinitely.

The deeper objective was not merely stabilizing markets but consolidating supranational control over monetary policy. Through the BIS, G10 central banks coordinated with the IMF and World Bank to impose a single financial governance model across Latin America. Once adopted, these frameworks became prerequisites for access to credit, development financing, and even trade - embedding nations into a self-reinforcing dependency loop where sovereignty became conditional on compliance.

This model also created an enduring geopolitical lever for the U.S. and its allies. Countries that resisted IMF-BIS prescriptions - such as Peru under Alan García, who attempted unilateral debt limits - were swiftly punished through capital flight, currency manipulation, and diplomatic isolation until compliance was restored. The message was clear: in the emerging financial order, sovereignty was negotiable, liquidity was conditional, and Basel was law.

By the early 1990s, Latin America had been effectively restructured. The BIS had achieved three strategic outcomes:

1.   Protected Western financial institutions from systemic collapse.

2.   Standardized Latin American banking systems under Basel rules.

3.   Integrated the region into global trade and capital flows on terms set in Basel, Washington, and New York, not in Buenos Aires, Mexico City, or Brasília.

The Latin American debt crisis was not an accident; it was a stress test for a new model of financial technocracy. The BIS proved it could quietly manage systemic shocks, enforce policy compliance through interbank leverage, and expand its influence without ever appearing in headlines. Sovereignty became a variable inside a global liquidity model, subordinate to the priorities of unelected institutions.

The template established in the 1980s was replicated repeatedly - in Asia during the 1997 financial crisis, in Greece during the Eurozone collapse, and globally during the 2008 meltdown. In each case, the BIS coordinated behind the scenes, the IMF enforced austerity, and debtor nations were folded deeper into a centralized monetary architecture where local policy autonomy was sacrificed for "stability."

Latin America's lost decade wasn't just an economic tragedy. It was a demonstration of how crisis becomes leverage. Through the BIS, Western financial elites perfected a system where debt is weaponized, sovereignty is conditional, and recovery comes with invisible chains - chains still locked firmly in place today.

14

Silicon Valley's First Empire

Bill Gates is often celebrated as the visionary founder of Microsoft, a pioneer who helped bring personal computing into homes and offices around the world. But the real story of Gates and Microsoft is far more complex - and far more deliberate. Beyond clever engineering and savvy business strategy, Microsoft became the first digital empire, securing dominance not simply by competing but by engineering dependency: locking users, governments, and corporations into proprietary ecosystems that transformed software into an instrument of control. Gates built more than an operating system - he helped create the foundation for the digital enclosure, where access, identity, and eventually even behavior would be mediated through private infrastructure.

When Gates founded Microsoft in 1975 with Paul Allen, the company entered a computing landscape still dominated by hardware giants like IBM, DEC, and Hewlett-Packard. Gates quickly understood something most of his competitors didn't: the future wasn't in machines; it was in the operating systems that would run them. Control the operating system, and you control the entire software stack - applications, file formats, and ultimately user habits. That insight shaped Microsoft's central strategy: own the standard, own the future.

In 1980, Gates struck the deal that defined his empire: Microsoft licensed its MS-DOS operating system to IBM for its first personal computer. Crucially, the license was non-exclusive, allowing Microsoft to sell MS-DOS to other manufacturers while IBM tied itself to Gates' platform. Within a few years, MS-DOS became the default operating system for the booming PC market, giving Microsoft leverage over software developers who now had to design around its standards or risk irrelevance. It was the first stage of Gates' ecosystem lock-in strategy - and it worked.

As computing evolved into graphical interfaces, Microsoft moved aggressively to cement its dominance with Windows, launched in 1985 and refined through the early 1990s. Windows became the "universal gateway" for interacting with digital environments, embedding Microsoft as the mediator between people and information. To deepen this grip, Gates pursued an aggressive campaign of bundling and exclusion: integrating Microsoft Office directly into Windows, cutting off competing software vendors from technical documentation, and leveraging proprietary file formats to force compatibility dependency. If your school, office, or government used Microsoft Word or Excel, you had no real choice but to adopt Windows too.

By the mid-1990s, Microsoft had achieved what was effectively a digital monopoly. Over 90% of the world's personal computers ran Windows, and Office became the default productivity suite globally. Gates used this dominance to dictate market behavior: software vendors were pressured into exclusive contracts, hardware manufacturers were coerced into pre-installation deals, and emerging competitors were either acquired, undermined, or crushed outright. When Netscape tried to challenge Microsoft with its web browser, Gates integrated Internet Explorer directly into Windows - free, pre-installed, and impossible to remove. This move triggered a landmark U.S. antitrust case in 1998, but by then, Microsoft's control was already entrenched.

What made Gates' monopoly different from industrial giants of the past was that Microsoft didn't just control products - it controlled infrastructure. Proprietary file formats like .doc and .xls became the invisible chains binding users, corporations, and even governments to Microsoft's platforms. Courts, schools, defense agencies, and hospitals standardized around Microsoft software, creating a systemic dependency where switching costs were prohibitively high. Over time, Microsoft became not just a technology vendor but a gatekeeper of digital life, embedding its systems so deeply that entire economies ran on its proprietary code.

This dependency wasn't limited to productivity software. Microsoft aggressively expanded into enterprise servers, networking, and identity systems, positioning itself as the backend for governments and corporations alike. Through frameworks like Active Directory, Microsoft became a central hub for user authentication and permissions - in essence, controlling who gets access to what in digital environments. This shift quietly made Microsoft infrastructure foundational to digital identity management, a precursor to today's emerging debates over centralized authentication, biometrics, and programmable access.

Gates' strategy aligned closely with the emerging ambitions of supranational institutions and financial elites seeking to integrate economies into a unified, digitally mediated framework. By the late 1990s, Microsoft was collaborating with governments, NGOs, and the IMF/World Bank development arms to "bridge the digital divide" in developing nations - but always on Microsoft's terms. Low-cost software licensing deals, hardware partnerships, and "educational initiatives" introduced Microsoft infrastructure into classrooms and agencies globally, ensuring generational dependence on proprietary systems.

When Gates shifted from Microsoft's day-to-day operations into the Bill & Melinda Gates Foundation in 2000, many assumed he was retreating from corporate strategy to focus on philanthropy. But the Foundation became an extension of the same model: invest in digital infrastructure projects around health, education, and finance that inevitably rely on Microsoft systems or affiliated partners. Initiatives like ID2020, launched in partnership with the Rockefeller Foundation, Accenture, and Microsoft, aimed to build digital identity frameworks linked to healthcare, financial access, and citizenship services - centralizing personal data into systems controlled by a handful of corporations and supranational agencies.

Critics argue that Gates' philanthropic endeavors operate as strategic influence laundering: positioning Microsoft-friendly infrastructure as benevolent while embedding it into national and global governance frameworks. During the COVID-19 pandemic, Gates' Foundation emerged as a central funder of vaccine research, digital contact-tracing systems, and health surveillance platforms, often tied to proprietary software ecosystems and cloud partnerships. Microsoft's Azure cloud services quietly became the backend for numerous pandemic response systems worldwide, deepening dependency under the guise of crisis management.

This dual role - Gates as philanthropist and Microsoft as infrastructure provider - reflects a broader digital technocracy emerging over the past three decades. Through proprietary standards, platform dominance, and public-private partnerships, Microsoft positioned itself at the heart of:

• Digital identity ecosystems - powering authentication frameworks for governments, corporations, and global NGOs.

• Cloud infrastructure - controlling data flows and storage through Azure, integrated with AI and security systems.

• Global education and development policy - embedding Microsoft tools into classrooms and public services in partnership with the UN, IMF, and World Bank.

• Algorithmic governance - supplying tools and platforms for data collection, modeling, and policy enforcement under "sustainable development" initiatives.

Gates didn't just build software. He helped create the digital rails upon which modern governance, commerce, and communication now operate. In doing so, he blurred the line between corporate power and public infrastructure, setting the stage for a future where digital dependency equals compliance.

Microsoft's monopoly was never only about market share. It was about establishing control points - over file formats, over access, over identity, over data - and then embedding those control points into the policy frameworks of governments and supranational institutions alike. Once dependency is engineered, leverage becomes effortless: security patches, software licenses, and cloud services turn into invisible levers of influence.

Bill Gates' empire illustrates a larger shift in power from nations to networks, from parliaments to platforms. Microsoft's dominance created the infrastructure for digital governance, where the operating system doesn't just manage computers - it manages societies. And in the age of cloud computing, biometric IDs, and AI-driven policymaking, the dependency Gates built has only deepened.

He didn't just dominate an industry. He rewired the architecture of control.

Steve Jobs is remembered as a visionary - a perfectionist who redefined personal computing, music, phones, and media. But behind the celebrated mythology of innovation lies a deeper truth about his impact: Jobs didn't just build products; he engineered psychological ecosystems designed to capture attention, create dependency, and shape behavior. Where Bill Gates locked the world into proprietary infrastructure, Jobs mastered the other half of the equation - the human interface, blending technology with design psychology to hardwire emotional attachment into devices. Through Apple, he helped pioneer a model of technological addiction that now permeates every layer of modern life.

From the earliest days at Apple, Jobs understood something that most of his competitors didn't: people don't buy hardware; they buy feelings. When Apple launched the Macintosh in 1984, Jobs framed it not as a machine but as a personal companion - simple, intuitive, and "designed for humans, not engineers." The now-iconic "1984" Super Bowl ad positioned Apple as the liberator of individuality against Orwellian conformity, transforming the purchase of a computer into an act of identity expression. This marketing sleight of hand marked the beginning of Apple's defining strategy: use aesthetics, simplicity, and symbolism to bypass rational decision-making and anchor technology into the psyche.

Jobs' obsession with design wasn't superficial. Every pixel, curve, and interface element was curated to evoke a sense of intimacy and control.

Buttons were rounded because sharp edges subconsciously signal danger. Icons mimicked familiar objects - a trash can, a folder - triggering recognition and comfort. The Macintosh introduced graphical metaphors like "desktops" and "windows" to lower cognitive friction, pulling people deeper into digital environments by making them feel natural, even inevitable. Jobs realized early on that design could reduce resistance to technological adoption by making users feel at home inside a machine.

This philosophy intensified with the arrival of the iPod in 2001 and the iPhone in 2007 - products that redefined not just industries but behavioral norms. Jobs didn't sell features; he sold transformations. The iPod's iconic tagline, "1,000 songs in your pocket," reframed music ownership into personal empowerment. The iPhone was marketed not as a tool but as an extension of the self, seamlessly merging communication, entertainment, identity, and commerce into a single device. By positioning technology as an appendage of personal expression, Jobs blurred the boundary between user and machine - a psychological shift with profound consequences.

At the core of Apple's strategy was dopamine design - the intentional crafting of interfaces and experiences to trigger reward pathways in the brain. While Jobs wasn't a neuroscientist, he intuitively grasped principles later exploited by Silicon Valley behavioral engineers: variable rewards, micro-feedback loops, and sensory cues that keep users hooked. Every click, swipe, and tap delivers subtle hits of novelty or achievement. Smooth scrolling, haptic vibrations, and carefully engineered sounds reinforce subconscious pleasure, creating habit loops that are difficult to break.

Apple's walled-garden ecosystem amplified this dependency. Devices, operating systems, and services were designed to integrate seamlessly - but only with each other. Buy an iPhone, and suddenly iTunes manages your music, iCloud stores your memories, and the App Store becomes your gateway to software. Each component is optimized to deliver convenience and aesthetic satisfaction, but the underlying strategy is psychological lock-in: once inside the Apple ecosystem, switching feels like losing part of yourself.

Jobs also mastered scarcity as psychological manipulation. Limited product runs, controlled release cycles, and secrecy around new features cultivated anticipation and status signaling. Owning the latest Apple device became synonymous with belonging to a cultural elite - a subtle hierarchy engineered through design and marketing. The annual keynote events, carefully choreographed by Jobs, functioned as ritualistic spectacles, blending corporate announcements with emotional theater to create tribal loyalty among users.

By the late 2000s, Apple had transformed consumer behavior on a global scale. Devices became personal portals, constantly tethering individuals to digital environments. The iPhone, in particular, reconfigured attention itself: notifications, infinite scrolling, and app integrations normalized continuous partial focus, fragmenting cognitive bandwidth and accelerating dependency. What Jobs set in motion has evolved into today's attention economy, where corporations compete to hijack neural pathways for profit.

The addiction wasn't accidental. Apple's Human Interface Guidelines - the internal "bible" for app developers - codified behavioral design principles that exploit psychological vulnerabilities. Recommendations included limiting cognitive load, using animation to guide focus, and employing color theory to trigger specific emotional responses. For example, notification badges were deliberately rendered in red - a color evolutionarily associated with urgency and danger - creating an unconscious compulsion to respond. Jobs framed these decisions as enhancing user experience, but the cumulative effect was behavioral conditioning on a mass scale.

Even Apple's minimalist hardware design served deeper psychological goals. The smooth glass, brushed aluminum, and absence of visible screws convey trust and inevitability - the device feels complete, untouchable, and permanent. Its simplicity reduces decision fatigue, pulling users into a frictionless cycle where Apple's defaults become personal norms. Jobs understood that to shape societies, you don't need to dictate behavior; you design the environment where choices are made.

Jobs' influence extends beyond Apple. His success in merging psychology, aesthetics, and engineering became the template for the entire technology sector. Companies like Facebook, Google, TikTok, and Amazon adopted - and intensified - the behavioral techniques Apple pioneered. Infinite scroll, push notifications, "like" buttons, and gamified metrics all descend from Jobs' insistence that technology must evoke emotion, not just utility.

Critically, this psychological integration of technology set the stage for algorithmic governance. As smartphones became extensions of identity, vast data streams about location, preferences, behavior, and biometrics began flowing into corporate and governmental systems. Jobs didn't create surveillance capitalism, but by normalizing always-on, always-connected devices, Apple helped make it possible. The very tools designed to "empower" users became sensors, feeding machine learning models that now shape advertising, finance, education, and even policy-making.

Jobs' genius was in making control feel like liberation. Through exquisite design and carefully orchestrated emotional cues, Apple cultivated voluntary dependency. People weren't coerced into adopting these systems; they lined up overnight to embrace them. This psychological integration is what makes modern technological addiction so effective - it doesn't feel imposed from above; it feels chosen.

But choice, in this context, is engineered. The environments we inhabit, the defaults we accept, the dopamine loops we engage with - all were designed upstream, not discovered organically. Jobs' legacy, beyond innovation, is the normalization of technological dependency: a world where identity, attention, and autonomy are mediated through platforms that anticipate, guide, and increasingly predict our every move.

Steve Jobs didn't just change technology. He rewired how humans relate to it - and, by extension, how we relate to ourselves.

Larry Ellison, the billionaire co-founder of Oracle Corporation, rarely gets discussed in the same breath as Bill Gates or Steve Jobs, but his influence on modern governance is arguably deeper and more structural. While Gates built the operating systems and Jobs engineered the interfaces, Ellison quietly built the databases - the invisible backbone of information control. Today, Oracle's systems underpin everything from financial markets and tax collection to military intelligence, law enforcement, biometric surveillance, and population registries. In doing so, Ellison created something unprecedented: the digital substrate for state-level control, where governments and corporations manage society through the architecture of data itself.

When Ellison launched Oracle in 1977, his vision wasn't just to create better software - it was to organize knowledge. Inspired by a classified CIA project called "Oracle" (from which the company took its name), Ellison set out to build the world's most efficient relational database systems - technology capable of ingesting vast volumes of structured data, querying it in real time, and producing actionable intelligence. What began as a military-funded experiment soon became the central nervous system of governments, banks, and corporations worldwide.

Oracle's rise coincided with the digital transformation of governance in the 1980s and 1990s, when governments began modernizing systems for taxation, social benefits, identity management, and security. Ellison positioned Oracle databases as mission-critical infrastructure, aggressively courting contracts with the Pentagon, intelligence agencies, and federal departments. By the mid-1990s, Oracle powered backend systems for:

- The U.S. Department of Defense - managing logistics, supply chains, and classified data.
- The IRS - tracking tax compliance, auditing processes, and revenue streams.
- FBI and CIA intelligence databases - indexing criminal records, surveillance data, and informant networks.
- State-level identity registries - digitizing driver's licenses, voter rolls, and passport systems.

Ellison didn't just sell software - he embedded Oracle's architecture deep into the mechanics of statecraft. Once a government built its core infrastructure on Oracle systems, switching became prohibitively expensive and operationally risky. This strategy created institutional lock-in on a massive scale: if you control the databases, you control the rules of interaction within them. Oracle became the default backend of governance, quietly shaping how states collect, store, and interpret information about their citizens.

As Oracle's reach expanded, so did its strategic integration with law enforcement and security agencies. The company developed specialized products for national security operations, including real-time intelligence platforms that could aggregate and cross-reference data from multiple sources: financial transactions, criminal records, immigration databases, and biometric systems. These tools enabled governments to construct comprehensive profiles of individuals - from travel history to political affiliations - integrating once-separate datasets into unified monitoring frameworks.

One of Oracle's most profound impacts has been in the rise of biometric and digital identity systems. Ellison was an early proponent of centralized identification frameworks, advocating publicly in the wake of 9/11 for national ID cards linked to Oracle-powered databases. Over the past two decades, Oracle technology has become a core component of large-scale population registries, including:

• India's Aadhaar program - the world's largest biometric ID system, storing data on over 1.4 billion people.

• U.S. REAL ID infrastructure - integrating driver's licenses, passports, and law enforcement databases.

• Global migration control systems - powering border security tools used by the EU, DHS, and Interpol.

Ellison's vision was clear: in the 21st century, identity would be data, and Oracle would manage the infrastructure that defines it. This positioning placed Oracle squarely at the heart of algorithmic governance, where decisions about access - to services, borders, financial systems, and even movement - are mediated through database queries.

Oracle's dominance also extends into finance and commerce, where its databases serve as the backbone for stock exchanges, payment systems, and corporate ERP platforms. Most global Fortune 500 companies run critical operations on Oracle systems, from energy giants and telecom firms to defense contractors and pharmaceutical conglomerates. By linking public and private datasets across sectors, Oracle quietly enabled a data convergence model where governments, corporations, and supranational institutions share overlapping access to information infrastructures.

This convergence has profound implications for sovereignty. Through Oracle, data governance becomes de facto globalized:

• Multinational corporations and NGOs can integrate seamlessly with state systems.

• Central banks and tax authorities can cross-reference compliance in real time.

• Security agencies can monitor individuals across borders through standardized formats.

• Supranational institutions - from the IMF to the WEF - gain leverage by integrating policies into platforms Oracle already dominates.

Ellison's empire thrives precisely because Oracle doesn't present itself as political. The databases are "neutral," but the power they grant is anything but. Whoever controls the database architecture controls who sees what, who gets flagged, who gets excluded, and who gets prioritized. Oracle's technology has enabled:

• Predictive policing frameworks, integrating crime statistics, social data, and surveillance footage.

• Public health tracking, linking vaccination registries, genomic data, and medical records.

• Behavioral analytics, fusing consumer, financial, and social datasets for targeted policy interventions.

Increasingly, these systems are connected to AI-driven decision engines - many also powered by Oracle - that automate judgments previously made by humans: approving loans, assigning risk scores, flagging "suspicious" travel patterns, or determining access to welfare. The deeper Oracle embeds itself, the more it becomes the invisible policymaker, shaping outcomes not by writing laws but by designing the infrastructure through which laws are enforced.

Ellison himself has been unusually candid about Oracle's ambitions. In interviews, he has openly stated his belief that data, not oil, is the true foundation of power in the 21st century. By controlling the systems where data lives and moves, Oracle has positioned itself as an indispensable mediator between governments, corporations, and citizens - a private company functioning as public infrastructure, but without public oversight.

This is the quiet brilliance - and danger - of Oracle's dominance. Unlike Microsoft, Oracle doesn't compete for your attention. Unlike Apple, it doesn't seek your loyalty. Its power comes from being unseen yet unavoidable, the digital substrate beneath statecraft, commerce, and social organization. Oracle doesn't just manage information; it defines the frameworks within which information becomes power.

Larry Ellison didn't just build a software company. He built the global database of governance, where identity, security, and control converge. Through Oracle, he created the architecture that makes state-level monitoring scalable, corporate integration seamless, and individual autonomy conditional.

The code runs quietly. But it runs everything.

The public story of Google begins in a Stanford University dorm room in 1996, where two Ph.D. students - Larry Page and Sergey Brin - built a search engine prototype called BackRub that evolved into the Google we know today. But behind the sanitized origin myth lies a deeper, more coordinated story involving the CIA, DARPA, Stanford research labs, and the venture capital arms of U.S. intelligence. Google didn't just emerge from Silicon Valley's entrepreneurial chaos; it was incubated inside a nexus of military research, predictive modeling, and surveillance infrastructure, designed to manage information flows on a planetary scale.

The roots of this integration stretch back to the Cold War, when the U.S. intelligence community began investing heavily in computational linguistics, networked systems, and data-mining tools to gain strategic advantage. The Defense Advanced Research Projects Agency (DARPA), created in 1958 in response to the Soviet launch of Sputnik, became the central hub for funding early internet protocols, machine learning research, and large-scale behavioral modeling. Projects like ARPANET, the proto-internet, were explicitly designed to facilitate real-time information sharing among research institutions tied to defense objectives. Stanford became one of DARPA's premier nodes - a testing ground where academic innovation blurred seamlessly into military priorities.

By the 1980s and 1990s, Stanford's Digital Library Project, where Page and Brin began their work, was heavily funded by agencies aligned with national security imperatives. Through DARPA, the Office of Naval Research, and later the Massive Digital Data Systems (MDDS) initiative - a CIA- and NSA-backed program - research into search, indexing, and information retrieval was integrated into broader objectives around predictive modeling and behavioral analysis. Page and Brin's algorithm, PageRank, wasn't just an academic exercise; it directly addressed MDDS objectives: how to index massive datasets, predict relationships, and surface relevant results dynamically.

At the same time, the CIA and NSA were building their own venture arms to accelerate technological innovation. In 1999, the CIA launched In-Q-Tel, a private investment vehicle tasked with funding emerging technologies relevant to intelligence work. Among its early focuses were search, geospatial mapping, and natural language processing - domains where Google was rapidly becoming a leader. While Google's direct funding ties to In-Q-Tel remain obscured by non-disclosure agreements, its early acquisition of technologies funded by intelligence venture arms - including satellite imaging, facial recognition, and deep web indexing - suggests alignment from the outset.

Google's infrastructure design itself reflects this integration. The company pioneered massively distributed data storage systems that allowed information to be indexed, retrieved, and ranked at unprecedented speed and scale. But those same systems also made it possible to map relationships between data points, users, and behaviors - capabilities highly prized by DARPA-funded research programs into predictive social modeling. By analyzing not just content but patterns - search queries, click-throughs, location histories - Google became a de facto real-time population monitoring tool, providing insights into human intention at scale.

In the early 2000s, as Google scaled globally, its partnership with defense and intelligence agencies deepened. Through contracts with DARPA, the NGA (National Geospatial-Intelligence Agency), and later the NSA, Google provided infrastructure and analytic tools for mapping, satellite imaging, and threat detection. The acquisition of Keyhole Inc. in 2004 - a startup funded by In-Q-Tel that became the foundation of Google Earth - cemented Google's integration with geospatial intelligence frameworks. What began as consumer-facing tools doubled as strategic military assets, supporting surveillance, targeting, and logistics operations worldwide.

Meanwhile, Google's rapid dominance over search made it the default gateway to information globally, effectively turning the company into an unofficial extension of state power. Through programs revealed by whistleblowers years later - like the NSA's PRISM initiative - Google became a core node in the post-9/11 surveillance architecture, granting intelligence agencies streamlined access to user data. This wasn't a one-way extraction; Google actively collaborated with agencies to refine models, improve data pipelines, and scale infrastructure to meet national security objectives.

DARPA's influence was especially pivotal in shaping Google's ambitions beyond search. Projects in machine learning, natural language processing, and artificial intelligence were seeded with DARPA funding, producing tools that now underpin not only Google's commercial empire but also U.S. military strategy. When Google acquired DeepMind in 2014, it extended its dominance into reinforcement learning and predictive modeling - technologies that DARPA and the Department of Defense are now integrating into battlefield simulations, drone targeting systems, and algorithmic decision-making frameworks for statecraft itself.

Critically, the integration of CIA, DARPA, and Google reflects a larger shift: the privatization of intelligence capabilities. By embedding data collection, behavioral modeling, and algorithmic inference within consumer platforms, surveillance became decentralized - routed through "neutral" private companies rather than overtly governmental systems. Search engines, email clients, and cloud storage providers became passive collection mechanisms feeding into predictive analytics pipelines operated jointly by corporations and intelligence agencies.

This integration set the stage for a feedback loop of influence:

• DARPA funds research at Stanford and other universities to solve national security problems.

• Those solutions - like PageRank - are spun out into private companies like Google.

• Google's platforms collect data at unprecedented scale, enriching datasets used by DARPA and the intelligence community.

• In-Q-Tel and other venture arms strategically invest in startups that complement Google's capabilities, ensuring alignment.

• The resulting infrastructure - search, mapping, biometrics, AI - becomes dual-use, serving both commercial markets and state power simultaneously.

The end result is a converged ecosystem where the lines between public and private, civilian and military, innovation and surveillance, effectively vanish. Google operates as a consumer brand but functions structurally as a node within the U.S. defense-intelligence architecture, shaping not just how information is accessed but how it is classified, ranked, and interpreted. What you see - and don't see - online increasingly reflects upstream priorities set by models optimized not only for ad revenue but also for strategic objectives defined in collaboration with intelligence frameworks.

This was never accidental. The flow from CIA-funded Stanford research, to DARPA-driven infrastructure, to Google's global dominance, represents the intentional outsourcing of state power into private platforms - platforms that shape reality by controlling the information environment itself. Today, Google is not simply an index of the internet; it is the filter through which modern knowledge flows, tightly integrated with systems of surveillance, behavioral prediction, and, increasingly, algorithmic governance.

The "search box" isn't neutral. It's the interface layer of a vast, converged architecture linking academia, private enterprise, and state power. Behind every query, every recommendation, every map coordinate, lies an infrastructure born of defense-funded research, optimized for population-scale modeling, and tightly aligned with the interests of institutions that built it.

What appears to be a convenience - free search, free email, free maps - is, in reality, the most powerful data-collection and influence engine ever created. Google didn't just organize the world's information; it organized the frameworks of control that govern it.

PART V - THE DIGITAL TAKEOVER (2000–2015)

The data economy, behavioral engineering, and early AI.

15

Surveillance Capitalism Goes Live

Google began as a search engine, but it has evolved into something much larger and far more consequential: a global prediction machine. Under the surface, Google's algorithms were never simply about "organizing the world's information." They were built to model, predict, and influence human behavior at scale, turning every query, click, and scroll into signals feeding machine-learning systems designed not just to understand what you want but to shape what you'll do next. Over time, Google learned to weaponize these predictive capabilities - first for profit, then for power - transforming from a search company into the central nervous system of behavioral manipulation in the digital age.

From the moment you interact with Google Search, Maps, Gmail, YouTube, or Chrome, you're training its predictive engines. Every keystroke, location ping, and video view refines a dynamic profile that maps not just who you are but how you think, what you desire, and where you're going. Initially, these models served one purpose: maximize ad revenue. Google's early dominance came from AdWords and AdSense, systems that auctioned access to your attention in milliseconds based on probabilistic models predicting your likelihood to click. The better the predictions, the more valuable the advertising space - turning data collection into the foundation of Google's empire.

But these algorithms didn't just forecast behavior; they began shaping it. By 2010, Google's ranking systems weren't just reflecting online trends - they were creating them. Search results, YouTube recommendations, and Google News curation quietly steered billions of users toward specific narratives, products, and viewpoints. Over time, the system learned that by subtly manipulating information hierarchies - what appears first, what's buried, what's omitted entirely - it could nudge population-scale behavior without users ever realizing they were being guided.

Nowhere is this clearer than in YouTube's recommendation engine, one of the most powerful behavioral tools ever built. Trained on trillions of data points, it predicts what you're most likely to watch next and serves it instantly, optimizing for engagement time rather than well-being. This algorithm alone drives over 70% of all watch time on the platform. It doesn't just observe user preferences; it shapes them, keeping people in closed loops of emotional triggers, outrage cycles, or comforting echo chambers designed to maximize clicks and ads. What began as personalization evolved into persuasion at planetary scale.

Behind the veneer of free services, Google has effectively built an attention market where your consciousness is the commodity. The Surveillance Capitalism model - coined by scholar Shoshana Zuboff - is perfected here: extract behavioral data, feed it into proprietary algorithms, and sell prediction products to advertisers, corporations, and increasingly, governments. Google's profits are no longer about "ads" in any simple sense; they come from turning users into predictable nodes within a behavioral network, refining models that tell third parties not just what you want now but what you'll want before you know it yourself.

These predictive capabilities are no longer limited to commerce. Through partnerships with intelligence agencies, law enforcement, and defense contractors, Google's models are integrated into systems of population-scale surveillance and social management. For example:

• Google Cloud and the Pentagon's Project Maven: using AI to analyze drone footage for automated targeting and battlefield intelligence.

- Real-time location datasets provided to law enforcement, often bypassing warrants, through apps like Google Maps and Android telemetry.
- Health data integration through acquisitions like Fitbit and partnerships with hospital networks, creating predictive models for insurance, pharmaceuticals, and care access.
- Financial scoring and fraud detection leveraging cross-linked behavioral data to assess "risk" in transactions, credit, and mobility.

In each of these domains, the same underlying machine-learning systems trained on billions of daily interactions are repurposed to forecast future behavior - of individuals, groups, or entire populations. These capabilities are marketed as innovation, efficiency, and security, but they enable an unprecedented asymmetry of power between those who control the data flows and those being modeled by them.

Google's integration into the U.S. national security apparatus deepens this dual-use dynamic. Through DARPA-funded research, CIA-linked investments, and strategic partnerships with agencies like the NSA and NGA, Google's predictive systems function both commercially and geopolitically. Its search algorithms, advertising models, and AI engines form part of a feedback loop of influence:

- Data extracted from users trains models.
- Models produce behavioral predictions.
- Predictions inform algorithmic outputs - search rankings, video recommendations, content suppression.
- Those outputs modify behavior, generating new data that validates the model's assumptions.

This feedback loop doesn't just predict; it creates reality. The visibility of ideas, the prominence of political narratives, the virality of cultural trends - all mediated through opaque ranking algorithms optimized for engagement, profit, or policy alignment. When a billion people see Google as the "neutral" gateway to knowledge, its ability to shape perception quietly becomes structural power.

In the background, Google's AI research, led by divisions like Deep-

Mind and Google Brain, is pushing predictive capabilities even further. DeepMind's reinforcement learning systems - trained on games, logistics, and human interactions - aren't just solving chess or Go; they're refining frameworks for modeling human decision-making itself. These tools feed back into Google's commercial platforms but also inform DARPA-led projects on autonomous decision systems, predictive policing, and battlefield simulations. The boundary between advertising optimization and behavioral control infrastructure has effectively disappeared.

The weaponization of prediction operates on two levels:

1. Profit - maximizing engagement, shaping consumption, and extracting ever more granular behavioral data.

2. Governance - integrating predictive tools into security, finance, health, and communication infrastructures, enabling soft control without overt coercion.

Most users still experience Google as benevolent convenience - the search box, the directions, the infinite videos. But beneath that surface lies a closed-loop architecture designed to refine human beings into predictable, manipulable patterns, feeding a system that increasingly manages societies like dynamic datasets rather than self-determining populations.

Prediction, in this context, isn't neutral. It's a tool of power. The same algorithm that guesses what ad you'll click can guess which protest you'll join, which video will keep you compliant, or which narrative will shift public sentiment just enough to legitimize policy decisions. By controlling the levers of visibility, relevance, and recommendation, Google has transformed the internet into a behavioral laboratory - one where consent isn't revoked because it's never explicitly asked.

What began as search has evolved into social steering. Google doesn't just know what you're thinking; it quietly decides what you'll think about next.

Facebook began as a social network, but it quickly evolved into something far more ambitious - and dangerous. What started in a Harvard dorm room in 2004 as a platform to connect students became the largest behavioral laboratory in human history, designed to extract personal data, map identities, and engineer dopamine-driven engagement loops at planetary scale. Facebook didn't just connect people; it reconstructed social life inside an algorithmic system, where attention is commodified, identity is weaponized, and politics is subtly manipulated through invisible levers of influence.

From the start, Facebook's model relied on psychological dependency. Its early growth strategy focused on exclusivity - first limiting access to Ivy League schools, then opening gradually to select universities, and later to the public. This created a sense of status and scarcity that conditioned users to seek belonging within the platform. Once users were inside, Facebook's engineers applied behavioral design principles to keep them there. Drawing from neuroscience, persuasive technology, and social psychology, Facebook became a pioneer in dopamine loop engineering:

• Variable rewards: Likes, comments, and notifications deliver unpredictable feedback, stimulating the brain's reward pathways and encouraging compulsive checking.

• Social comparison triggers: Algorithms amplify content designed to provoke envy, outrage, or validation-seeking, increasing emotional engagement.

• Infinite scrolling: The absence of natural stopping cues eliminates decision fatigue, creating a frictionless environment where users lose track of time.

• Push notifications: Timed pings are optimized to exploit peaks of boredom, loneliness, or distraction, maintaining constant re-engagement.

These mechanisms transformed Facebook into a neural slot machine, keeping users hooked while silently collecting behavioral exhaust - every click, pause, and interaction feeding predictive models. The longer you stayed, the more data Facebook harvested, and the more accurately it could predict and manipulate future actions.

By 2010, Facebook had shifted from being just a social network to becoming the central identity graph of the internet. Unlike Google, which modeled intent through search queries, Facebook mapped who you are: your relationships, interests, habits, personality traits, and affiliations. Every friend added, group joined, or page liked fed into a high-dimensional profile capable of predicting not just what you'll buy but what you'll believe, who you'll vote for, and how you'll react to emotionally charged narratives.

This identity mapping created unprecedented power - and unprecedented vulnerability. When Facebook opened its API to third-party developers, millions of apps harvested user data, building an ecosystem of shadow profiling where advertisers, political campaigns, and intelligence contractors could access psychographic insights at scale. One of the most infamous examples was the Cambridge Analytica scandal: a single personality-quiz app captured data on over 87 million users, which was then used to design micro-targeted political campaigns during the 2016 U.S. election and Brexit referendum. Facebook claimed ignorance, but the architecture that enabled this wasn't a flaw - it was a feature.

Behind the surface of birthday posts and vacation photos, Facebook became a behavioral prediction marketplace. Advertisers and political actors weren't just buying demographics; they were buying algorithmically optimized influence campaigns. Using real-time A/B testing and reinforcement learning, Facebook's ad tools identified which messages - fear, hope, outrage, belonging - would move specific individuals or groups most effectively. This wasn't generic persuasion; it was personalized manipulation, invisible to the public and untraceable by regulators.

At the core of this system is the News Feed algorithm, introduced in 2006 and continuously refined. The News Feed doesn't simply display posts chronologically; it curates them based on engagement probability, prioritizing content likely to provoke emotional responses. Studies later revealed that the algorithm disproportionately amplifies content that triggers anger, fear, and tribal identity, because these emotions drive longer sessions and more clicks. In 2012, Facebook even ran a covert "emotional contagion" experiment on nearly 700,000 users, deliberately manipulating their feeds to test whether altering emotional tone could shift mood and behavior. The result? It could - and did.

By optimizing for engagement above all else, Facebook unintentionally (or perhaps inevitably) became a radicalization engine. Outrage, conspiracy theories, and hyper-partisan narratives rose to the top because the algorithm's single metric of success was "time on platform." Former executives, like Chamath Palihapitiya and Sean Parker, later admitted that Facebook knowingly exploited "human vulnerability" to keep users locked into addictive cycles while externalizing the social costs - political polarization, mental health crises, and declining trust in institutions.

Simultaneously, Facebook aligned itself with governments, militaries, and intelligence networks, deepening its role in algorithmic governance. Its AI-driven moderation systems - initially marketed as safeguards against misinformation and hate speech - also enable policy-driven censorship, where content visibility is shaped by partnerships with state agencies and NGOs. During elections and crises, Facebook routinely prioritizes narratives that align with "trusted" institutional partners while downranking or removing dissenting perspectives. Under the guise of "safety," the platform became an information choke point that can throttle debate at planetary scale.

Facebook's global expansion compounded its influence. In many developing nations, its "Free Basics" initiative offered subsidized access to the platform as a gateway to the internet - but only Facebook-approved content and services were accessible. For millions of users, Facebook became the internet itself, granting the company unprecedented cultural leverage and direct control over the flow of information in emerging economies.

By the mid-2010s, Facebook had quietly morphed into Meta, a company openly investing in neuro-marketing, augmented reality, and metaverse technologies. These moves signal an evolution beyond platforms toward full-spectrum behavioral immersion - not just predicting actions but shaping the environments where choices occur. The company's acquisitions of Instagram, WhatsApp, and Oculus consolidated massive cross-platform datasets, enabling Meta to track identity, attention, and social dynamics across multiple digital realms simultaneously.

The power Facebook wields today rests on three pillars:

1. Dopamine Architecture

By exploiting neural reward loops, Facebook engineers compulsive usage patterns, creating digital dependencies that make disengagement psychologically difficult.

2. Identity Mapping

Through relentless data aggregation, Facebook builds psychographic models capable of predicting individual choices, vulnerabilities, and responses with astonishing precision.

3. Political Influence

By controlling information hierarchies, Facebook shapes perception, public discourse, and even democratic outcomes, often invisibly and without accountability.

What makes Facebook uniquely dangerous is not just the volume of its data but the integration of emotion, identity, and influence inside a single algorithmic framework. Where Google predicts intent, Facebook engineers it by restructuring the social context in which decisions are made. Where Microsoft locks institutions into infrastructure, Facebook locks minds into feedback loops optimized for manipulation.

The result is a platform that doesn't just reflect society but rewires it - fragmenting communities, amplifying conflict, and normalizing algorithmic curation as the arbiter of reality. Users aren't customers; they're test subjects in a perpetual experiment where the end goal is maximum behavioral predictability, whether for selling products, steering elections, or enforcing consensus.

Facebook was marketed as a tool of connection, but it has become an engine of control. It maps identities, predicts behaviors, and nudges decisions while keeping users hooked inside dopamine-driven loops. Its real product isn't social networking; it's behavioral influence at planetary scale - sold to the highest bidder, licensed to political actors, and increasingly integrated into governance itself.

Amazon presents itself as the ultimate consumer convenience machine - the "everything store" where speed, efficiency, and frictionless commerce define the experience. But behind the public-facing retail empire, Amazon has quietly built one of the most powerful infrastructures of control on Earth, positioning itself as an unofficial extension of state power. Through its logistics networks, data centers, surveillance platforms, and deep integration with the U.S. defense and intelligence apparatus, Amazon has evolved far beyond e-commerce. It now operates as a shadow government - managing critical systems for finance, communication, cloud computing, and national security - while remaining almost entirely outside the reach of democratic oversight.

When Jeff Bezos founded Amazon in 1994, his stated ambition was to dominate online retail. But Bezos had a larger vision from the start: own the rails of digital infrastructure. While competitors fought over margins on books and electronics, Amazon quietly built an integrated empire spanning logistics, data storage, AI, and financial processing. Today, Amazon Web Services (AWS) - not the retail arm - generates the bulk of the company's profit, hosting the backbone of the modern internet. Governments, banks, hospitals, streaming platforms, intelligence agencies, and entire national infrastructures run on AWS servers, making Amazon the central nervous system of digital society.

This control over infrastructure gave Amazon unprecedented leverage, but Bezos went further: he fused Amazon's growth with U.S. state power. In 2013, Amazon secured a $600 million contract to provide secure cloud services to the CIA, establishing AWS as the preferred vendor for intelligence agencies. This deal marked a turning point: Amazon became the cloud provider for the U.S. security state, hosting classified data and analytical tools for the CIA, NSA, Department of Defense, and dozens of federal agencies.

The partnership deepened with the Pentagon's $10 billion JEDI contract (Joint Enterprise Defense Infrastructure), designed to centralize

military data and battlefield intelligence within a unified cloud platform. While Microsoft eventually won the contested bid, AWS already
controlled many of the systems feeding into JEDI and remains the dominant vendor for U.S. defense applications. From predictive maintenance for fighter jets to global troop logistics, Amazon's infrastructure
increasingly mediates the operational capabilities of the U.S. military.

Parallel to defense contracts, Amazon has embedded itself within domestic surveillance architectures. Its subsidiary Ring - marketed as a
consumer home security system - operates as a decentralized neighborhood surveillance grid, sharing user footage directly with local law enforcement through private-public partnerships. Amazon also owns
Rekognition, one of the most advanced facial recognition systems in
the world, which has been quietly deployed by police departments, federal agencies, and border authorities despite widespread concerns about
bias, accuracy, and civil liberties violations. Through these tools, Amazon has effectively privatized elements of policing and border security,
functioning as an unregulated extension of state enforcement.

AWS's dominance extends beyond U.S. borders. Governments worldwide - from the U.K. Home Office to the Australian Tax Authority to
the Singapore Ministry of Defense - rely on Amazon's infrastructure
for everything from biometric databases to tax collection systems. This
means Amazon sits at the center of global identity governance: passports, driver's licenses, criminal records, and immigration systems are increasingly processed, stored, and cross-referenced on AWS servers. For
supranational bodies like the World Bank, UN, and WHO, Amazon
provides cloud integration for health registries, financial tracking, and
population management programs.

This entanglement creates a profound sovereignty problem: when the
infrastructure of governance is outsourced to a private corporation,
control flows upward, away from parliaments and toward opaque systems designed by Amazon engineers and optimized for Amazon's interests. The company can technically see, store, or process vast amounts of
classified and personal data - including medical records, financial histo-

ries, and biometric identifiers - yet its internal governance is answerable only to its shareholders and select federal partners.

Meanwhile, Amazon's logistics empire - warehouses, fulfillment centers, and its global delivery network - has become essential for supply chain stability. Through its integration with defense and disaster response frameworks, Amazon coordinates delivery of military-grade equipment, emergency medical supplies, and critical infrastructure components during crises. In effect, the company has made itself too big to fail, ensuring any regulatory challenge risks destabilizing systems the state itself depends on.

Adding to this, Amazon wields data asymmetry as a weapon. The company collects and cross-links datasets at scales few can rival: consumer purchasing patterns, streaming preferences, device telemetry, Alexa voice data, geographic mobility through delivery routes, and even biometric data via Amazon One, its palm-based payment and authentication platform. These datasets, when combined with AWS's integration into government systems, provide Amazon - and its institutional partners - with planetary-level visibility into populations, consumption, and behavior.

Amazon also operates as a gatekeeper of censorship and content moderation, controlling critical infrastructure for communication platforms, streaming services, and social media. When Amazon abruptly de-platformed Parler in 2021 by cutting off its AWS hosting, it demonstrated the extent of its meta-governance power: the ability to erase entire political ecosystems from the internet by flipping a switch. No legislation, no due process - just unilateral corporate action with global consequences.

This fusion of corporate infrastructure and state power creates a hybrid governance model:

• Amazon builds and owns the infrastructure that powers commerce, communication, defense, and identity.

• The U.S. government integrates Amazon systems into its intelligence, surveillance, and military apparatus.

• Global institutions adopt Amazon frameworks, ensuring harmonized data standards and centralization.

• Citizens and governments become dependent on AWS-hosted systems, unable to operate outside Amazon's ecosystem without catastrophic disruption.

Bezos' long-term vision is even more expansive. Amazon is investing heavily in satellite-based internet infrastructure through Project Kuiper, seeking to connect global populations directly to Amazon's networks, bypassing national telecom providers entirely. Combined with its AI research, drone logistics, and biometric authentication systems, Amazon is steadily consolidating control over the pipes, the platforms, and the data that constitute modern governance.

Amazon is not just a retailer. It is the operating system for statecraft, functioning as an unelected layer of power beneath governments but above citizens. Through Pentagon contracts, surveillance platforms, and global infrastructure dominance, Amazon has positioned itself as an indispensable partner to institutions that manage war, law, finance, and identity. Yet unlike governments, it operates in complete opacity.

The result is a quiet inversion of sovereignty: where states once governed corporations, corporations like Amazon now govern states - not through elections or legislation, but through control of the systems upon which governance depends.

Amazon doesn't need to pass laws to shape society. It writes the code, owns the servers, manages the logistics, and supplies the intelligence tools. In doing so, it has become something far more potent than a tech giant: a shadow government, invisible to most, yet embedded in the architecture of modern power.

16

Biosecurity as the New Governance

B ill Gates' second act has been sold as a pivot from tech titan to philanthropist, but behind the public narrative of altruism lies a carefully constructed health empire - one built through vaccines, patents, and institutional capture. Through the Bill & Melinda Gates Foundation (BMGF), Gates has leveraged his wealth and influence to position himself at the center of global health governance, effectively transforming public health into a privately managed enterprise where decisions impacting billions flow through unelected networks tied to his funding, his partnerships, and his strategic control of intellectual property.

When Gates launched the Foundation in 2000, his stated goal was "improving health and reducing inequity." But from the outset, the BMGF's strategy mirrored the same lock-in model that made Microsoft dominant: control the infrastructure, set the standards, and build dependency. In software, Gates locked users into proprietary ecosystems. In health, he is doing the same with vaccines, patents, and supranational partnerships that centralize decision-making above the level of national sovereignty.

Building the Vaccine Empire

The BMGF became one of the world's largest funders of vaccine research and distribution, investing billions into programs like Gavi, the Vaccine Alliance (founded in 2000) and the Coalition for Epidemic Preparedness Innovations (CEPI) in 2017. Gates' Foundation effectively bankrolls and directs these bodies, which coordinate with the WHO, pharmaceutical companies, and national governments to set global vaccination priorities. While publicly framed as humanitarian, these networks operate on a public-private partnership model that prioritizes intellectual property protection and centralized procurement - ensuring that decisions about which vaccines get developed, funded, and distributed are made within small, Foundation-aligned circles.

Gavi, headquartered in Geneva but funded heavily by Gates, functions as the operational arm of Gates' influence. It negotiates vaccine prices with manufacturers, allocates donor funds, and establishes distribution pipelines - but its board includes executives from Pfizer, GlaxoSmithKline, and other pharmaceutical giants who benefit directly from these deals. By steering Gavi's agenda, Gates effectively sets de facto global vaccine policy, often bypassing the voices of recipient nations themselves.

CEPI, co-founded by Gates in partnership with the World Economic Forum, focuses on "pandemic preparedness" but operates as an innovation gatekeeper. By funding specific platforms - such as mRNA technology - and locking development into patent-protected ecosystems, CEPI ensures that control over next-generation vaccines remains concentrated in a handful of corporations, often those already partnered with the BMGF.

Patents Over People

One of the most controversial aspects of Gates' influence is his staunch defense of pharmaceutical patents, especially during global health emergencies. During the COVID-19 pandemic, Gates opposed calls from developing nations and humanitarian groups to waive intellectual property rights on vaccines, arguing instead for controlled licensing through proprietary channels. This decision delayed vaccine production in the Global South, reinforcing dependency on Western suppliers and keeping billions in potential profits aligned with Gates-funded partners.

Critics argue this mirrors Microsoft's playbook: use proprietary systems to dominate markets, then force everyone else to operate inside your architecture. By funding vaccine research and simultaneously backing patent-protection regimes, the Gates Foundation sits on both sides of the equation - shaping supply while indirectly benefiting from its corporate alliances.

Capturing Global Health Governance

Gates' power in public health comes not only from funding but from institutional capture. Through billions in grants, the BMGF has become the second-largest donor to the World Health Organization (WHO) after the U.S. government, giving it outsize influence over WHO priorities, agenda-setting, and emergency response protocols.

This influence extends beyond WHO. Gates' Foundation funds countless universities, public health departments, NGOs, and scientific journals, shaping research agendas and controlling the narrative around vaccines, nutrition, and disease prevention. In effect, Gates has created a closed-loop influence system:

- Fund the research.
- Influence the regulators.
- Shape the media narrative.
- Control the intellectual property.
- Partner with governments for rollout.

By embedding itself across every layer of global health, the Gates Foundation ensures alignment with its strategic vision - one centered on techno-centric, pharmaceutical-first solutions over systemic reforms like clean water, food sovereignty, or decentralized care models, which receive comparatively less attention and funding.

The Pandemic as Proof of Concept

COVID-19 revealed just how consolidated Gates' influence had become. From the earliest days of the pandemic, Gates-funded organizations coordinated vaccine development, manufacturing contracts, and distribution pipelines. Gavi and CEPI played central roles in creating COVAX, the global vaccine-sharing initiative, while Gates simultaneously promoted frameworks tying vaccine access to digital identity systems through initiatives like ID2020.

Microsoft, meanwhile, positioned its Azure cloud infrastructure to handle health data, vaccine passports, and digital authentication systems in partnership with Gavi, the WHO, and national governments. This fusion of biometric ID, vaccination status, and digital infrastructure signaled a shift toward programmable access to services, where inclusion in social and economic systems increasingly depends on participating in centralized health databases.

Engineering Dependency Through "Philanthropy"

The Gates Foundation frames its model as generosity, but its outcomes often mirror monopoly dynamics:

• Centralized standards: Gates-funded bodies establish vaccine platforms, pricing strategies, and patent protections that lock nations into specific suppliers.

• Dependency cycles: Low-income countries reliant on donor-funded vaccines remain tethered to external procurement rather than developing domestic manufacturing capacity.

• Data consolidation: Gates-funded programs integrate biometric identity, immunization records, and health tracking into interoperable systems managed by private tech partners.

• Narrative control: Through media grants and research funding, dissenting perspectives on vaccine governance, intellectual property, or decentralized health models are marginalized.

In this sense, Gates' health empire isn't separate from Microsoft's legacy - it's Microsoft 2.0: a proprietary, centralized architecture for global health governance, built on patents instead of code but optimized for the same outcome: structural control.

A De Facto Health Czar Without a Mandate

Unlike governments or international bodies, Gates' Foundation faces no electoral oversight, no parliamentary checks, and no public accountability. Yet its funding decisions shape the priorities of entire regions, influencing everything from pandemic response strategies to nutritional guidelines and vaccine passports. Gates didn't just become a major player in public health; he became one of its primary architects, using private wealth to dictate systems that affect billions of lives.

This isn't philanthropy in the traditional sense. It's strategic influence-building - a process of embedding control inside the infrastructure of health systems globally, using donor funding as leverage to align public policy with private objectives.

Bill Gates 2.0 didn't abandon monopolistic ambition; he simply changed the domain. Instead of software ecosystems, the product is vaccines, patents, and data. Instead of operating systems for PCs, it's operating systems for populations - centralized frameworks managing identity, access, and biological compliance, all under the guise of benevolence.

Gates built a fortune by owning the tools of the digital world. Now, through global health, he's positioning himself to own the tools of the biological one.

Gavi, the Vaccine Alliance, was founded in 2000 with heavy seed funding from the Bill & Melinda Gates Foundation, but the real story isn't philanthropy - it's control. On paper, Gavi exists to increase vaccine access and "save lives," but in practice, it functions as a privatized planetary health governance network, dictating vaccine priorities, negotiating procurement deals, and locking entire nations into frameworks designed upstream by a small group of unelected actors aligned with corporate and philanthropic interests.

Gavi sits at the intersection of private wealth, supranational institutions, and pharmaceutical monopolies. Its board includes representatives from Pfizer, GlaxoSmithKline, Johnson & Johnson, the Gates Foundation, the World Bank, UNICEF, and donor governments. This composition gives Gavi the ability to set global vaccination policies while directly aligning those policies with corporate profit models. It doesn't just fund vaccine access - it manages the rules of participation, deciding which technologies get prioritized, which companies get contracts, and how nations access supplies.

Countries working with Gavi must sign long-term agreements governing procurement, data-sharing, and pricing standards. These agreements bypass parliamentary oversight in most cases and become effectively binding frameworks. Low-income nations are given subsidized access to vaccines, but those subsidies are tied to platforms, patents, and supply chains controlled by a small handful of Western pharmaceutical giants - the same corporations represented on Gavi's board. Instead of fostering local production and sovereignty, Gavi entrenches dependency cycles: health systems reorganize around Gavi-approved pipelines, and when subsidies expire, countries are locked into pricing structures and procurement systems they no longer control.

The Gates Foundation's influence over Gavi cannot be overstated. Gates' funding gave him permanent seats at the policymaking table, where his preferences shape not only which vaccines are prioritized but also which technologies receive billions in investment. Gates' aggressive backing of proprietary platforms like mRNA ensures that entire nations now base their vaccination strategies on technologies owned and licensed by companies directly tied to Gates-funded initiatives. Through Gavi, these choices ripple outward into WHO policy, where Gates' role as the second-largest funder gives him indirect leverage over official global health guidelines without ever holding an elected mandate.

The COVID-19 pandemic exposed how deeply consolidated this power has become. Alongside CEPI, also co-founded by Gates, Gavi became one of the architects of COVAX, the global vaccine distribution program. COVAX claimed to ensure equitable access, but in practice, wealthier nations bypassed it entirely with direct purchase agreements, while Gavi-dependent countries were left at the back of the line. Gavi enforced contracts protecting corporate intellectual property, even as billions of people waited for doses. Calls from the Global South to suspend vaccine patents under the TRIPS Agreement were actively opposed by Gates and his aligned institutions, preserving monopoly control during a global emergency.

But Gavi's influence extends beyond vaccines into data, identity, and governance. Through its partnership in ID2020, launched with Microsoft and the Rockefeller Foundation, Gavi promotes linking vaccination records to digital identity systems that can integrate with banking, travel permissions, and access to social services. Under the guise of efficiency, Gavi is helping construct interoperable biometric databases tied to vaccine compliance - systems that could easily become programmable access controls governing participation in economic and civic life. For many low- and middle-income countries, participation in these frameworks is no longer optional. Vaccine procurement, identity management, and data integration now come bundled, reshaping sovereignty into compliance.

What emerges is not a humanitarian alliance but an unelected governance layer, where private actors wield authority traditionally reserved for governments and parliaments. Gavi doesn't legislate, but its agreements become binding policy. It doesn't regulate, but its frameworks dictate regulatory standards. It isn't a government, but it makes decisions that affect entire populations, often beyond the reach of any democratic accountability.

Philanthropy here isn't charity; it's leverage. By using donor funding to set the rules, Gates and his aligned institutions effectively dictate the future of global health. Publicly, Gavi markets "vaccines for all," but structurally, it creates centralized systems where supply, identity, and data governance converge. A small network of corporations, foundations, and supranational agencies controls the rails, while billions of people - and the governments meant to represent them - are left dependent on pipelines they didn't design and cannot change.

This is planetary health policy designed from the top down, managed through private institutions, and insulated from democratic challenge. Gavi functions as the operational core of that system, building a framework where compliance is enforced not by governments but by infrastructure - and where access to medicine, identity, and participation increasingly flows through the same digital gateways.

Anthony Fauci's career at the helm of the National Institute of Allergy and Infectious Diseases (NIAID) inside the U.S. National Institutes of Health (NIH) spans more than four decades, but his real role goes far beyond science or public health. Over time, Fauci transformed NI-AID into a gatekeeping institution - one that determines which research gets funded, which narratives dominate policy, and which voices are silenced. Under his leadership, the NIH evolved from a scientific funding body into a regulatory chokepoint tightly integrated with pharmaceutical companies, supranational health agencies, and political power structures. Fauci's influence cannot be measured simply in terms of infectious disease research; his tenure reshaped the architecture of global health governance itself.

Fauci took over NIAID in 1984, during the early years of the HIV/AIDS crisis, at a time when the institute controlled a massive and growing portion of federal biomedical research funding. NIH, and NIAID in particular, sits at the center of the U.S. scientific ecosystem - controlling tens of billions annually in grants that determine which laboratories thrive, which technologies advance, and which careers survive. For researchers and universities, alignment with NIH priorities is not optional; it's existential. This structure gave Fauci enormous leverage: by steering grant funding, he could effectively shape the direction of biomedical science worldwide.

This funding power became the foundation for a network of policy-aligned influence. Laboratories that challenged prevailing narratives or proposed alternative treatments often found their grants cut or renewal requests denied. Conversely, institutions and scientists that stayed within the NIH-approved paradigm were rewarded with continuous funding, prestigious publications, and seats at advisory tables. Over decades, this created an ideological monoculture within biomedical research, where deviation from official policy meant professional marginalization.

NIAID's dominance also extends into drug development pipelines. While the NIH presents itself as a neutral scientific body, it operates in tight coordination with the pharmaceutical industry, particularly through the system of public-private partnerships. Fauci's institute routinely funds early-stage research for vaccines, antivirals, and therapeutics, only to hand intellectual property rights and later-stage trials to private corporations. This structure socializes research costs through taxpayer dollars while privatizing profits through licensing agreements and patents.

Nowhere was this more apparent than during the COVID-19 pandemic. The NIH, under Fauci's leadership, co-held the intellectual property rights on key technologies underlying the mRNA vaccines developed by Moderna. While NIAID-funded researchers helped invent the spike protein stabilization techniques that made these vaccines possible, the NIH licensed those patents to pharmaceutical companies under agreements largely shielded from public scrutiny. Fauci publicly presented vaccine rollout as a purely humanitarian effort while NIH quietly negotiated royalty arrangements - blurring the line between regulator, funder, and profit participant.

Fauci's role as gatekeeper became even more controversial with his involvement in gain-of-function research - experiments designed to enhance the transmissibility or lethality of pathogens to study potential pandemic threats. While Fauci repeatedly denied funding such work, documents later revealed NIH-supported grants routed through the non-profit EcoHealth Alliance to the Wuhan Institute of Virology, directly tied to studies manipulating coronaviruses. The funding mechanisms were legal but opaque, illustrating how Fauci's NIH could shape sensitive research agendas behind closed doors, bypassing open public debate on risks and ethics.

At the same time, Fauci's influence extended well beyond NIH into global health governance networks. Through partnerships with the WHO, the Gates Foundation, CEPI, and Gavi, Fauci became a central node in a transnational decision-making web. During COVID-19, these relationships allowed NIH-backed priorities - from vaccine-first strategies to digital health surveillance frameworks - to cascade globally, bypassing national legislatures and regulatory bodies. Countries around the world aligned their policies with NIH-approved guidance not through democratic deliberation but because funding, supply chains, and international coordination were already integrated into Gates-led and NIH-linked systems.

Media narratives reflected this centralization of authority. Fauci became the face of "The Science," an archetype promoted as the singular voice of reason while dissenting views from credentialed experts were censored, deranked, or deplatformed. Social media companies partnered directly with NIH and allied agencies to "combat misinformation," creating feedback loops where approved narratives were amplified while alternative hypotheses were labeled conspiratorial, regardless of their scientific merit. NIH wasn't simply funding research; it was managing consensus across academia, media, and policy simultaneously.

This power structure reveals the NIH not as a neutral arbiter of science but as an operational hub where public health, corporate profit, and political influence converge. Under Fauci, the institute's priorities consistently reflected a pattern:

• Centralize control over funding pipelines to enforce alignment.

• Tie regulatory approval to patent-protected products owned by NIH-aligned partners.

• Shape global narratives by coordinating directly with supranational institutions and private foundations.

• Normalize digital health surveillance and identity frameworks linked to vaccination programs.

Fauci's tenure also highlights the growing entanglement of health and security policy. Beginning in the early 2000s with the anthrax scares and post-9/11 biodefense funding, NIH took on an expanded role in national security planning. Fauci was instrumental in framing emerging infectious diseases as security threats, unlocking billions in defense-linked research budgets and tightening relationships between NIH, DARPA, and the Department of Homeland Security. This securitization of public health further blurred the boundary between scientific neutrality and policy enforcement.

By the time Fauci retired in 2022, he had become one of the most powerful unelected officials in the United States - not just because he advised presidents or managed crises but because he controlled the operating system of biomedical science. Through the NIH, Fauci effectively determined what counted as "legitimate research," who received resources, and which narratives dominated global discourse. At the same time, his institute sat inside a vast public-private architecture linking governments, corporations, NGOs, and supranational bodies into a single coordinated framework for planetary health governance.

The NIH under Fauci exemplifies how gatekeeping institutions function in the technocratic era: they set the priorities, fund the aligned actors, marginalize dissent, and synchronize global systems without requiring overt legislative control. On the surface, this looks like expertise-driven governance. In reality, it creates a closed-loop ecosystem of influence where a handful of individuals and organizations control the flow of money, research, regulation, and narrative simultaneously.

Anthony Fauci did not just manage NIAID; he built an enforcement mechanism for a broader infrastructure - one where science, politics, and profit converge. The NIH became less a research institute and more an architectural chokepoint, shaping how health policy is decided and executed worldwide while insulating its decision-makers from democratic accountability.

Event 201, held on October 18, 2019, in New York City, was presented publicly as a pandemic preparedness exercise. In reality, it functioned as a biosecurity rehearsal for coordinated planetary crisis management - not simply responding to a health emergency, but stress-testing governance, information control, and economic continuity under the pretext of a viral outbreak. Organized by the Johns Hopkins Center for Health Security in partnership with the Bill & Melinda Gates Foundation and the World Economic Forum (WEF), Event 201 brought together corporate executives, government officials, intelligence-linked NGOs, and media leaders to simulate a global pandemic scenario. Its timing - just months before COVID-19 emerged - and its content reveal how deeply public-private power networks were already preparing frameworks for managing populations, information flows, and economies at planetary scale.

The exercise simulated a novel coronavirus outbreak originating from animal reservoirs, spreading globally through human-to-human transmission, ultimately overwhelming health systems and disrupting trade, finance, and political stability. But Event 201's focus wasn't on hospital capacity or vaccine logistics alone. Its working sessions centered on synchronizing authority across governments, corporations, and supranational bodies to control not just disease but behavior, markets, and narrative coherence.

Participants included representatives from the Gates Foundation, WEF, Johnson & Johnson, Merck, Lufthansa Group, the U.S. Centers for Disease Control (CDC), the Chinese CDC, the United Nations Foundation, Edelman PR, NBCUniversal, and other nodes of influence. Missing were elected legislators, grassroots health organizations, or voices outside elite policymaking circles. The event wasn't designed to democratize pandemic response - it was designed to centralize it.

One of Event 201's core scenarios dealt with coordinated information management. In breakout discussions, participants debated strategies to combat "misinformation" and "disinformation" during the simulated pandemic. The proposals included collaboration between governments, tech companies, and traditional media to identify and suppress narratives deemed harmful to "public trust." In practical terms, this meant developing pre-agreed censorship protocols, leveraging social platforms like Facebook, Google, and Twitter to throttle or remove dissenting voices, while ensuring "trusted messengers" - often institutional partners tied to funding networks - dominated information environments.

A second major theme was financial and trade stabilization. Event 201 modeled cascading economic disruption from lockdowns, labor shortages, and supply-chain collapse. Participants called for using central banks, IMF facilities, and multinational corporations to coordinate liquidity injections, maintain resource flows, and secure intellectual property rights in emergencies. In these simulations, pandemic response was framed not as a public-health challenge but as an opportunity to restructure economic dependencies around central institutions and private stakeholders, with minimal transparency and no democratic input. Vaccine development and distribution were also heavily emphasized. Event 201 assumed vaccines would become the critical bottleneck in resolving the crisis and discussed advance market commitments (AMCs) - financial mechanisms guaranteeing pre-purchased contracts for vaccine manufacturers, funded by governments but brokered by entities like Gavi and CEPI, both founded and heavily funded by the Gates Foundation. These arrangements ensured pharmaceutical companies would bear minimal financial risk while maximizing control over intellectual property, pricing, and global distribution channels.

Perhaps the most revealing discussions, however, revolved around behavioral governance. Event 201 highlighted the need to maintain population compliance during extended restrictions, resource shortages, and health mandates. Participants proposed leveraging digital platforms, biometric IDs, and integrated data systems to track vaccination status, manage mobility permissions, and model citizen sentiment in real time. Proposals aligned closely with initiatives like ID2020, launched by Gavi, Microsoft, and the Rockefeller Foundation, which seeks to integrate digital identity with health records, financial access, and service eligibility - effectively creating programmable gateways into economic and civic participation.

What makes Event 201 especially significant is not simply that it anticipated a coronavirus pandemic months before COVID-19 but that its policy blueprints mirrored what later unfolded in reality:

- Lockdowns, school closures, and restrictions on gatherings.
- Rapid emergency authorization of vaccines under AMCs, with centralized procurement through Gavi and CEPI.
- Coordination between Big Tech and governments to moderate "harmful" information.
- Integration of vaccine compliance into emerging frameworks for digital identity and mobility controls.
- A parallel centralization of financial decision-making under the IMF,

BIS, and World Bank to stabilize capital flows.

Critics argue that the similarity between Event 201's scenarios and subsequent pandemic responses is coincidental, but this overlooks how the same actors who staged the exercise also executed its solutions. The Gates Foundation, Gavi, CEPI, WHO, WEF, and major pharmaceutical companies didn't just predict the playbook; they wrote it, rehearsed it, and deployed it - using the crisis to accelerate pre-existing agendas around digital health governance, biotech expansion, and supranational coordination.

Event 201 wasn't an isolated simulation; it was part of a broader series of pandemic strategy exercises dating back nearly two decades. Programs like Dark Winter (2001), Clade X (2018), and the Global Health Security Agenda had already tested scenarios involving biosecurity threats, data-driven population management, and cross-border resource coordination. Event 201 synthesized these threads into a comprehensive framework that positioned unelected foundations and corporate boards as de facto decision-makers for planetary emergencies.

What's critical to understand is that these simulations aren't about preparing nations for unpredictable crises. They're about engineering predictable responses. By consolidating authority into closed, pre-aligned networks of global stakeholders, the outcomes of future emergencies become less dependent on democratic processes and more controlled by technocratic infrastructures. Event 201 revealed how health emergencies can function as catalysts for reorganizing governance, commerce, and individual freedoms at planetary scale, while framing these shifts as necessary and inevitable.

The pandemic that followed was unprecedented in scale, but the solutions were not improvised - they were scripted upstream. Event 201 shows how public-private partnerships now act as the real policy architects during crises, using rehearsals to align key stakeholders, stress-test their strategies, and ensure that when emergencies hit, control flows toward the same small network of institutions managing vaccines, data, media, and finance.

Event 201 wasn't about saving lives; it was about consolidating systems. It modeled how to manage information, regulate movement, secure corporate assets, and normalize digital ID systems - all under the cover of emergency response. The blueprint it established has now become the baseline for future planetary governance.

17

Peter Thiel and the Palantir State

Palantir was founded in 2003 by Peter Thiel, Alex Karp, and a team of engineers with early funding from In-Q-Tel, the CIA's venture capital arm. Publicly, it branded itself as a cutting-edge data analytics company capable of "solving the world's hardest problems." But behind the marketing, Palantir has quietly built the core infrastructure for predictive governance - a system where individual behavior, social patterns, and population dynamics are modeled in real time to anticipate threats before they occur.

This isn't about policing in the traditional sense. Palantir operates at the nexus of surveillance, machine learning, and algorithmic decision-making, building platforms that integrate data from hundreds of sources - financial transactions, criminal records, biometric databases, travel histories, social media, health registries, and even private communications where authorized - into a single, unified environment. Within that environment, predictive models flag anomalies and probabilities: who's likely to commit a crime, where unrest might emerge, which networks pose potential "threat vectors." The result is a quiet shift from reactive governance to pre-crime governance.

Palantir's flagship platform, Gotham, was initially deployed in the U.S. intelligence community during the post-9/11 War on Terror. The company pitched Gotham as a tool to connect the dots between disparate datasets to identify terrorist networks. But its capabilities quickly expanded. By integrating watchlists, geolocation data, and social graphs, Palantir enabled agencies like the CIA, NSA, and Department of Defense to model relationships at scale and generate probability scores for targeting decisions. Those same techniques soon migrated into domestic law enforcement under the banner of predictive policing.

Cities like Los Angeles, Chicago, and New Orleans quietly adopted Palantir systems to predict where crimes were likely to occur and which individuals were most likely to be involved - either as perpetrators or victims. Officers received risk heat maps, neighborhood profiles, and suspect lists based on algorithmic outputs rather than investigations. Police were instructed to increase patrols in "high-probability zones," intervene early with flagged individuals, and maintain constant surveillance on algorithm-identified networks.

Proponents argue this makes policing "smarter." But critics warn it creates self-reinforcing feedback loops:

• More patrols in algorithm-flagged neighborhoods generate more arrests.

• Those arrests feed back into the model, reinforcing bias in future predictions.

• Over time, entire communities become locked into permanent high-risk status - not because of what they've done but because of what the system predicts they might do.

Palantir's role extends far beyond local police. Through contracts with Immigration and Customs Enforcement (ICE), Palantir's systems have powered mass deportation campaigns by linking DMV data, utility bills, court filings, and social media activity to identify and track undocumented individuals. In the pandemic era, Palantir built Tiberius, a platform used by the U.S. government to manage vaccine distribution, integrating demographic, health, and geospatial datasets to coordinate resource allocation. These same capabilities, designed ostensibly for efficiency, establish frameworks where health compliance, immigration status, and social identity converge inside single, integrated monitoring environments.

Internationally, Palantir has positioned itself as a key contractor for intelligence agencies, militaries, and supranational bodies like NATO and Europol. In war zones from Afghanistan to Ukraine, its platforms model battlefield logistics, predict insurgent activity, and manage civilian displacement flows. In financial hubs, Palantir tools are used to flag "suspicious transactions," cross-referencing global banking systems, corporate registries, and crypto exchanges with watchlists maintained by agencies like the Financial Action Task Force (FATF).

At its core, Palantir is building the operational backbone for pre-crime governance:

• Integrating real-time surveillance feeds from CCTV, license plate readers, drones, and facial recognition systems.

• Linking biometric ID frameworks like Aadhaar in India or REAL ID in the U.S. to social graphs and mobility data.

• Cross-mapping health, financial, and behavioral datasets into unified digital identity profiles.

• Feeding this data into machine learning systems that continuously update risk predictions for individuals, communities, and even entire nations.

This shift has profound implications for personal autonomy and sovereignty. In the Palantir model, probability becomes policy. If the system assigns you a high-risk score based on your associations, location history, or online activity, you can be flagged for increased surveillance, denied resources, or targeted for intervention - often without any due process. Your "threat profile" isn't adjudicated in court; it's computed upstream by proprietary algorithms hidden from public scrutiny.

These platforms are sold as neutral tools, but their outputs reflect the biases baked into their inputs. Historical policing data, financial inequality, and geopolitical agendas shape how the system identifies "risk." At scale, this creates an invisible framework of algorithmic stratification, where certain populations - often already marginalized - are subjected to intensified scrutiny while others remain largely invisible to enforcement. Palantir's integration with broader global governance architectures amplifies its reach. Its platforms are increasingly connected with initiatives backed by the World Economic Forum, WHO, and Gavi, linking predictive analytics to pandemic response, climate migration forecasting, and financial compliance systems tied to ESG scoring. As more sectors adopt Palantir-powered infrastructure - from border control to disaster relief to digital identity verification - the company positions itself as the invisible intermediary between citizens, corporations, and governments. The trajectory is clear: predictive policing is only the beginning. As Palantir layers machine learning onto unified data ecosystems, governance shifts from responding to actions to managing probabilities, and eventually to engineering behavior itself. By controlling the platforms that integrate surveillance, health, finance, and identity, Palantir is helping construct the foundation for a continuous compliance grid - a world where deviations from modeled norms are flagged in real time, and intervention becomes automated.

This isn't science fiction; it's already operational. In cities, your location history, transaction patterns, and social affiliations can trigger algorithmic alerts long before any crime is committed. In airports, Palantir-powered watchlists and facial recognition systems decide who gets flagged for secondary screening. In finance, predictive models determine whether your transfers are "high-risk." In pandemics, these same systems assess compliance with lockdowns, mask mandates, and vaccination schedules, feeding into risk dashboards used by governments and NGOs alike.

Palantir isn't just another contractor; it's building the hidden operating system of modern governance. The state still passes laws, but Palantir's platforms increasingly define how those laws are enforced, who gets targeted, and which behaviors are preemptively managed. Through partnerships with intelligence agencies, supranational institutions, and global corporations, it sits quietly at the heart of a shift from rule-based governance to algorithmic prediction and control - where freedom itself becomes conditional on what the system believes you might do.

Palantir's pitch was "connect the dots." In practice, it has connected everything.

The CIA's venture capital arm, In-Q-Tel, was founded in 1999 as a "bridge" between Silicon Valley startups and U.S. intelligence agencies, but its real function is far broader. In-Q-Tel operates as the financial bloodstream of the technocracy, seeding private companies with defense-aligned funding, steering technological innovation toward surveillance, control, and behavioral prediction - while disguising these projects as neutral market-driven breakthroughs. By quietly investing in startups that build the infrastructure of data integration, biometric tracking, predictive analytics, and autonomous decision-making, In-Q-Tel has created a pipeline where cutting-edge civilian technology is co-opted early, shaped upstream, and ultimately embedded into both state power structures and corporate governance models worldwide.

Unlike traditional government funding mechanisms, In-Q-Tel operates as a private, nonprofit venture fund. Its portfolio companies aren't formally government contractors - they're dual-use innovators developing products for consumers and corporations, but designed from inception to integrate seamlessly into intelligence and defense architectures. This structure gives the CIA plausible deniability while embedding spy-grade tools deep inside private markets and public infrastructure.

From its earliest investments, In-Q-Tel targeted technologies critical to population-scale information control:

• Palantir - Data fusion and predictive analytics, now powering intelligence operations, predictive policing, and global compliance systems.

• Keyhole Inc. - Satellite imaging platform acquired by Google in 2004 and converted into Google Earth, a CIA-seeded tool disguised as consumer software while simultaneously serving the National Geospatial-Intelligence Agency (NGA).

• Recorded Future - Machine learning platforms for open-source intelligence and predictive modeling of geopolitical events and social movements.

• Basis Technology - Natural language processing and translation software used to index and monitor global communication streams.

- Digital Reasoning - Cognitive analytics systems capable of scanning massive text datasets to detect sentiment, intent, and emerging narratives.

Through In-Q-Tel, these companies receive early-stage funding, privileged access to classified problem sets, and intelligence community testing environments. In return, their products are shaped to align with the surveillance, data-integration, and behavioral-modeling needs of agencies like the CIA, NSA, DHS, and FBI - and later deployed at planetary scale via Big Tech partnerships.

This isn't passive investment; it's strategic preemption. By financing startups before they dominate their sectors, In-Q-Tel ensures that data infrastructure, identity frameworks, and predictive algorithms are designed to be interoperable with state systems. Google's search architecture, Facebook's social graphs, Amazon's cloud dominance, and Microsoft's identity frameworks are not separate stories - they are pieces of an integrated, intelligence-aligned ecosystem seeded deliberately through these pipelines.

In-Q-Tel doesn't stop at domestic intelligence; its influence extends across supranational governance structures. The World Bank, NATO, the World Economic Forum (WEF), and Gavi increasingly rely on tools built by In-Q-Tel-backed companies to manage digital identity programs, pandemic compliance frameworks, climate migration modeling, and ESG-based financial scoring systems. This integration creates a globalized technocratic architecture where the same platforms simultaneously serve corporate markets, government surveillance, and policy enforcement at international scale.

One of In-Q-Tel's deepest areas of investment is biometric and digital identity infrastructure. Companies funded by the agency have pioneered systems for facial recognition, iris scanning, gait analysis, and DNA storage - tools now integrated into border control regimes, vaccine verification frameworks, and digital ID projects like ID2020. Once these platforms are adopted, sovereignty begins to dissolve: national governments become dependent on interoperable technologies designed upstream by unelected actors, creating soft compliance to global-ized systems without the need for treaties or legislation.

In-Q-Tel has also been heavily involved in next-generation communica-tion and AI research. Investments in natural language processing, ma-chine translation, and sentiment analysis feed directly into programs for real-time information dominance - the ability to monitor narratives as they emerge and suppress them before they metastasize. Through part-nerships with Google, Meta, and Twitter, intelligence-linked platforms can throttle information flows, derank dissent, and amplify "trusted" narratives without leaving visible fingerprints of state censorship.

During the pandemic, these pipelines became fully operational. In-Q-Tel-backed companies provided health compliance dashboards, predic-tive outbreak modeling, and vaccination logistics platforms used by governments and supranational agencies alike. Palantir's Tiberius sys-tem integrated health, mobility, and demographic data to manage U.S. vaccine distribution while sharing outputs across intelligence networks. Simultaneously, biometric-linked vaccine passports - built with In-Q-Tel-supported infrastructure - were normalized through programs like Gavi's COVAX and ID2020, tying health status to economic and civic participation.

In-Q-Tel's influence reveals a quiet strategic convergence:

• Seed civilian technologies early so they align with intelligence priori-ties from inception.

• Integrate platforms into global governance frameworks, ensuring supranational interoperability.

• Normalize deployment via consumer markets, app ecosystems, and public-private partnerships.

• Leverage crises - pandemics, terrorism, climate shocks - to accelerate adoption of compliance-driven infrastructure.

In this way, In-Q-Tel acts less like a venture fund and more like a tech-nocratic command center disguised as innovation. The companies it funds don't just build products; they create the rails of control: plat-forms through which identity, mobility, finance, health, and information are increasingly managed. Governments adopt these tools because they're efficient and cheap, corporations integrate them because they're scalable and standardized, and citizens use them because they're convenient - all while the architecture of surveillance and influence becomes seamless, invisible, and irreversible.

By embedding CIA-backed technologies into the DNA of global digital infrastructure, In-Q-Tel has effectively privatized the tools of governance while centralizing control. Platforms born in secrecy now manage airports, borders, payment systems, vaccine registries, predictive policing programs, and AI-driven censorship - all under the guise of "innovation."

What emerges is not a patchwork of separate institutions but a single technocratic stack, where unelected intelligence-linked networks control the systems that define modern life. Through In-Q-Tel, predictive policing, digital identity, biometric databases, pandemic modeling, and financial scoring are being stitched together into an integrated governance framework - managed privately, enforced algorithmically, and largely immune to democratic oversight.

The CIA no longer needs to build its own tools or maintain overt control of domestic systems. In-Q-Tel ensures that the entire technological ecosystem evolves toward surveillance-first architectures by default, creating the infrastructure for preemptive governance on a planetary scale. This is not venture capital in the traditional sense. It's a strategic weapon - shaping the technological substrate through which power, identity, and compliance are defined in the 21st century.

In 2001, a small Silicon Valley startup called Keyhole Inc. developed a revolutionary technology: a 3D geospatial visualization platform capable of stitching together satellite imagery, aerial photography, and mapping data into an interactive, zoomable model of the planet. To the public, it was marketed as innovation for digital cartography. But behind the scenes, Keyhole was funded and shaped by In-Q-Tel, the CIA's venture capital arm, as part of a strategic effort to develop next-generation reconnaissance tools for U.S. intelligence and military operations.

What later became Google Earth began as a classified surveillance asset, and its journey from battlefield infrastructure to consumer app illustrates how intelligence-driven technology pipelines shape planetary governance under the guise of convenience.

Keyhole was founded by John Hanke, a former U.S. defense analyst who had previously worked on military simulations and satellite data integration. The company's flagship platform, EarthViewer 3D, used advanced image-compression algorithms and cloud-streaming techniques to deliver high-resolution, real-time satellite imagery directly to end-users over the internet - a capability previously limited to classified military systems. This made it immediately valuable to U.S. intelligence agencies seeking to integrate geospatial intelligence (GEOINT) into targeting operations, battlefield simulations, and population monitoring after 9/11.

Recognizing the potential, In-Q-Tel provided early funding and positioned Keyhole as a direct contractor for the National Geospatial-Intelligence Agency (NGA) and the Defense Department. EarthViewer became a quiet backbone for U.S. operations in Iraq and Afghanistan, providing analysts and commanders with interactive, 3D battlefields where troop movements, drone feeds, and logistical pipelines could be visualized in real time. Its architecture also enabled integration of multiple classified datasets:

- Live drone surveillance layered over satellite imagery.
- SIGINT intercepts mapped geographically to identify communications clusters.
- Infrastructure models highlighting power grids, transportation corridors, and choke points.
- Population overlays derived from census data, social media, and local intelligence sources.

From the outset, EarthViewer wasn't designed for consumer convenience; it was designed to dominate environments by fusing data into operational insights.

Then came the pivot. In 2004, Google acquired Keyhole Inc. for a reported $35 million. At first glance, the acquisition looked like a natural extension of Google's ambition to "organize the world's information." But the deeper story reveals a seamless handoff between intelligence-backed innovation and private-sector consolidation. Google didn't just buy Keyhole's tech; it absorbed its contracts, datasets, and strategic relationships with U.S. defense and intelligence agencies.

Within a year, EarthViewer was rebranded as Google Earth and released to the public for free. Millions downloaded it, marveling at the ability to virtually "fly" anywhere on the planet, zooming in on cities, landmarks, and even private residences. But as the user base exploded, Google was simultaneously expanding its role as an intelligence partner:

• The NGA became one of Google's earliest enterprise clients, integrating Google Earth into classified workflows.

• Google began maintaining dual-use infrastructures, developing consumer-facing features while enhancing restricted-access capabilities for defense and surveillance applications.

• The platform's global popularity generated an unprecedented crowdsourced intelligence layer, as millions of users voluntarily uploaded geotagged photos, location data, and annotations, effectively populating Google's geospatial datasets for free.

Keyhole's military DNA remained embedded in the platform's architecture. Google Earth enabled real-time updating of satellite imagery and integration of high-resolution feeds from third-party providers contracted through defense agencies. Governments worldwide quickly adopted Google Earth as a civilian-friendly reconnaissance tool - but behind that adoption was the quiet normalization of planetary-scale geospatial surveillance.

By 2010, Google Earth's capabilities were being used not just for navigation or urban planning but for:

• Drone targeting and mission planning integrated directly into defense networks.

• Border enforcement by DHS and international agencies managing migration flows.

• Environmental monitoring tied to climate policy frameworks managed by the UN and World Bank.

• Disaster response modeling, coordinated through NGOs that shared their datasets with government-linked repositories.

Crucially, Google's open-facing geospatial products became intertwined with emerging predictive governance frameworks. By combining Earth's imagery with Palantir's data fusion platforms and machine learning models from Google AI, intelligence agencies could simulate urban unrest, track infrastructure vulnerabilities, and forecast population movements under stress scenarios like pandemics or natural disasters.

This integration accelerated during the COVID-19 era, when Google Earth data pipelines were quietly merged into health-compliance dashboards and mobility tracking systems. Combined with Android location telemetry and cloud-based biometric databases, Google's geospatial infrastructure provided real-time mapping of population behavior, feeding into predictive models shared between corporations, governments, and supranational agencies like the WHO and WEF.

The acquisition of Keyhole thus marked a larger strategic convergence:

• Intelligence-funded startups like Keyhole prototype dual-use technologies under defense contracts.

• Big Tech absorbs these startups, embedding their capabilities inside consumer-friendly platforms.

• Public adoption generates massive data streams, enhancing the same systems used by intelligence agencies.

• Governments and global institutions normalize reliance on privately owned infrastructures for surveillance, security, and policy execution.

What appears to be neutral innovation - "free mapping for everyone" - actually functions as distributed reconnaissance. With Google Earth and its associated APIs powering platforms like Google Maps, Waze, and Android services, Google now maintains a near-total geospatial monopoly, aggregating location data from billions of devices into a single planetary interface. This isn't just about seeing the world; it's about managing it.

Keyhole's transition into Google Earth demonstrates how In-Q-Tel's pipelines quietly reshape the foundations of governance and commerce: intelligence-backed technologies are sanitized, scaled, and normalized through consumer adoption until they become critical public utilities. Once society depends on them, the underlying systems - location telemetry, satellite integration, population overlays - can be repurposed for predictive policing, digital ID enforcement, and compliance modeling without public debate.

Google Earth was never simply a map. It is a geospatial control platform, seeded by the CIA, scaled by Big Tech, and now embedded into the operational fabric of governments, militaries, and supranational institutions worldwide. The architecture of planetary surveillance was built in plain sight - disguised as convenience, powered by consent, and monetized through the data we volunteer.

The blueprint established by Keyhole has since been replicated across sectors: health, identity, finance, and communication - each one seeded through similar CIA-backed pipelines and absorbed into the Big Tech–intelligence ecosystem. Google Earth was the first mainstream interface to this architecture. It won't be the last.

PART VI - THE AI GODS (2015–PRESENT)

The Fourth Industrial Revolution goes live.

18

Klaus Schwab's Great Reset

COVID-19 wasn't just a pandemic; it was a global stress test - a controlled shock to the system that accelerated decades of centralization in governance, technology, and finance. On the surface, it appeared to be a public health emergency. Beneath it, COVID-19 acted as a catalyst, triggering the deployment of pre-engineered frameworks for supranational control - consolidating decision-making power into the hands of a tightly aligned network of corporations, unelected foundations, intelligence-linked NGOs, and global governance bodies.

The policies rolled out during COVID weren't improvised. They were based on simulation playbooks like Event 201 (October 2019), Clade X (2018), and Dark Winter (2001), which had already rehearsed everything from lockdown scenarios and mass vaccination strategies to information control and supply chain modeling. When the World Health Organization declared a global emergency, the infrastructure for planetary coordination - vaccines, data sharing, financial levers, and behavioral compliance - was already designed, tested, and waiting. COVID was the trigger that moved these mechanisms from prototype to operational reality.

Lockdowns were the first instrument of centralization. With coordinated messaging across governments, supranational agencies, and corporate media, societies were placed into unprecedented states of suspension. Businesses were closed, movement restricted, and populations placed under regulatory regimes enforced algorithmically through apps, QR codes, and geofencing. In many nations, compliance with mandates was managed digitally - smartphones became control interfaces, where vaccine status, mobility permissions, and emergency alerts converged into unified frameworks.

These controls weren't temporary. COVID normalized the digitization of compliance, collapsing once-separate domains - health records, identity systems, financial transactions, and social access - into interoperable platforms controlled by private-public partnerships. Programs like ID2020 and the EU Digital COVID Certificate became templates for integrating biometric identity, vaccination status, and economic participation into single, programmable gateways. In less than two years, what had been positioned as "optional" conveniences became mandatory prerequisites for work, travel, and even social interaction.

At the heart of this centralization were the same actors rehearsed during Event 201:

• Gavi and CEPI, both founded and funded by the Gates Foundation, coordinated global vaccine procurement through the COVAX facility, setting price points, distribution priorities, and eligibility frameworks for nearly 200 nations.

• The WHO, heavily funded by Gates and aligned NGOs, issued guidelines adopted wholesale by governments, bypassing democratic debate or legislative scrutiny.

• Big Tech platforms - Google, Meta, Twitter, Microsoft, Amazon - integrated directly with health authorities to manage "trusted information" pipelines, controlling which narratives were amplified and which were silenced.

• Palantir, contracted by multiple governments, operated dashboards combining health data, mobility tracking, and predictive analytics to manage resource allocation and enforce compliance.

• Financial institutions like the IMF and World Bank provided pandemic relief loans contingent on adopting centralized frameworks for health verification and digital infrastructure integration.

What COVID exposed was the growing alignment between private tech monopolies and supranational governance. Google, Amazon, Microsoft, and Apple became the operational arms of pandemic response, providing cloud storage for vaccination registries, facial recognition systems for access control, and predictive dashboards for "pandemic management." Public health became inseparable from data infrastructure, creating an interdependency where governments outsourced operational control to unelected corporate stakeholders.

Meanwhile, financial centralization accelerated in lockstep. Governments printed unprecedented volumes of money while simultaneously pushing populations toward cashless systems, ostensibly to reduce viral transmission. Digital payment rails, biometric authentication, and mobile wallets became defaults for accessing economic life. These pipelines converge with initiatives like Central Bank Digital Currencies (CBDCs), currently being piloted in over 100 countries, where programmable money can be tied directly to compliance frameworks - effectively merging financial sovereignty with behavioral governance.

The pandemic also weaponized crisis psychology to condition populations into accepting expanded surveillance and reduced freedoms. Contact-tracing apps, once marketed as voluntary, became tied to employment, schooling, and mobility. Private corporations - airlines, event organizers, employers - were deputized as enforcers of policy through digital access controls, pushing public regulation into private hands where constitutional protections no longer applied. This outsourcing of enforcement normalized a corporate governance model where technology companies became the de facto regulators of daily life.

Perhaps the most profound shift came through information control. COVID allowed for unprecedented coordination between governments, Big Tech, and media to manage narratives in real time. Social platforms throttled dissenting perspectives, labeling them "misinformation" even when voiced by credentialed experts. Fact-checking networks funded by Gates-aligned foundations and NGOs created centralized arbiters of truth, collapsing the Overton window around a narrow set of institutionally sanctioned narratives.

By mid-2021, the pandemic had revealed the shape of an emerging architecture:

• Health sovereignty collapsed into supranational coordination through WHO, Gavi, and CEPI.

• Digital identity frameworks tied to biometric verification and vaccine status became normalized.

• Financial control systems, from digital wallets to programmable currencies, began integrating with health compliance data.

• Predictive governance platforms - powered by Palantir, Google, and Microsoft - modeled population movement, sentiment, and risk in real time.

• Speech governance infrastructures embedded into social media platforms created harmonized narrative control at planetary scale.

COVID was not the cause of this transformation; it was the accelerant. The infrastructures had been developed incrementally for decades - through initiatives like In-Q-Tel pipelines, Gavi's procurement frameworks, WHO treaty alignments, and Event 201 rehearsals - but the pandemic created the political, psychological, and economic environment necessary for their rapid deployment. Under the cover of emergency response, the groundwork was laid for persistent governance through crises, where public health, climate, financial instability, and "disinformation" can all justify similar frameworks of control.

What began as a health crisis became a global systems upgrade, shifting authority from nation-states toward a networked technocratic order that operates across borders, answerable not to voters but to its funding networks, institutional partnerships, and proprietary technologies. COVID normalized the convergence of health, finance, identity, and surveillance into a single digital infrastructure - one capable of managing populations at scale through algorithmic governance and programmable access.

The emergency has ended. The architecture remains.

ESG - Environmental, Social, and Governance scores - are sold to the public as a tool for building a more "sustainable" economy. The narrative frames them as benevolent: a way to encourage companies to act responsibly, protect the planet, and respect human rights. In reality, ESG scoring functions as a mechanism of financial coercion - a soft-control architecture where corporations, banks, and entire nations are graded, rewarded, or punished based on their alignment with centralized policy agendas. Far from being a grassroots movement for ethical capitalism, ESG has evolved into a global compliance system controlled by unelected bodies, supranational institutions, and financial cartels with the power to grant or deny access to capital, markets, and legitimacy.

At its core, ESG consolidates financial influence under a small network of asset managers, banks, and governance bodies, turning them into de facto regulators of private and public life. Companies are scored based on their carbon emissions, diversity metrics, political stances, and adherence to "sustainability goals" set by organizations like the World Economic Forum (WEF), United Nations (UN), and International Monetary Fund (IMF). These scores are used by institutional investors to decide where trillions in capital flows, effectively forcing corporations into alignment without passing a single law. Governments can't legislate ESG directly in many regions, but they don't need to - capital allocation itself becomes the enforcement mechanism.

The three pillars of ESG hide its deeper function:

• Environmental: Ostensibly about carbon neutrality and conservation, but in practice, ESG environmental metrics funnel investment into preselected industries - renewable energy giants, carbon credit markets, and "green infrastructure" tied to World Bank and IMF-backed frameworks. This creates a controlled transition economy, where capital migrates away from traditional energy systems and into financialized "sustainable assets" dominated by a small set of global institutions.

• Social: Framed around human rights and equality but largely designed to enforce ideological compliance. Companies and, increasingly, nations are scored based on workforce diversity quotas, political statements, social justice activism, and alignment with "approved narratives." Dissent from these standards risks reputational downgrades and, more importantly, restricted access to credit and investment.

• Governance: Marketed as corporate ethics but engineered to standardize data transparency requirements and integrate real-time monitoring systems into business operations. These systems are designed upstream by private standards bodies, ensuring compliance is measured, scored, and enforced algorithmically across supply chains and financial markets.

The most powerful aspect of ESG is its integration into financial chokepoints. Major asset managers like BlackRock, Vanguard, and State Street - collectively controlling over $20 trillion in assets - have embedded ESG frameworks into their investment strategies. Companies failing to meet "sustainability" benchmarks risk divestment, shareholder revolt, and exclusion from major stock indexes. At the nation-state level, credit ratings agencies are beginning to incorporate ESG compliance into sovereign risk models, effectively pressuring entire countries to adopt policy agendas dictated not by their citizens but by transnational financial networks.

This creates a cascading leverage structure:

• Corporations comply with ESG mandates to retain investor access and avoid capital flight.

• Governments rewrite policy to remain attractive to ESG-driven capital markets and avoid reputational downgrades.

• Banks integrate ESG metrics into lending decisions, forcing small businesses and municipalities into alignment or risk exclusion from financial services.

• Consumers are nudged into compliance indirectly, as ESG-driven policies reshape product availability, pricing, and even personal creditworthiness.

The shift toward ESG coincides with the planned rollout of Central Bank Digital Currencies (CBDCs) and programmable finance infrastructures. Once financial rails are fully digitized, ESG scores can be tied directly to real-time behavioral compliance. For corporations, that means instant penalties for exceeding carbon caps, failing diversity benchmarks, or resisting "approved" governance frameworks. For individuals, it signals a potential future where personal access to loans, mortgages, or even payment platforms could be influenced by personalized carbon scores, travel patterns, and "social impact metrics."

COVID-19 accelerated the ESG agenda dramatically. Under the cover of "building back better," governments and financial institutions tied pandemic recovery funds to green transition requirements and social governance reforms. The European Union's Green Deal and WEF's Great Reset framework openly framed ESG as the roadmap for restructuring global economies around climate compliance and social responsibility standards. Trillions in stimulus and debt relief were conditioned on adopting these frameworks, effectively outsourcing sovereignty to ESG-aligned institutions and their scoring methodologies.

The World Economic Forum, one of the loudest champions of ESG integration, pitches it as the foundation of "stakeholder capitalism" - the idea that corporations exist to serve not just shareholders but society at large. In practice, this model elevates CEOs into unelected policymakers, granting them the power to shape global supply chains, labor practices, and political stances under the guise of "corporate responsibility." Through ESG, boards and asset managers become extensions of global governance, bypassing democratic processes entirely.

Meanwhile, ESG's environmental metrics have spawned entire synthetic financial markets like carbon credits, biodiversity offsets, and emissions futures. These markets are dominated by institutions tied to the same stakeholders setting ESG standards, creating closed-loop profit mechanisms. The entities defining sustainability also control the financial instruments monetizing it - effectively turning climate narratives into collateral for global debt expansion.

For nations and corporations alike, ESG compliance isn't optional - it's financial survival. Countries resisting ESG-driven policy agendas risk exclusion from global capital markets and trade finance systems dominated by Bank for International Settlements (BIS)-aligned central banks. Companies refusing to adopt ESG frameworks face investor divestment campaigns coordinated by BlackRock and its peers, public "name and shame" strategies, and systemic downgrades on credit ratings. The pressure operates less like regulation and more like financial blackmail: comply or get cut off from the flows of capital that define modern economies.

This convergence of ESG metrics, digital financial infrastructure, and supranational policy objectives points toward an emerging global compliance architecture:

• Centralized bodies set policy-aligned scoring frameworks based on climate, social, and governance agendas.

• Asset managers, banks, and rating agencies act as private enforcement arms.

• Programmable financial tools like CBDCs create real-time, automated compliance tied directly to ESG metrics.

• Governments and populations are coerced into adopting standards they didn't vote for and can't challenge.

ESG isn't about ethics, sustainability, or accountability. It's a system designed to financialize morality and turn corporate, national, and individual behavior into programmable variables managed by unelected stakeholders. Through ESG scores, the flow of capital - and by extension, the functioning of economies themselves - becomes contingent on alignment with the narratives and priorities of global technocratic elites. This is governance without legislation and regulation without representation. The mechanisms are quiet, but the leverage is absolute.

The Internet of Things (IoT) was marketed as convenience - smart homes, wearable devices, connected cars, personalized healthcare, and seamless automation. But as billions of sensors now blanket the planet, each streaming data into centralized systems, IoT has evolved into something far more consequential: the foundation for real-time population modeling, where every human being, every device, and every interaction feeds into predictive engines that construct digital twins - algorithmic replicas of you, continuously updated, scored, and simulated. Paired with artificial intelligence, these systems are quietly building behavioral shadows for every person on Earth, designed not just to predict what you'll do next but to shape the choices available to you before you make them.

At its core, IoT turns the physical world into a sensor network. Smartphones, fitness trackers, smart speakers, vehicles, biometric wearables, payment terminals, and even refrigerators constantly generate high-frequency telemetry: location data, heart rate, sleeping patterns, purchases, speech, and keystrokes. In isolation, these datasets look benign. In aggregate, they create a granular map of human life, where context, intention, and future behavior can be inferred with extraordinary precision.

This data becomes exponentially more powerful when combined with AI-driven analytics. Machine learning models trained on trillions of data points don't just interpret your past actions - they simulate possible futures. Using probabilistic modeling, AI can predict what you'll buy, who you'll meet, where you'll travel, what content will trigger emotional responses, and even which ideological narratives you're most susceptible to. These models evolve constantly, ingesting fresh data from IoT streams, refining their simulations of you in real time.

The result is the rise of digital twins for humans - algorithmic replicas designed to mirror your identity, preferences, vulnerabilities, and decision patterns. These twins don't just represent you; they increasingly stand in for you in systems you don't see:

• Credit scoring and financial access: AI models built on digital twins assess your risk profile, loan eligibility, and fraud probability - often before you even apply.

• Health monitoring and insurance: Data from wearables, genetic tests, and medical IoT devices inform predictive health models that can price policies or preemptively restrict treatments.

• Targeted influence operations: Digital twins are used by advertisers, political campaigns, and intelligence agencies to test messaging strategies against simulated populations, optimizing persuasion before deployment.

• Predictive policing: Palantir and other In-Q-Tel-backed platforms integrate IoT data, surveillance feeds, and behavioral profiles into "risk scores," flagging individuals and communities for increased monitoring or intervention.

As these systems expand, you become less relevant than the data shadow trailing behind you. AI models trained on your patterns make decisions about your access to financial products, employment, healthcare, mobility, and even information flows - without you knowing the variables being scored or the thresholds triggering exclusion. It's governance by proxy simulation, and it's largely invisible.

Global institutions and Big Tech have quietly built the infrastructure for scaling this architecture:

• IoT ecosystems: Apple, Google, Amazon, and Huawei dominate consumer IoT, embedding surveillance into daily life under the banner of convenience.

• Cloud monopolies: AWS, Microsoft Azure, and Google Cloud host the petabyte-scale datasets feeding digital twin models, tightly integrated with government contracts.

• AI frameworks: OpenAI, DeepMind, and DARPA-funded research develop reinforcement learning systems capable of simulating complex human-environment interactions in real time.

• Digital identity programs: Initiatives like ID2020 and the EU Digital Identity Wallet link biometric identifiers and behavioral data into interoperable profiles, ensuring twin models remain persistent across jurisdictions and applications.

These frameworks are converging into predictive governance systems, where decisions once made reactively are now modeled and executed preemptively. Governments, corporations, and supranational bodies increasingly rely on AI-simulated populations to plan urban development, allocate resources, deploy police forces, or anticipate "social unrest." In these scenarios, your digital twin interacts with countless others in algorithmic simulations of society, and policy decisions are adjusted in real time based on predicted outcomes - even before events occur.

COVID-19 accelerated this shift dramatically. Lockdowns normalized health telemetry via wearables, QR codes, and vaccine passport apps, embedding IoT-driven compliance infrastructure into daily life. Contact-tracing frameworks and mobility dashboards tied personal identity to real-time location data, which was then fed into predictive outbreak models operated by Palantir, Google, and the WHO. The pandemic demonstrated how IoT, AI, and digital twins could be rapidly deployed to manage populations dynamically, using algorithmic feedback loops to enforce behavioral norms under emergency protocols.

The implications are enormous. Digital twins move us toward a model where autonomy becomes conditional:

- Access to services, travel, employment, and finance can be automatically restricted if your twin flags a "risk pattern."
- Behavioral nudging - via content curation, location-based prompts, or social incentives - can steer you toward preferred choices without explicit coercion.
- Population-scale simulations enable policy prototyping, where governments test restrictive measures on modeled societies before enforcing them on real ones.
- Algorithmic stratification emerges, creating scored hierarchies of trust, compliance, and opportunity based on opaque variables hidden deep inside proprietary systems.

This isn't speculative. Global forums like the World Economic Forum openly discuss digital twin programs for entire populations, merging IoT infrastructure, biometric registries, and AI models into continuous governance frameworks. In parallel, the healthcare industry is developing "digital twin patients" for predictive medicine, while insurance providers are piloting real-time premium adjustments based on behavioral telemetry. Corporations and governments alike are investing in synthetic population modeling, where individual twins are stitched together into macro-level simulations used to test policies, pricing, and propaganda strategies before they ever reach you.

This is the quiet convergence of surveillance, identity, and simulation. With IoT as the sensor layer, AI as the inference engine, and digital twins as the behavioral proxy, human autonomy is gradually subordinated to algorithmic prediction. Once your twin exists in the system, you are no longer just observed - you are modeled, managed, and manipulated in ways you cannot see or contest.

In this emerging paradigm, your choices matter less than the predicted outputs generated by your behavioral shadow. Governments and corporations will increasingly act on the twin, not the person, bypassing consent entirely. The twin becomes the real locus of governance - an invisible construct owned and updated by entities you don't control, feeding decisions that shape the limits of your reality.

IoT promised convenience. AI promised intelligence. Together, they've delivered a new architecture of continuous compliance, where freedom becomes less about what you choose and more about what the system expects you to choose. The twin knows you better than you know yourself - and in this infrastructure, the twin wins every time.

The World Economic Forum didn't need to govern during COVID - it had already built the frameworks, drafted the scripts, and installed the actors. Governments didn't invent their own responses; they ran plays written years in advance under the banner of "multistakeholder governance" and "global coordination." When the emergency hit, WEF's networks - unelected, unaccountable, and operating outside the constraints of national sovereignty - stepped in and filled the vacuum. What followed looked like a chaotic collection of national policies. In reality, it was the deployment of a single operating system for crisis management, tested, rehearsed, and refined long before anyone heard the term "social distancing."

The first move was narrative capture. From the earliest days of the outbreak, the WEF positioned itself not as an observer but as the central node for "public-private cooperation" in pandemic response. Through its long-standing ties with the World Health Organization, the Gates Foundation, CEPI, and Gavi, the Forum had already assembled the architecture of planetary health policy. COVID simply activated it. Within weeks, hundreds of corporations, NGOs, and government agencies were participating in WEF-coordinated "action platforms," where policies, talking points, and strategies were aligned behind closed doors. No votes. No hearings. No debate.

The Great Reset became the ideological wrapper. Announced mid-pandemic, it offered leaders a ready-made narrative: the crisis wasn't just a catastrophe; it was an "opportunity" to remake the world. Everything from stimulus spending to vaccine mandates to digital identity programs could now be justified as part of "building back better." Green transitions, universal health frameworks, ESG compliance, and centralized data infrastructures were bundled together into a single package and sold as inevitabilities, not options. It wasn't just about health - it was about using the pandemic to accelerate pre-existing agendas under the cover of emergency response.

Then came the operational tools. The Forum had spent years promoting digital identity frameworks, biometric systems, and "interoperable" data standards. When lockdowns began, these tools were rapidly deployed under the guise of safety. WEF-backed pilots like CommonPass demonstrated how cross-border travel could be tied to digital health credentials, integrating test results and vaccine status into a single scannable QR code. That blueprint became the template for countless national "vaccine passport" systems, all designed around the same centralized logic: control access to mobility and services through private, standardized gateways.

Health policy was only the first layer. COVID also gave WEF-aligned institutions leverage over financial architecture. Pandemic relief packages, IMF-backed lending, and corporate bailouts came with "conditions" tied to sustainability metrics and ESG compliance. Stakeholder capitalism - WEF's pet project - became operational reality, elevating corporate boards into de facto policymakers. CEOs of the largest banks, asset managers, and tech monopolies now sat at the same table as heads of state, setting frameworks that redefined who could operate, who could transact, and under what terms. Governments didn't dictate these terms; they adopted them.

Meanwhile, the Forum was heavily involved in shaping information control. As debates over vaccines, mandates, and treatments erupted, the WEF convened its partners - Big Tech platforms, media conglomerates, NGOs, and regulators - to "combat misinformation." In practice, this meant harmonizing content moderation guidelines across borders and platforms, ensuring that narratives aligned with institutional priorities. Posts, videos, and entire accounts disappeared not through legislation but through coordinated enforcement between companies and unelected "stakeholders." The censorship wasn't chaotic; it was synchronized.

All of this was justified by the need for "global coordination." The WEF argued that no single nation could handle a pandemic, and it used that premise to install systems that operate above national sovereignty:

• Digital health credentials became de facto passports.

• Vaccine procurement was centralized through entities like Gavi and CEPI, both tightly aligned with WEF partners.

• Predictive analytics platforms like Palantir's dashboards merged population health data with real-time mobility tracking.

• Global ESG frameworks ensured that compliance extended into finance, energy, and resource allocation far beyond healthcare.

These systems were sold as temporary responses, but their design was permanent. Interoperable ID frameworks, behavioral tracking, biometric registries, and centralized resource management didn't vanish when restrictions lifted. The pandemic normalized infrastructure for continuous governance through crises - where emergencies justify policy first, and democratic consent, if it arrives at all, comes later.

What happened during COVID wasn't spontaneous. It was the acceleration of a model the WEF had been refining for decades: convene unelected actors, align narratives, test digital control systems through pilot programs, and synchronize private infrastructure with public policy. By embedding itself into governments, corporations, NGOs, and supranational institutions simultaneously, the Forum created a system where control doesn't require passing laws - it emerges from dependency.

Countries didn't follow identical rules because they were told to. They followed them because the systems they relied on - supply chains, financial flows, travel permissions, vaccine procurement pipelines, even information channels - were all running through the same WEF-aligned infrastructure. Step out of line and you risked losing access to the rails that keep your economy, your healthcare system, and your population moving.

COVID proved the model works. Governance no longer needs to look like overt power; it hides in the agreements, platforms, and data standards that everyone depends on but nobody voted for. Once deployed, these systems rarely retreat. The frameworks for digital identity, health credentials, synchronized censorship, and ESG-driven financial compliance remain intact, waiting for the next declared crisis - pandemic, climate, cybersecurity, or otherwise.

COVID didn't create centralized governance. It revealed how far it had already advanced, and it handed the WEF its greatest proof of concept: an emergency so total, so global, that people accepted a restructuring of society as if it were inevitable. The laws of sovereignty didn't change. The architecture beneath them did.

19

The New Technocratic Kings

Elon Musk has been marketed as a visionary, a rebel outsider challenging entrenched power structures - but when you strip away the narrative, Musk is building something far more aligned with the emerging technocratic architecture than most people realize. Through Neuralink, Starlink, and his colonization rhetoric, Musk is laying the groundwork for a fully integrated control system that spans earth, orbit, and eventually off-world infrastructure. He doesn't operate outside the system; he's helping design its next layer, where human cognition, communication, and mobility converge inside digital frameworks owned by private interests - interests that answer to no one.

Neuralink is Musk's most ambitious project, openly pitched as a cure for disease, disability, and human limitation itself. The narrative promises restored mobility for paraplegics, treatments for Alzheimer's, and eventually, cognitive enhancement. But beyond the glossy PR, Neuralink represents the first serious attempt to normalize direct integration between human neural activity and digital networks - a brain-computer interface designed to collect, interpret, and eventually manipulate the most private layer of human existence: thought itself. Neuralink's long-term goals are not limited to restoring function; they explicitly aim to merge humans and AI to prevent what Musk frames as "machine dominance." In his worldview, our only defense against artificial intelligence is to become part of it.

That's the sales pitch. But in practice, Neuralink is developing a real-time cognitive data pipeline, where sensors embedded in the brain translate neural signals into structured digital outputs. Once this link is operational, every thought, intention, and emotional state has the potential to be recorded, decoded, and modeled. The risks here go far beyond privacy violations. A fully integrated Neuralink system would enable bi-directional influence: the ability to read neural states and, eventually, to stimulate or suppress them. In the wrong hands - corporate, governmental, or supranational - this isn't therapy; it's compliance engineering at the neural level.

Parallel to Neuralink is Starlink, Musk's satellite internet constellation, now comprising thousands of low-Earth-orbit satellites blanketing the globe with high-speed connectivity. Publicly, Starlink is pitched as bridging the "digital divide," bringing internet access to rural communities, developing nations, and disaster zones. But the infrastructure has far deeper implications. Starlink isn't just a network; it's the communications backbone for next-generation governance systems, particularly where terrestrial infrastructure is absent or politically unreliable.

Starlink's contracts with the Pentagon, NATO, and intelligence-linked agencies reveal its other purpose: battlefield dominance. In Ukraine, Starlink became a critical platform for coordinating military operations, drone targeting, and encrypted intelligence exchanges. In effect, Starlink demonstrated how private communications infrastructure can replace state-owned systems entirely, bypassing sovereign control and placing global connectivity in the hands of a single corporate entity. The implications extend beyond warfare. By monopolizing satellite broadband at planetary scale, Starlink is positioning itself as the default infrastructure for digital identity, IoT integration, and real-time surveillance - a platform for managing populations through persistent, location-aware connectivity.

Musk's Mars narrative frames him as an anti-establishment pioneer, breaking humanity free from Earth-bound politics and centralized systems. In reality, his Mars rhetoric functions as a long-term blueprint for extraterrestrial technocracy. The vision isn't just colonizing Mars; it's about owning the rails of off-world infrastructure: communications, energy grids, life-support ecosystems, and mobility systems - all proprietary, all Musk-controlled. Mars is sold as human liberation but designed as dependency. If every dome, habitat, and airlock runs on Tesla batteries, SpaceX supply chains, and Starlink connectivity, Musk's companies effectively become planetary governance structures outside any national jurisdiction.

In this sense, Musk's projects form a single architecture rather than three separate ventures:

• Neuralink builds the human interface layer, mapping the brain into readable, programmable code.

• Starlink builds the network substrate, providing uninterrupted planetary communications and data exchange at military and civilian scales alike.

• SpaceX's Mars program extends this architecture beyond Earth, setting the precedent for proprietary governance over off-world settlements.

Layered together, these systems create the foundations for closed-loop control ecosystems. Neuralink produces cognitive data streams; Starlink provides the rails for instantaneous transmission; AI-driven behavioral models process and simulate individuals and populations; and the hardware built to "liberate" humanity from Earth binds those populations to private infrastructure instead.

COVID accelerated this convergence. As centralized governance pushed health passports, biometric registries, and satellite-linked compliance platforms, Starlink emerged as the backbone of network continuity, bypassing traditional terrestrial infrastructure in regions where governments lacked capacity or alignment. Neuralink, meanwhile, positioned itself as part of a longer-term "human upgrade" narrative, selling integration with machines as the inevitable next step for managing existential risks - pandemics, climate change, AI itself. The pandemic normalized dependency on private platforms, and Musk's systems slotted perfectly into that ecosystem.

The broader context matters. The World Economic Forum, DARPA, and supranational coalitions like the OECD have openly promoted brain-computer interfaces, satellite-based governance, and off-world infrastructure as pillars of the coming technocratic order. Musk packages these goals as visionary rebellion against the establishment, but the pipelines he's building - neural telemetry, low-orbit network dominance, private colonization frameworks - are perfectly aligned with the objectives of the very elite structures he claims to oppose.

The danger isn't Musk himself. It's the normalization of dependency on private infrastructure to mediate identity, cognition, communication, and survival. Starlink's control over digital rails, Neuralink's access to neural activity, and SpaceX's monopoly on off-world habitats all bypass democratic oversight entirely. These aren't tools of liberation; they're the scaffolding for privatized governance, where access to communication, cognition, and even breathable air is contingent on corporate compliance frameworks.

The narrative sells freedom, but the architecture builds control. Neuralink promises to "unlock human potential" while tethering thought to proprietary interfaces. Starlink delivers "internet for all" while consolidating global communications into a single privately owned system. Mars is framed as humanity's "escape" from failing institutions while setting up new forms of dependency in a jurisdiction where no checks or balances exist.

Musk isn't dismantling centralized control. He's extending it - vertically, across domains, into spaces where no sovereignty yet exists. Neuralink maps the mind. Starlink claims the skies. SpaceX claims the frontier. Together, these projects sketch the blueprint for the next phase of technocracy: an ecosystem where autonomy dissolves, choice collapses into algorithms, and governance shifts upward into infrastructures nobody voted for.

This isn't rebellion. It's integration. And most of the world won't realize it until they're inside the system - when connection, cognition, and survival itself all flow through rails they don't own and can't escape.

Sam Altman has successfully positioned himself as the public face of "responsible AI," but beneath the rhetoric, his projects - OpenAI, AGI governance initiatives, and Worldcoin - are building the scaffolding for planetary-level control systems. Altman speaks in visionary terms about artificial general intelligence (AGI) saving humanity, but the infrastructure he's constructing points in a different direction: the fusion of machine intelligence, biometric identity, and programmable finance, managed by unelected institutions and enforced through private networks. OpenAI writes the algorithms, AGI governance frameworks dictate the rules, and Worldcoin provides the verification layer to ensure everyone falls in line. Altman presents these as separate projects. They are not. They are pieces of a single system.

OpenAI began as a nonprofit research lab in 2015, supposedly founded to democratize artificial intelligence and prevent corporate monopolies from controlling the technology. But within a few years, Altman transformed it into a hybrid for-profit structure, accepting billions in investment from Microsoft and integrating directly with Azure's cloud infrastructure. This "pivot" gave OpenAI access to planetary-scale compute power while effectively binding its core models - GPT, Codex, DALL·E, and beyond - to private corporate rails. OpenAI now serves as both AI arms dealer and gatekeeper, licensing models to Big Tech giants and governments alike while holding back full releases under the justification of "safety."

That safety narrative is critical. Altman has used the threat of uncontrolled AGI as a lever to shape global AI governance. He calls for international regulatory bodies, modeled on frameworks like the IAEA for nuclear weapons, to "coordinate" AI development and enforce safety thresholds. On the surface, this looks like altruism. In practice, it establishes a centralized regulatory chokepoint where a small network of corporations, NGOs, and supranational agencies will dictate the rules of machine intelligence for the entire planet. The same players developing the most powerful AI systems are lobbying to define the limits, set the permissions, and control access to the compute infrastructure required to build competitive alternatives.

AGI governance isn't about preventing existential risk; it's about securing dominance over the tools that will govern existence itself. As AI evolves from language models into multi-modal, agentic systems capable of autonomous planning, real-time adaptation, and integration with IoT infrastructure, whoever controls these models controls the simulation layer of society. Governments, corporations, and financial systems are already outsourcing decision-making to OpenAI's products: fraud detection, predictive policing, content moderation, loan approvals, and resource allocation are increasingly managed by algorithms trained and fine-tuned in opaque, privately owned systems. Altman's public statements about "aligning AGI with human values" obscure the deeper reality: alignment is defined upstream, by those with access to the data, the models, and the servers.

Enter Worldcoin, Altman's most ambitious - and troubling - venture. Marketed as a digital identity solution and "universal basic income" project, Worldcoin asks people to scan their irises using proprietary "Orbs" in exchange for tokens on a blockchain-based network. Ostensibly, the goal is to create a global proof-of-personhood system to distinguish humans from AI. In reality, Worldcoin represents an attempt to build a planetary biometric registry, linking unique biological signatures to digital wallets, payment rails, and, eventually, access to services. Under the guise of protecting humanity from "deepfakes" and synthetic identities, Worldcoin lays the groundwork for programmable inclusion: a framework where your ability to transact, travel, or participate in civic life is mediated through a private platform - one directly connected to OpenAI's emerging AGI ecosystem.

This isn't speculation. Altman himself has stated that OpenAI's success will drive massive labor displacement, requiring new systems for distributing value and managing resource access. Worldcoin is marketed as that solution: a tokenized income stream tied to biometric verification, issued globally, and eventually interoperable with central bank digital currencies (CBDCs). Once your identity, wallet, and access permissions are unified under a single authentication layer, compliance is no longer enforced by law or coercion; it's enforced by design. If your credentials aren't recognized, you're locked out of the system - instantly and automatically.

Altman frames Worldcoin as decentralized and "for the people," but the structure tells another story. The hardware is proprietary. The identity database is privately managed. The distribution algorithm is centrally controlled. And the network's early adopters skew heavily toward regions in the Global South, where populations are enticed into scanning their irises with little transparency about how their biometric data will be stored, protected, or monetized. Far from democratizing finance, Worldcoin is building the rails for a privately owned planetary identification regime.

The synergy between OpenAI, AGI governance, and Worldcoin becomes clear when you follow the architecture:

• OpenAI develops the cognitive engines capable of simulating reality, managing complexity, and predicting human behavior at planetary scale.

• AGI governance frameworks concentrate decision-making power in small networks of corporations and supranational bodies under the pretense of "safety."

• Worldcoin supplies the verification layer - a single source of truth for who is "real," who is "authorized," and who can participate in the digital economy.

When combined, these pieces converge into a closed-loop control system. Neural telemetry from IoT devices, biometric authentication via Worldcoin, predictive modeling through OpenAI, and behavioral nudging orchestrated through platforms like Microsoft, Google, and Meta - all stitched together under "safety standards" defined by private committees in partnership with global governance bodies like the WEF, IMF, and United Nations. The infrastructure isn't theoretical; it's already operational, just fragmented. Altman's projects aim to unify it.

COVID proved how rapidly such frameworks can be deployed under emergency conditions. Health passports, biometric registries, and mobility-linked digital identities were normalized in less than two years. The same logic now extends into AI: "safety," "misinformation control," and "proof of humanity" become the pretexts for embedding new rails of identity, access, and behavioral management into everyday life. Worldcoin's pitch slots perfectly into this paradigm - a programmable identity wallet tied to AGI-governed platforms and globally harmonized rulesets.

Altman presents himself as a steward of humanity's future, but what's being built isn't stewardship; it's infrastructure for algorithmic sovereignty. When the systems deciding your creditworthiness, employment eligibility, and legal standing are governed by AI models owned by private companies - and when your identity and wallet exist on a biometric ledger operated outside any democratic oversight - sovereignty shifts quietly, irreversibly, away from individuals and nations alike.

OpenAI's models are the cognitive layer. AGI governance provides the permissioning layer. Worldcoin installs the identity layer. Together, they create a planetary architecture where participation itself becomes conditional - not on laws debated and voted on, but on rulesets written upstream by unelected actors with opaque incentives. Altman calls it progress. In practice, it's the scaffolding of a digital caste system.

This isn't about AI replacing humanity. It's about AI managing humanity, one verified biometric and one programmable transaction at a time. The rails are being built in plain sight, marketed as empowerment, while they embed a deeper form of dependence into the very structure of daily life. By the time the system is complete, opting out won't just be difficult. It will be impossible.

Yuval Noah Harari has become one of the loudest intellectual evangelists for the emerging technocratic order. From his TED talks to World Economic Forum stages, Harari openly promotes a vision where humans are "hackable animals," stripped of privacy, autonomy, and even individuality. He doesn't hide it. To Harari, the old liberal notions of free will and sovereignty are obsolete in the face of exponential data collection, machine learning, and biometrics. In his view, the future will belong to those who control data about bodies, brains, and behavior - and everyone else will be managed by the algorithms that model them. Harari presents himself as a historian explaining trends, but his language often reads less like detached analysis and more like advocacy. He frames human agency as a myth, suggesting that with enough biometric inputs, continuous monitoring, and computational power, people can be reduced to predictable, programmable patterns. He argues that once you can capture someone's heart rate, stress levels, neural activity, and digital footprints in real time, you don't need to guess their motivations or choices - the system will know them better than they know themselves. In this worldview, freedom isn't taken from you; it simply becomes irrelevant.

When Harari speaks of "hacking humans," he's referring to integrating vast data ecosystems into unified, predictive models. Every device you carry, every IoT sensor you pass, every biometric scan you submit - all of it funnels into the infrastructure he celebrates: networks capable of mapping your physiology, psychology, and decisions continuously. Harari openly praises the power of combining AI, genomics, behavioral data, and ubiquitous sensors to create "digital doubles" of individuals - dynamic models that simulate you in real time and anticipate your choices before you make them.

For Harari, this isn't hypothetical. He frames COVID-19 as the moment that "surveillance went under the skin," where health passports, wearable telemetry, and biometric-linked identity systems normalized real-time monitoring of populations. In his lectures, he describes a future where the ultimate authority isn't God or governments but algorithms. He openly states that once enough biometric and behavioral data is captured, the system won't just predict human actions - it will direct them. Choice collapses into computation.

Harari also believes this transformation will produce a new hierarchy of power, one where humanity splits into "useless classes" and "upgraded elites." Those with access to cognitive enhancement, AI integration, and biometric feedback loops will become augmented decision-makers, while the majority will be managed by automated systems optimized for efficiency and stability. In his vision, democracy as we know it becomes unworkable - not abolished, just irrelevant - replaced by data-driven governance administered by technocratic institutions and private infrastructures.

This ideology dovetails perfectly with the agenda of organizations like the World Economic Forum, where Harari is a frequent speaker. He doesn't hide his belief that nation-states are outdated and that sovereignty will inevitably migrate upward into global governance frameworks enforced by technology. To Harari, pandemics, climate change, cyber risks, and financial instability are collective problems that require planetary coordination, and he insists this can't happen without centralized control of data and identity.

But beneath the surface of inevitability lies design. The architecture Harari describes already exists in fragments, built quietly by the same networks he advises:

• Biometric identity systems like Worldcoin, ID2020, and India's Aadhaar create permanent, interoperable digital profiles for every human being.

• IoT and sensor networks track behavior, mobility, and environment in real time, feeding data into centralized models.

• AI-driven simulations build predictive "digital twins" for individuals and populations, enabling algorithmic policy tested on synthetic societies before being imposed on real ones.

• Health surveillance frameworks - normalized under COVID - merge personal data, biometrics, and digital credentials into continuous compliance platforms.

Harari doesn't apologize for any of this. He celebrates it. He claims humanity will trade its outdated notions of privacy and autonomy for "personalized optimization," where algorithms make better decisions than individuals ever could. In his words, humans become hackable not because they lose freedom, but because they "choose" convenience, safety, and efficiency over sovereignty - unaware that these choices are engineered upstream.

At the core of Harari's ideology is the idea that data = destiny. Whoever controls the most intimate datasets - your genome, your neural patterns, your biometrics, your behavior - controls you. And yet he rarely acknowledges the power imbalance this creates. In his lectures, he openly concedes that data consolidation will concentrate unprecedented control into the hands of a few corporations, governments, and supranational bodies. But instead of framing this as a threat, he frames it as inevitability. To Harari, resisting this transformation is futile; the only question is who builds the system and who gets excluded from it.

This fatalistic framing serves a purpose. By declaring sovereignty obsolete and free will an illusion, Harari disarms resistance to the very infrastructures being built today. He normalizes the integration of biometric surveillance, algorithmic governance, and centralized data control by framing them as evolutionary steps rather than deliberate policy choices. His vision encourages populations to accept algorithmic management as progress and to see those who resist as irrational, outdated, or dangerous.

Harari's ideology aligns seamlessly with broader technocratic ambitions. Underneath his polished academic persona is a worldview where:

•   Individuals don't own their data - institutions do.

•   Decisions are outsourced to predictive models operating above human comprehension.

•   Citizenship dissolves into compliance with private infrastructures governing identity, finance, and mobility.

•   Inequality is locked in, as "enhanced" elites move beyond traditional governance while the masses are managed like subsystems.

For Harari, this is the next logical stage of history. For the rest of us, it's a roadmap to algorithmic feudalism - a world where data replaces land as the new resource, and human beings become tenants inside systems they don't own, controlled by rules they didn't write. Once humanity becomes hackable, autonomy no longer matters. The algorithms decide, and your only "freedom" is to comply.

This isn't a forecast. It's a framework. Harari and the institutions he serves are pushing societies toward a model where identity, behavior, and biology are continuously harvested, scored, and optimized. Whether framed as inevitable or sold as benevolent, the outcome is the same: a permanent system of predictive governance, where your future is calculated before you live it - and dissent is eliminated not by force, but by code.

20

Carbon Credits, CBDCs, and Digital Slavery

Mark Carney has quietly become one of the most influential architects of the financial technocracy - a system where programmable money, carbon markets, and global ESG frameworks converge to control not just economies but human behavior itself. While politicians debate budgets and central bankers tweak interest rates, Carney operates upstream, redesigning the financial infrastructure that defines what can be bought, where wealth flows, and who gets access. Through his roles at the Bank of Canada, the Bank of England, the UN Special Envoy on Climate Action and Finance, and as a central player in the World Economic Forum's financial transformation agenda, Carney is building the rails for a system where money, identity, and carbon footprints merge into a single programmable framework.

Carney presents his vision as a climate solution. He argues that preventing environmental catastrophe requires "rewiring global finance" to redirect trillions into sustainable energy, carbon-neutral infrastructure, and "green innovation." But beneath the rhetoric of saving the planet lies a structural shift: the replacement of free-market dynamics with policy-driven allocation of capital, enforced not by laws but by the infrastructure of programmable finance. Carney's climate agenda isn't about environmental stewardship - it's about using climate policy as leverage to install centralized control mechanisms over economies, corporations, and individuals alike.

His central project has been building the global carbon markets. As head of the Taskforce on Scaling Voluntary Carbon Markets (TSVCM) - created in partnership with the WEF - Carney has been instrumental in designing a standardized system for measuring, pricing, and trading carbon emissions across the planet. The pitch is simple: create a global marketplace where every ton of carbon emitted carries a cost, pushing corporations and nations toward net-zero targets. But in practice, these markets act as compliance frameworks disguised as markets. Companies that fail to meet emissions targets face penalties, reputational downgrades, and restricted access to capital - while those aligned with carbon accounting standards are rewarded with favorable financing and investor flows.

The catch is that Carney's network sets the rules. Through the Glasgow Financial Alliance for Net Zero (GFANZ), Carney has assembled over $150 trillion in managed assets under a unified pledge to enforce net-zero compliance across lending and investment. These aren't government mandates; they're private-sector ultimatums enforced by the biggest asset managers on Earth - BlackRock, Vanguard, State Street, and their peers. If your company, industry, or even nation doesn't align with GFANZ targets, you risk being excluded from global capital markets altogether. Access to financing, insurance, and credit rating stability now depends on adopting Carney-approved sustainability frameworks. This is where programmable money enters the picture. Carney has been one of the most prominent advocates for central bank digital currencies (CBDCs) - state-backed digital currencies designed to replace cash with fully traceable, programmable transactions. He frames CBDCs as tools for modernizing payments and increasing financial inclusion, but the integration with carbon markets exposes their real function: enforcing behavioral compliance in real time.

Imagine a future where every purchase is logged, scored, and cross-referenced against carbon budgets. Under Carney's model, programmable money can automatically restrict transactions that exceed your personal emissions quota or penalize you with dynamic pricing based on your carbon profile. Fly too often, drive too far, or consume outside approved thresholds, and the system can instantly adjust your spending power - not through taxation or legislation but through code at the currency level. What begins as "incentivizing sustainability" quickly becomes algorithmic rationing.

Tying carbon markets to programmable money also creates the infrastructure for personalized ESG scoring. Corporations already receive ESG scores based on environmental and social compliance, but the architecture Carney promotes extends that scoring down to the individual. Through IoT sensors, smart meters, digital ID frameworks, and biometric-linked wallets, every person's consumption patterns can be monitored, assessed, and regulated. Access to services, credit, or even cross-border travel could become contingent on maintaining an acceptable personal "impact profile." In Carney's system, financial sovereignty dissolves into conditional access, where compliance with sustainability goals and governance norms determines your participation in the economy.

COVID-19 provided the perfect proving ground for this infrastructure. Stimulus payments, small business bailouts, and vaccine passport systems all converged on digital rails that integrated identity, health data, and eligibility criteria into centralized frameworks. Carney and his allies within the WEF used the crisis to push "green recovery" mandates, tying access to funding and global supply chains to net-zero commitments. Once populations accepted QR codes, conditional access, and digital credentials under pandemic pretexts, the groundwork was laid for embedding the same mechanisms into climate and financial governance.

Carney's alignment with the World Economic Forum's "stakeholder capitalism" agenda cements his role in this transformation. In stakeholder capitalism, corporations are elevated beyond serving shareholders to act as policy enforcers, implementing ESG-aligned mandates across labor practices, supply chains, and consumer interactions. This framework bypasses legislatures entirely. Carney's system doesn't require passing unpopular climate laws or building public consensus. It operates through capital control - forcing compliance by making participation in the global economy contingent on adhering to centrally defined sustainability standards.

This isn't environmentalism. It's the construction of a planetary compliance architecture:

• Carbon becomes the currency of control, with emissions tracked, priced, and penalized in real time.

• CBDCs become the mechanism of enforcement, embedding policy rules directly into programmable money.

• ESG scoring becomes the algorithmic gatekeeper, determining access to credit, mobility, and opportunity.

• Asset managers act as private regulators, bypassing democratic processes and dictating policy through investment flows.

In this system, sovereignty - corporate, national, or individual - becomes irrelevant. What matters is interoperability with Carney's standards. Align with the frameworks, and you gain access to capital, markets, and mobility. Step outside them, and you're quietly frozen out of the rails that govern economic life.

Mark Carney isn't pitching this as coercion. He presents it as inevitable progress - a necessary evolution of capitalism to "save the planet" and "stabilize markets." But once programmable money, carbon tracking, and ESG scoring converge, the mechanisms of compliance will be built into the infrastructure itself. No elections. No appeals. No opting out. Code enforces policy automatically.

What Carney is constructing isn't just a financial reset; it's a behavioral operating system for humanity. Carbon markets measure you. CBDCs control you. ESG scoring ranks you. And global capital decides whether you belong inside or outside the system. Once this framework is live, freedom won't disappear suddenly. It will fade quietly, replaced by programmable participation inside an economy you no longer control.

The Bank for International Settlements (BIS) and the International Monetary Fund (IMF) are at the center of a quiet financial revolution - the construction of a globally integrated system of central bank digital currencies (CBDCs). This isn't about modernizing payments or making transactions "faster and cheaper," as the official narrative claims. It's about building the digital control architecture for a new monetary order - one where currency itself becomes programmable, every transaction is traceable, and access to financial participation can be granted or revoked at the level of code.

For decades, the BIS has operated as the "central bank of central banks," coordinating policy frameworks for the global financial system. The IMF, meanwhile, manages sovereign debt, monetary assistance, and structural adjustment programs for nearly every nation on Earth. Now, these two institutions are working hand in glove to accelerate the shift toward CBDCs - positioning themselves as the architects of a unified global settlement layer. Individually, each wields enormous influence. Together, they're designing the infrastructure that will govern how money moves, who can use it, and under what conditions.

The BIS began quietly laying the groundwork years ago through Project Helvetia, Project Dunbar, and Project mBridge - experimental platforms testing cross-border CBDC interoperability between major central banks. These pilots demonstrated not just the feasibility of CBDCs but their programmable potential: the ability to attach conditions directly to the currency. Under these systems, a transaction isn't merely approved or denied; it can be shaped. Funds can expire after a set period, be restricted to specific goods, or be blocked entirely based on regulatory or behavioral criteria.

At the same time, the IMF has been preparing its own digital infrastructure for integrating CBDCs into global financial flows. Its key tool is the International Monetary and Financial Committee's Integrated Policy Framework (IPF), which establishes standards for monetary coordination and capital mobility. This allows the IMF to weave CBDCs into its lending programs, debt restructuring agreements, and crisis response mechanisms - effectively ensuring that any nation seeking assistance aligns its digital currency with BIS/IMF-defined interoperability rules.

Once CBDCs are standardized, cross-border settlement becomes frictionless - but so does centralized control. The BIS has been explicit in its reports: the goal is a unified platform where multiple central banks can transact directly over shared rails, bypassing commercial intermediaries and removing the last remnants of national monetary independence. Every transaction - between banks, corporations, and eventually individuals - moves through an integrated global clearing system. In practice, that means monetary sovereignty is quietly surrendered to unelected technocrats operating above national governments.

Programmable money is the real endgame. The BIS frames programmability as a feature to "enable innovation" and "ensure compliance," but the implications are profound:

• Governments could automatically block purchases deemed harmful to "climate goals," public health, or national security.

• Social policies - from tax rebates to welfare payments - could be locked to approved vendors or time-limited, enforcing behavioral nudges by code.

• Individual spending could be tracked, scored, and regulated seamlessly across borders, creating a financialized compliance grid at planetary scale.

The IMF's role makes this architecture inescapable. For decades, the Fund has leveraged debt dependency to push structural reforms on developing nations. Now, as CBDCs roll out, nations will increasingly be compelled to adopt IMF-approved interoperability frameworks in exchange for access to capital markets and crisis financing. Those that refuse risk exclusion from international settlement networks - effectively cutting them off from trade, aid, and global liquidity.

This integration also ties directly into ESG frameworks and carbon markets. The BIS has been explicit about linking CBDCs to real-time emissions tracking and sustainability-linked finance, embedding climate compliance into the very structure of money. Under this model, every transaction is cross-referenced against carbon budgets or environmental impact scores:

- Fuel purchases could trigger dynamic pricing or quota restrictions.
- Travel could require pre-authorized "carbon allowances."
- Investments in non-ESG-compliant sectors could be blocked at the settlement layer.

Once these controls are hardwired into CBDCs, policy enforcement moves from legislation to automation. There's no debate, no appeal, no opt-out - the code executes policy at the point of transaction. In this model, financial inclusion becomes conditional compliance: your participation in the economy depends on meeting the standards defined upstream by BIS committees, IMF frameworks, and their aligned private partners.

The BIS is also positioning CBDCs to absorb and unify digital identity systems. Through pilot projects, it's testing the integration of biometric verification, Know-Your-Customer (KYC) data, and real-time risk scoring into digital wallets. The objective is a seamless infrastructure where your identity, financial history, health records, and even carbon footprint are tied to your programmable currency. This convergence mirrors the goals of WEF-aligned initiatives like ID2020 and the EU's Digital Identity Wallet, ensuring interoperability between identity frameworks and financial rails.

COVID-19 served as an accelerant. Emergency stimulus programs normalized digital wallet infrastructure. Vaccine passport frameworks primed populations for identity-linked permissions. Supply chain disruptions justified centralizing liquidity controls, and global debt spikes drove more nations under IMF management. The "green recovery" narrative created alignment between climate compliance, programmable payments, and supranational governance. By the time CBDCs become mainstream, the operational playbook for controlling populations through financial infrastructure will already be tested and accepted.

Carney's climate-linked carbon markets, Gavi's health credential systems, Palantir's predictive modeling platforms, and BIS/IMF's CBDC rails aren't separate projects; they're converging layers of the same architecture. The BIS writes the rules for money. The IMF enforces adoption through debt and liquidity. WEF-aligned ESG frameworks set the behavioral conditions. And Big Tech provides the platforms, wallets, and identity verification systems to make it all seamless.

This isn't monetary innovation - it's financial governance without representation. Once CBDCs are integrated into a single global clearing layer, individual and national autonomy dissolve into a managed grid of programmable access. Opting out won't just be inconvenient. It will mean exclusion from trade, services, travel, and eventually, economic existence itself.

The BIS calls it interoperability. The IMF calls it inclusion. In practice, it's the operating system for planetary-scale compliance - an invisible infrastructure of control where policy isn't debated, it's embedded. The next monetary system won't just measure value. It will measure you.

The climate emergency has become one of the most powerful tools for accelerating technocratic governance. Unlike wars or pandemics, which come and go, climate change is framed as permanent crisis - a never-ending state of emergency that justifies sweeping restructurings of finance, energy, mobility, and individual behavior on a planetary scale. The narrative is carefully engineered: existential fear meets utopian promise, paired with prepackaged solutions designed not by elected governments but by a tightly aligned network of supranational institutions, private corporations, and unelected stakeholders.

At its core, the "climate emergency" narrative shifts the balance of power upward - away from local decision-making and toward global coordination frameworks. Bodies like the United Nations, the World Economic Forum (WEF), the International Monetary Fund (IMF), and the Bank for International Settlements (BIS) position themselves as indispensable arbiters of planetary survival. Nation-states are portrayed as too small and fragmented to act effectively, paving the way for centralized institutions to dictate policies, financial flows, and behavioral norms in the name of saving the Earth.

The narrative also reframes carbon - an invisible molecule - into the primary unit of social and economic governance. Through frameworks like the Paris Agreement and the UN Sustainable Development Goals (SDGs), emissions are transformed into measurable "budgets" and tradable assets, creating a global carbon economy where every transaction, industry, and individual becomes a data point to be monitored, priced, and regulated. This isn't environmentalism. It's the construction of a compliance-based economic system hidden beneath the language of sustainability.

Institutions like the BIS, IMF, and Mark Carney's Glasgow Financial Alliance for Net Zero (GFANZ) are already embedding climate compliance directly into the financial system. Carbon emissions are treated as financial liabilities, scored, traded, and settled using ESG frameworks that tie capital access to behavioral alignment. Under this model, corporations must demonstrate adherence to "net-zero" targets or risk losing investor support, access to credit, and stock index eligibility. For nations, failure to comply can trigger downgrades in sovereign credit ratings or restrictions on IMF-backed financing. These aren't recommendations - they are ultimatums enforced through control of liquidity and capital markets.

Once carbon metrics are baked into central bank digital currencies (CBDCs) - a core focus of BIS and IMF pilot programs - compliance will move from policy into code. Programmable money enables automated enforcement of climate-linked restrictions:

- Purchases of fuel, meat, or high-emission products could be capped or denied at the transaction level.
- Airline tickets might require carbon allowances before being issued.
- Personal energy usage could trigger dynamic pricing penalties tied to ESG-linked financial rails.
- Individual "carbon scores" could determine access to loans, insurance rates, and even eligibility for certain jobs or benefits.

These mechanisms are sold as empowering consumers to "make sustainable choices," but in reality, they are tools for behavioral engineering. With CBDCs, IoT integration, and unified digital identity frameworks, authorities - whether governmental or corporate - won't need to legislate restrictions. Policy will be enforced automatically, embedded into the infrastructure of payments, mobility, and consumption itself.

Climate-linked digital identity systems are already being tested globally. Programs like ID2020, the EU Digital Identity Wallet, and Worldcoin are designed to merge personal identity, transaction history, and biometric verification into interoperable profiles. Once these IDs integrate with carbon tracking, every purchase, movement, and online interaction can be cross-referenced against personal emissions budgets. Your "climate impact" will no longer be abstract; it will be scored and regulated in real time, feeding predictive governance models that manage populations algorithmically.

The technocratic architecture goes deeper still. IoT sensors embedded across cities, vehicles, and supply chains provide live data streams on energy consumption, transportation habits, and environmental conditions. These inputs feed into AI-driven simulations - "digital twins" of individuals, businesses, and entire societies - which model policy outcomes before implementation. Governments and corporations can test carbon taxes, rationing schemes, and behavioral nudges on simulated populations first, then deploy them seamlessly in the real world. This transforms climate policy from reactive to preemptive, justified by predictive models the public cannot audit or challenge.

COVID-19 demonstrated the playbook. Emergency declarations, digital passports, and movement restrictions were normalized under the justification of collective safety. The same infrastructure now being deployed for climate governance - identity-linked permissions, programmable incentives, and centralized control of mobility and consumption - was stress-tested during the pandemic. What was framed as temporary "crisis management" became proof of concept for a permanent compliance system.

Under this emerging regime, climate narratives provide cover for a vast reordering of economic and social structures:

• Finance is re-engineered: Trillions in investment flows are redirected toward ESG-compliant industries, while "non-compliant" sectors face capital starvation.

• Sovereignty dissolves: National policies are subordinated to global agreements enforced through supranational financial levers.

• Behavior becomes data: Every purchase, trip, and energy decision feeds your carbon profile, influencing your access to services and opportunities.

• Policy moves into infrastructure: Once carbon controls are programmed into currency, identity systems, and IoT platforms, opting out becomes nearly impossible.

This isn't speculation. Institutions like the WEF, BIS, IMF, and GFANZ are explicit about linking climate goals to financial access and personal freedoms. Carbon budgets are becoming the new social contracts, with programmable enforcement mechanisms replacing democratic negotiation. Under the guise of planetary survival, a centralized operating system for global population management is being installed - one where dissent isn't punished directly but rendered irrelevant by the architecture itself.

The danger isn't environmental stewardship; it's environmental pretext. The planet's health becomes the justification for a permanent emergency state, where top-down mandates override local autonomy and personal choice collapses into algorithmic enforcement. The narrative is designed to feel benevolent - save the Earth, save ourselves - while embedding a system that measures, predicts, and regulates human life at planetary scale.

Climate change is real, but the solutions being rolled out have less to do with protecting ecosystems than with restructuring civilization around compliance-by-design. The "climate emergency" isn't just a warning. It's a lever - one engineered to shift control from governments to unelected technocratic networks and to embed policy into the very code that runs economies, currencies, and identities.

When the architecture is complete, "sustainability" won't be a choice. It will be a condition of existence, continuously verified, scored, and enforced by systems you don't control. And like every previous phase of technocracy, it will arrive dressed as progress.

The infrastructure for carbon scoring is already being built, but its true power won't emerge until it fully converges with AI-driven social credit systems. This isn't environmental stewardship. It's the foundation for an algorithmic compliance grid where your carbon footprint, financial behavior, political alignment, and personal decisions are continuously monitored, scored, and regulated in real time. The "climate emergency" provides the justification, but the architecture being constructed goes far beyond emissions tracking. It's about merging identity, currency, and behavior into a single system of programmable control.

At the heart of this convergence is the carbon profile - a continuously updated record of your individual "climate impact." Every purchase, trip, meal, and online interaction generates emissions data that flows into global reporting frameworks being standardized by the BIS, IMF, WEF, and GFANZ. Banks and payment processors are already piloting tools that automatically estimate the carbon cost of each transaction: swipe your card, buy a flight, book a hotel, and your profile adjusts instantly. Under the surface, AI integrates this data into personalized emissions budgets defined by supranational policy frameworks.

This is the entry point for programmable money. As central bank digital currencies (CBDCs) roll out, the integration of carbon scoring into programmable payments creates a seamless mechanism for automated enforcement:

• Purchases exceeding your monthly carbon allowance could be blocked at the point of sale.

• "High-impact" items - fuel, meat, flights - could trigger dynamic pricing penalties built directly into the currency rails.

• Carbon overages might automatically deduct credits from your wallet or restrict unrelated transactions until compliance is restored.

• Access to services like loans, insurance, or housing could be preconditioned on maintaining an acceptable carbon score.

Once embedded in CBDCs, these controls don't require laws, regulators, or enforcement officers. The currency enforces policy automatically. There's no appeal, no debate, and no opting out.

The AI layer expands this from environmental compliance into full-spectrum behavioral scoring. Social credit systems already exist in fragments across multiple domains:

• Financial compliance: creditworthiness, anti-money-laundering risk, and fraud detection.

• Political trustworthiness: monitoring online activity for "misinformation" or "extremism."

• Health compliance: vaccine passports, mobility permissions, and biometric-linked status checks.

• Workplace loyalty: HR-managed reputation systems scoring "alignment" with corporate ESG goals.

Carbon scoring plugs directly into these frameworks. Combined with IoT sensors, digital IDs, and AI-driven analytics, the system doesn't just track what you buy; it models who you are - your preferences, risk profiles, and ideological leanings. That model becomes your digital twin, a constantly evolving simulation used to predict your future behavior and preemptively adjust your permissions and opportunities.

This isn't theoretical. Major institutions are already aligning these systems under the banner of climate finance and ESG compliance:

• GFANZ, under Mark Carney, coordinates $150 trillion in assets across banks, insurers, and asset managers, tying lending and investment flows to emissions data and sustainability disclosures.

• BIS pilots like Project mBridge are testing cross-border CBDC settlements, embedding carbon metrics into programmable currency rulesets.

• Big Tech platforms - Google, Mastercard, Microsoft, and Amazon - are rolling out consumer-facing "carbon calculators" and integrating them into digital wallets, payment gateways, and e-commerce platforms.

• WEF-aligned policy labs are drafting frameworks for personal carbon quotas that integrate biometric identity, IoT telemetry, and AI modeling into unified compliance dashboards.

Once these systems are linked, carbon becomes the Trojan horse for a much larger AI-governed social credit system. On the surface, you're rewarded for "sustainable choices": taking public transit, eating plant-based diets, installing energy-efficient appliances. But the same datasets also feed into ideological trust scoring - assessing your political alignment, social influence, and information consumption. Viewed through predictive AI models, environmental compliance becomes inseparable from social and behavioral compliance.

Here's how the merge looks in practice:

• Step 1: Carbon as baseline identity - Your personal carbon profile is tied to your digital ID and wallet, accessible by banks, governments, and platforms.

• Step 2: Programmable currency - CBDCs integrate emissions thresholds into payment infrastructure, creating automated enforcement without visible regulators.

• Step 3: AI-driven risk modeling - Machine learning models ingest environmental, social, and behavioral data, assigning you dynamic "trust scores."

• Step 4: Policy enforcement by proxy - Access to finance, mobility, information, and healthcare becomes conditional on maintaining acceptable scores across multiple dimensions.

The power of this system lies in its invisibility. You're not arrested or fined for dissenting or exceeding your carbon budget - you're simply denied participation. Bookings fail. Transactions decline. Search results disappear. Insurance premiums spike. Your influence score drops, reducing your visibility online and offline. The system nudges you toward approved behaviors without ever having to confront you directly.

COVID served as the prototype for this convergence. Vaccine passports normalized identity-linked permissions. Digital wallets for stimulus payments built the infrastructure for programmable disbursements. Health compliance dashboards demonstrated how predictive AI could manage populations dynamically in real time. The same architecture is now being repurposed for climate governance, folding carbon scoring into broader AI-driven frameworks for tracking and shaping behavior.

This trajectory transforms governance itself. Policy no longer operates through debate, legislation, or consent; it flows through data standards and algorithmic rulesets that operate beyond the reach of democratic oversight. Decisions about what you can buy, where you can travel, or whether you're considered "trusted" aren't made by parliaments or courts - they're embedded into financial infrastructure, identity frameworks, and AI models you'll never see.

The endgame is a global compliance architecture where environmental, financial, and ideological scoring merge into a single predictive governance system. It won't look like authoritarianism as we know it. It won't need police, checkpoints, or courts. Enforcement becomes ambient, seamless, and invisible - a digital feudalism managed by algorithms owned and operated by unelected technocratic networks.

The language will remain soft, optimistic, and progressive: sustainability, inclusion, equity, safety. But the underlying architecture is hard, centralized, and absolute. Once carbon scoring merges with AI-driven social credit, freedom stops being a right and becomes a score. Participation in society will no longer be assumed; it will be granted conditionally, maintained only by continuous, algorithmically verified compliance.

PART VII - THE MACHINE REVEALED

Exposing the networks and playbooks.

21

The Technocrat Family Tree

The thread linking the Rockefeller Foundation, the World Economic Forum (WEF), the World Health Organization (WHO), and the Bill & Melinda Gates Foundation isn't a conspiracy theory - it's a documented architecture of influence built over decades. Each of these institutions plays a distinct role, but together they form a vertical integration of power: the Rockefellers built the framework for technocratic governance, the WEF acts as its networking hub, the WHO provides institutional legitimacy, and Gates supplies funding and operational muscle. The common objective is clear - centralize authority over health, finance, and behavior under a unified, unelected framework disguised as multilateral "cooperation."

The Rockefeller Foundation set the stage in the early 20th century by reshaping medicine, public health, and education into standardized, centralized systems. Through its funding of the Flexner Report (1910), Rockefeller money reorganized medical schools, eliminating traditional and alternative practices in favor of pharmaceutical-based care - a model perfectly suited to the emerging industrial medicine complex they helped finance. Their early investment in the League of Nations' Health Organization, later absorbed by the WHO, laid the foundation for global health governance decades before most governments even considered such centralization. More importantly, the Rockefellers pioneered the "philanthropic capture model": use private foundations to fund institutions, define research priorities, and exert soft influence over international bodies without direct political accountability.

Fast-forward to 1971, when Klaus Schwab launched the World Economic Forum with direct intellectual and financial support from Rockefeller-backed think tanks. WEF positioned itself as the premier networking platform for public-private partnerships, bringing together heads of state, corporate executives, central bankers, and NGOs. But WEF wasn't simply a neutral convener; it served as the policy alignment hub where supranational agendas are shaped before filtering into national frameworks. Whether it's ESG scoring, digital identity infrastructure, or pandemic response protocols, WEF's annual Davos meetings create a consensus layer among elite stakeholders - and Rockefeller-aligned funding has been deeply embedded in this architecture from the beginning.

This is where the WHO enters the picture. Founded in 1948 and shaped heavily by Rockefeller-funded personnel and policy frameworks, the WHO gradually evolved into the global arbiter of health governance. For decades, it coordinated international disease tracking and vaccine programs, but its power expanded dramatically after the International Health Regulations (IHR) reforms of 2005 and again after 2020. These reforms gave the WHO authority to declare global health emergencies and recommend binding responses - from lockdowns to travel bans to vaccine mandates.

On paper, the WHO is a UN agency accountable to its 194 member states. In practice, it operates like a privately steered body due to its funding model. Less than 20% of its budget comes from assessed contributions by governments; over 80% comes from voluntary, earmarked donations dominated by private foundations and corporate-aligned NGOs. At the top of that list: the Bill & Melinda Gates Foundation and its proxy organization, Gavi, the Vaccine Alliance, both of which consistently rank among the WHO's largest funders - in some years surpassing entire sovereign nations.

Bill Gates' role goes beyond funding. Through the Gates Foundation, Gavi, and CEPI (Coalition for Epidemic Preparedness Innovations), Gates has operationalized Rockefeller-style influence over global health policy:

- Gavi negotiates vaccine procurement and distribution deals directly with governments and pharmaceutical companies, bypassing many local authorities.
- CEPI, co-founded by Gates and WEF at Davos in 2017, finances vaccine R&D while securing pre-purchase commitments from governments.
- Gates-aligned funding drives WHO policy priorities, shaping recommendations on everything from vaccination schedules to pandemic response protocols.

COVID-19 revealed how tightly these networks are integrated. The WHO declared the pandemic, Gates-funded Gavi and CEPI coordinated vaccine development and procurement, and the WEF convened the private-sector "solutions" playbook under the banner of the Great Reset. Rockefeller-backed institutions like the Johns Hopkins Center for Health Security - creators of the Event 201 pandemic simulation in October 2019 - fed directly into these response frameworks, modeling the exact protocols later adopted globally. Every layer reinforced the others:

- The WHO provided authority.
- Gates provided funding and distribution pipelines.
- The WEF provided corporate and political alignment.
- Rockefeller legacies provided the architecture of centralized control underpinning the entire system.

This integration doesn't stop at public health. It extends into digital identity frameworks, programmable finance, and carbon-based compliance systems. WEF-aligned initiatives like ID2020, funded by Gates and Gavi, explicitly link biometric identity to health records, payment systems, and access permissions. The WHO provides the global legitimacy for identity-linked vaccine certificates and mobility controls, while Gates' infrastructure supplies the technical backbone. At the same time, WEF drives ESG frameworks and carbon markets supported by Rockefeller-funded policy labs, and BIS/IMF pilot programs test integration with central bank digital currencies.

The result is a closed-loop control system masquerading as multilateral cooperation:

1. Rockefeller Foundation → built the structural blueprint for centralized governance via medical standardization, institutional capture, and global health frameworks.

2. WEF → creates elite consensus and public-private alignment on policy, technology, and finance.

3. WHO → supplies institutional authority to declare emergencies and impose global health protocols.

4. Gates Foundation & Gavi → finance and operationalize distribution systems, vaccine pipelines, and digital ID frameworks.

When these actors move in sync, nation-states lose autonomy. Decisions are made upstream, codified through WEF-aligned frameworks, funded by Gates and Rockefeller-style philanthropy, legitimized by WHO authority, and enforced through technology and finance controlled by their corporate partners. Governments implement policies, but they don't design them.

COVID was the proof of concept. The same network is now pivoting toward climate governance, digital identity systems, and financial compliance frameworks tied to carbon scoring and programmable currencies. The model doesn't change - only the justification does. Whether the crisis is pandemics, climate change, or "misinformation," the same vertical stack applies: unelected bodies define the problem, engineer the solutions, and deploy them through private infrastructure dressed as public policy.

This isn't a conspiracy of individuals. It's an ecosystem of power deliberately constructed over a century, starting with Rockefeller's institutional capture, scaled by Gates' funding, networked through WEF's alignment hubs, and enforced through WHO's declarations and public-private contracts. By the time policies reach the public, the choices have already been made.

Once digital IDs, programmable CBDCs, carbon quotas, and biometric health credentials are stitched together, the same network effectively controls who can transact, who can travel, who can work, and who can participate. And because these levers operate through private infrastructure rather than governments, democratic oversight becomes irrelevant. This is the new sovereignty: not of nations or citizens, but of networks - financial, technological, and institutional - aligned around shared goals and operated by unelected actors. Rockefeller built the skeleton. Gates provided the bloodstream. The WHO wears the mask of legitimacy. And WEF connects the brainstem to the muscles.

The pipeline linking RAND Corporation, DARPA, Google, and OpenAI isn't just a story of innovation. It's the architecture of a military-technocratic integration spanning six decades - a closed-loop ecosystem where government-funded research, private corporations, and elite-aligned institutions merge to create tools of population management, predictive modeling, and algorithmic control. Each phase has been sold as progress: RAND built the theories, DARPA operationalized them, Google privatized them, and OpenAI is now pushing them into a planetary-scale infrastructure. But the thread connecting them is constant: behavioral prediction, information dominance, and governance through data.

It starts with RAND Corporation after World War II. Founded in 1948 as a U.S. Air Force think tank, RAND pioneered systems theory and operations research, introducing the idea that human societies, markets, and conflicts could be modeled as complex systems governed by quantifiable inputs and outputs. RAND developed early predictive simulations for war gaming, social behavior, and economic stability - applying computation not just to weapons but to populations. This was the birth of algorithmic governance: using mathematics to forecast and shape human decision-making. RAND also laid the groundwork for network-centric thinking, conceptualizing the kind of interconnected information systems that would eventually evolve into the internet.

From RAND came DARPA - the Defense Advanced Research Projects Agency, founded in 1958 after Sputnik jolted U.S. defense policy into overdrive. DARPA took RAND's theoretical modeling and pushed it into operational infrastructure. Its mission was simple: build tools to ensure technological supremacy over adversaries, foreign and domestic alike. Within DARPA's early projects, three breakthroughs set the stage for everything to come:

• ARPANET (1969) - The prototype for the modern internet, designed not for consumer convenience but for distributed command-and-control during nuclear conflict. Every packet of information had to survive network disruptions - laying the foundations for total data survivability.

• Machine-assisted translation and early AI - Cold War intelligence demanded the capacity to analyze vast volumes of global communication. DARPA's AI research focused on natural language processing, sentiment detection, and predictive modeling long before "deep learning" became a buzzword.

• Cognitive modeling - DARPA funded experiments to quantify human perception, memory, and decision-making, with the goal of integrating this understanding into simulations capable of predicting population-level responses to policy and media campaigns.

DARPA's innovations weren't designed for open societies; they were tools for total information awareness. They created the protocols, databases, and predictive frameworks for large-scale monitoring - then quietly offloaded many of them into the private sector under the banner of "commercialization."

This is where Google enters. Founded in 1998 out of Stanford University's Digital Library Project, the company was seeded with grants from DARPA and the National Science Foundation. Its core algorithm - PageRank - was designed to solve information retrieval problems DARPA had been wrestling with for decades: how to index, categorize, and prioritize the world's knowledge at scale. What appeared to be a search engine was, from inception, a global intelligence tool disguised as a consumer product.

Key connections make the lineage clear:

• Google co-founder Sergey Brin's early funding came directly from DARPA-linked research grants.

• Google's initial data architecture was modeled on distributed systems designed for military intelligence handling classified communication streams.

• Google Maps' origin traces back to Keyhole Inc., a CIA- and In-Q-Tel-funded startup later acquired by Google in 2004 - repackaging satellite reconnaissance tools into consumer-facing platforms like Google Earth.

• Google's deep integration with U.S. defense and intelligence networks expanded over time, supplying cloud infrastructure to the CIA, Pentagon, and NSA while maintaining consumer dominance.

By the mid-2000s, Google wasn't just indexing the web; it was mapping humanity - search history, location telemetry, purchasing habits, biometric signatures, and social graphs. Through Android, Gmail, Maps, and Chrome, Google built the most comprehensive behavioral database in human history, merging DARPA's surveillance priorities with RAND's predictive modeling frameworks. But even this was just groundwork for what came next.

Enter OpenAI. Founded in 2015 under the banner of AI "democratization," OpenAI's origin story centers on altruism - preventing AGI from falling into the hands of "bad actors." Yet OpenAI's trajectory mirrors the same RAND-to-DARPA-to-Google playbook, only accelerated and scaled. Initially structured as a nonprofit, OpenAI pivoted into a capped-profit hybrid model, aligning itself with Microsoft's Azure platform while drawing on massive government and defense-related compute contracts to train models like GPT.

OpenAI's core innovation isn't generative AI itself; it's the integration of reinforcement learning, predictive modeling, and population-scale behavioral simulation. These systems don't just interpret data - they shape it. With billions of users generating conversational prompts, OpenAI is harvesting an unprecedented feedback loop on human thought, intent, and emotional response. Paired with DARPA-developed simulation frameworks and Google's behavioral data monopolies, OpenAI is effectively training planetary-scale digital twins of populations - predictive models used to simulate how individuals and societies will react to policy shifts, narratives, and economic shocks.

The real pipeline looks like this:

- RAND built the theory: systems thinking, war gaming, and modeling human behavior as data.
- DARPA operationalized the tools: the internet, early AI, cognitive modeling, and predictive simulations.
- Google privatized the infrastructure: global surveillance disguised as consumer convenience, fused with military-grade data pipelines.
- OpenAI is weaponizing the outputs: AGI aligned with behavioral governance systems designed to steer populations at scale.

When combined, these layers form the control stack for modern technocracy:

- IoT and biometric identity systems provide the sensor layer.
- Google, Meta, and Amazon manage the data aggregation layer.
- OpenAI models simulate populations and optimize persuasion strategies.
- BIS, IMF, and WEF-linked frameworks integrate these systems into financial, health, and climate governance.

COVID revealed the playbook in real time: predictive dashboards from RAND-modeled frameworks, DARPA-backed epidemiological simulations, Google's mobility data feeding global compliance systems, and OpenAI-adjacent AI tools used for information control. That was the beta test. The next phase integrates programmable currencies, digital IDs, carbon scoring, and AI-driven social credit into a single predictive governance infrastructure.

The narrative remains benign - innovation, democratization, safety - but the trajectory is unmistakable. RAND built the map. DARPA weaponized it. Google commercialized it. OpenAI is closing the loop, embedding algorithmic governance directly into platforms, currencies, and institutions. What emerges isn't a free market of ideas or technologies - it's a vertical stack of control, spanning research, infrastructure, and policy, owned and steered by networks you'll never vote for.

This isn't about AI replacing humans. It's about AI managing humans, guided by frameworks built decades ago for information dominance and now scaled to planetary reach. Once these systems converge - and they already are - opting out won't just be impractical. It will be impossible.

The story of the Club of Rome, the IPCC, ESG frameworks, and today's so-called "sustainability" agenda is a single unbroken arc - one that spans decades of policy engineering and psychological conditioning. It begins with a small elite group modeling planetary "limits," filters through scientific bodies designed to produce consensus narratives, migrates into financial systems through ESG scoring, and now manifests as a global compliance architecture disguised as environmental stewardship. What appears to be about saving the planet is, in practice, about building the rails for a technocratic economy, where access to resources, markets, and even personal freedoms is conditional upon alignment with "sustainability" mandates defined by unelected networks.

The Club of Rome laid the foundation in 1968, when a coalition of industrialists, academics, and policymakers gathered to solve what they framed as the existential challenge of human overconsumption. Their 1972 report, The Limits to Growth, used computer-based modeling to predict societal collapse without dramatic interventions to curb population and industrial activity. Presented as neutral science, the report established the narrative framework still in use today: humans are a threat to planetary stability, and centralized management of resources is the only solution. The Club's genius wasn't in its models - which have been repeatedly criticized for flawed assumptions - but in its ability to shift policy discourse from national sovereignty to planetary governance.

This shift paved the way for the Intergovernmental Panel on Climate Change (IPCC), founded in 1988 under the United Nations. On paper, the IPCC is a scientific body aggregating peer-reviewed research on climate change. In practice, it functions as a consensus manufacturer, synthesizing vast and complex data into simplified "summaries for policymakers" that governments adopt wholesale. These summaries, often written by committees influenced by political and corporate stakeholders, become the basis for binding international agreements like the Paris Accord. The IPCC doesn't set policy directly; it sets the scientific narrative that makes certain policy options - carbon pricing, emissions caps, population management - appear inevitable and non-negotiable.

From there, the agenda moves into financial control mechanisms, and this is where ESG frameworks enter. ESG - Environmental, Social, and Governance scoring - has become the de facto enforcement tool for sustainability mandates. Pushed heavily by the World Economic Forum, asset managers like BlackRock, and elite consortia like the Glasgow Financial Alliance for Net Zero (GFANZ), ESG frameworks convert planetary narratives into compliance metrics for corporations and, increasingly, entire nations. A company's access to investment, credit, and insurance now depends on demonstrating adherence to emissions targets, diversity quotas, and governance standards defined upstream by ESG gatekeepers - not by democratic institutions.

Through ESG, global financial flows are being weaponized to engineer corporate and social behavior. The largest asset managers, controlling tens of trillions in capital, collectively enforce alignment with "net-zero" objectives by threatening divestment or exclusion from major indexes. Sovereign wealth funds and IMF lending programs have begun embedding similar sustainability clauses into national financing agreements, compelling governments to adopt energy policies, infrastructure changes, and identity-linked digital compliance tools to remain viable in global markets. Under this system, "voluntary targets" rapidly evolve into financial mandates enforced by institutions no voter can influence.

But the real power of ESG lies in its convergence with technological enforcement mechanisms. Carbon scoring is being integrated into central bank digital currencies (CBDCs), allowing regulators - or algorithms - to automatically restrict or penalize transactions tied to emissions profiles. Smart meters, IoT sensors, and digital identity frameworks link individual consumption patterns to carbon budgets, creating the infrastructure for personal sustainability quotas enforced at the point of purchase. Combine this with real-time data from smart cities, behavioral tracking from Big Tech platforms, and predictive modeling powered by AI, and "sustainability" transforms from a policy goal into a continuous compliance regime.

This is no longer theoretical. The World Economic Forum openly frames "stakeholder capitalism" - their flagship model - as the backbone of the sustainability agenda. Under this framework, corporations aren't just economic actors; they become policy executors, embedding environmental and social mandates into products, supply chains, and customer relationships. The result is governance without legislation: algorithms, corporate policies, and financial incentives enforce rules once debated publicly in parliaments.

COVID-19 acted as the accelerant. Under the cover of "green recovery" and "build back better" narratives, trillions in stimulus were conditioned on ESG-aligned infrastructure investments and digital transformation projects. Vaccine passports, biometric identity frameworks, and QR-based access controls normalized identity-linked permissions. That same infrastructure is now being retrofitted for carbon budgeting and "sustainable consumption" tracking, expanding ESG scoring from corporations down to individual citizens. The pandemic served as the beta test; climate policy provides the permanent justification.

In the emerging model, "sustainability" is not an aspiration - it's a gateway into programmable participation:

• Carbon quotas regulate what you can buy, eat, or travel to, enforced by CBDCs and real-time emissions tracking.

• Personal ESG scores tie your financial, social, and political behavior into a unified risk profile.

• IoT-linked infrastructure monitors energy use, mobility, and consumption habits continuously.

• AI-driven predictive models simulate population responses, enabling preemptive policy enforcement before dissent can form.

The Club of Rome established the existential narrative. The IPCC provides the scientific consensus layer. ESG converts the narrative into enforceable financial policy. And the WEF integrates these tools into a single technocratic operating system, quietly transforming the meaning of governance itself. Decisions about energy, mobility, and even personal consumption are being outsourced to algorithms and unelected institutions. Governments remain implementers, not designers. Citizens become managed variables in data-driven "sustainability" simulations.

This isn't about protecting the environment. It's about embedding policy into infrastructure so deeply that opting out becomes impossible. The "sustainability technocracy" is being constructed to manage economies, societies, and individuals through code, incentives, and programmable constraints - replacing democratic negotiation with algorithmic enforcement.

The language remains soft: inclusion, equity, resilience, planetary stewardship. But behind it is a hard system of vertical integration:

- Narrative layer → Club of Rome and IPCC
- Policy layer → WEF and ESG frameworks
- Enforcement layer → programmable money, IoT, AI, and predictive modeling
- Compliance layer → corporations deputized as regulators through financial leverage

When these layers fully converge, "sustainability" stops being a choice and becomes a condition of participation in society. And because the agenda is distributed across institutions rather than concentrated in a single governing body, there's no single point of accountability - only the illusion of consensus and inevitability.

This is the genius of the design. By cloaking technocratic control in the language of planetary survival, the system converts fear into compliance and compliance into permanence. What began as a 1970s thought experiment on "limits to growth" has evolved into a global governance architecture where your ability to live, work, and transact depends on seamless integration into a framework you didn't vote for - one that measures, predicts, and regulates your existence in real time.

22

Case Studies in Global Control

C hina's social credit system is the closest thing humanity has seen to a live beta test for algorithmic governance. It's not speculation, it's not theory, and it's not some distant dystopian scenario - it's operational, it's expanding, and it's refining its control mechanisms in real time. What Beijing has constructed is not merely surveillance, nor just financial tracking, nor simple law enforcement. It's the convergence of all three into a single framework where compliance isn't requested - it's engineered.

At its heart, the system seeks to collapse the boundary between citizen and subject. Digital identity forms the foundation: your national ID, phone number, banking details, biometric data, travel records, online activity, and even genetic information are stitched together into a single interoperable profile. Everything you do, from paying bills to buying groceries to commenting online, feeds the system's score-keeping engines. Behavior becomes a data stream. That data stream is continuously evaluated, ranked, and assigned meaning based on criteria most people never see, by algorithms most people never question, within a process that offers no appeal.

This isn't about law; it's about code. It turns the entire population into variables in a vast predictive model. Forget due process, courts, and debates about right or wrong. In this model, the question isn't whether you've broken the law - it's whether your behavior aligns with government-defined "trustworthiness." And trustworthiness is a moving target, adjusted at will and updated across millions of profiles in seconds.

If the algorithm decides you've acted against policy, punishment isn't debated, it's executed - seamlessly and invisibly. You don't get arrested; you get excluded. Suddenly, you can't buy train tickets. Your children can't attend certain schools. Your mortgage application gets denied. One day you log into your banking app, and entire services are grayed out with no explanation.

The genius of the system - and its danger - is in its invisibility. Traditional repression relies on overt threats and physical enforcement, but China's design weaponizes subtlety. Compliance is manufactured by conditioning, not coercion. People begin policing themselves because the costs of stepping out of line are immediate and tangible. If you know your social credit score is tied to your ability to secure a loan, book a flight, or keep your job, you self-censor long before the state intervenes. And because everything is automated, there's no single official to appeal to and no transparent process to challenge. The punishment isn't loud, it's quiet - a locked door, an unavailable option, a transaction declined.

But the deeper ambition goes beyond punishment. The ultimate goal is prediction. By integrating facial recognition cameras, purchase histories, geolocation data, and biometric feeds, the system builds a living behavioral model of every individual. It doesn't just track what you've done - it anticipates what you might do. Combined with machine learning, this architecture allows the state to intervene before dissent materializes, to adjust incentives before noncompliance spreads, to manage populations proactively rather than reactively. It isn't about prosecuting crime after the fact; it's about shaping behavior before crime or protest even occurs.

And China isn't hiding its aspirations. This isn't a single monolithic database; it's a mesh of corporate-government partnerships stretching across sectors. State ministries, big tech giants like Alibaba and Tencent, banks, insurance providers, and municipal authorities all feed the network. What emerges is a federated control system - not one institution ruling all, but a shared infrastructure of governance where everyone, from the central bank to the supermarket chain, enforces the same behavioral norms. It is both centralized and distributed, top-down and bottom-up. The entire architecture is designed to make deviation costly, even dangerous, at every point of interaction with society.

The narrative pushed publicly frames this as safety, efficiency, and modernization. Officials tout reduced fraud, faster loan approvals, and "building trust" between citizens. But underneath, this is about obedience, not efficiency. Trust, in this model, flows in one direction: upward. The citizen trusts the state, not the other way around.

And it doesn't stop at China's borders. Pilot programs inspired by this model are emerging globally, often branded as "digital identity frameworks," "carbon scoring initiatives," or "financial inclusion programs." These appear in India's Aadhaar biometric identity system, the EU's digital ID wallets, and the World Bank's ID4D projects. In each case, the infrastructure mirrors the same architecture: tethering individuals to unified, interoperable IDs that connect payments, health records, mobility, and reputation into a seamless data-driven governance layer. What China has built today serves as the test bed - refining the tools, normalizing the concept, and proving its effectiveness at scale. Once perfected, it can be exported.

This is why China's social credit system matters far beyond Beijing. It signals a paradigm shift: from laws to algorithms, from governance to engineering, from persuasion to programming. When your rights, your access, and your freedom are mediated not by elected officials but by unseen code, sovereignty becomes an illusion. And because the model learns, it improves. Every fine-tuned parameter, every pilot city, every punished dissenter feeds the machine more data, sharpening its predictive precision and tightening its grip.

This isn't a Chinese experiment; it's the prototype of a new global operating system. The beta test is running. Everyone else is next.

COVID-19 revealed something unprecedented - not a pandemic in the biological sense, but a pandemic of governance, a stress test for control, and the unveiling of a new model where planetary policy is drafted, coordinated, and executed by unelected elites. What unfolded between late 2019 and 2021 was not merely emergency response; it was the first live demonstration of how supranational networks - public-private alliances, philanthropic foundations, transnational corporations, and NGOs - could synchronize the behavior of entire populations without relying on traditional legislative processes. The policies weren't debated in parliaments or voted on by citizens. They were aligned in boardrooms, summit sessions, and private networks long before the crisis reached its peak.

From the earliest days, coordination wasn't chaotic - it was already structured. The World Health Organization provided the authoritative declarations, but its funding sources and partnerships made it anything but politically neutral. With the Gates Foundation, Gavi, CEPI, and other WEF-aligned entities supplying capital, technical expertise, and policy frameworks, WHO's role was transformed into a central messaging hub for pre-agreed strategies. National governments didn't draft independent responses; they implemented templated policies distributed through standardized WHO playbooks and aligned through forums like the World Economic Forum, Gavi, the IMF, and transnational corporate lobbies. Lockdowns, mask mandates, school closures, and travel bans rolled out almost simultaneously across nations not because the virus behaved identically everywhere, but because the governing frameworks had already been harmonized.

The infrastructure enabling this didn't materialize in 2020 - it had been designed over decades. The WEF's "Global Risks" frameworks, Gavi's procurement systems, and the 2019 Event 201 tabletop exercise in New York, co-hosted by the WEF, Gates Foundation, and Johns Hopkins, simulated the very crisis that would unfold months later. The exercise wasn't predictive in the mystical sense; it demonstrated how institutional players could leverage a pandemic to align financial, health, and technological responses across borders. When COVID hit, the protocols weren't improvised; they were activated.

Power migrated upward. The crisis justified the sidelining of local governance and democratic processes in favor of top-down directives from global bodies. Public-private "task forces" blurred lines between state authority and corporate enforcement, allowing multinational tech platforms, financial institutions, and pharmaceutical giants to act as de facto policy executors. Algorithms became enforcers: social media throttled dissenting narratives under "misinformation" protocols coordinated through partnerships between WHO, WEF, and Big Tech. Censorship wasn't legislated; it was harmonized.

Meanwhile, vaccine procurement revealed the leverage point: control over supply chains equals control over governments. Through Gavi, CEPI, and COVAX - all deeply interwoven with WEF and Gates Foundation funding - wealthy nations secured early access while developing nations were locked into dependency frameworks that forced alignment with centralized policy in exchange for doses. Health sovereignty was effectively replaced by health dependency. At the same time, digital credentialing systems, piloted under the guise of vaccine passports, introduced infrastructure for interoperable biometric ID frameworks - laying rails for future population-level permissions tied to health, finance, and mobility.

And above it all, the narrative was carefully engineered. "Build Back Better," "The Great Reset," and "One Planet, One Health" became unifying slogans pushed through Davos sessions and adopted wholesale by national governments. These weren't grassroots ideas; they were branding campaigns for a pre-existing agenda to consolidate governance at the planetary scale. Trillions in stimulus were directed through ESG-aligned investment frameworks, making recovery conditional on compliance with "sustainability" mandates defined by unelected entities.

This was the proof of concept: crises justify synchronization. Policy doesn't need parliaments when global infrastructures bypass them entirely. COVID allowed elites to test digital identity systems, programmable health credentials, and AI-assisted mobility controls, while conditioning populations to accept central coordination as natural and necessary. The narrative was "emergency," but the deeper play was normalization - normalizing the idea that unelected actors can set universal policy because "the science" demands it, and that noncompliance is not a political disagreement but a public health threat.

The framework didn't dissolve when lockdowns ended. The infrastructure remains, awaiting the next declared crisis: pandemic, climate emergency, financial collapse, or cyberattack. Each response is designed to trigger the same alignment mechanisms - bypassing sovereignty, dissolving borders, and embedding unelected influence deeper into the mechanics of daily life. COVID was not the final goal; it was the rehearsal. Once policies are harmonized at this scale, reversing them becomes nearly impossible. National governments find themselves trapped in dependency cycles where access to vaccines, financial liquidity, or critical technologies depends on adherence to frameworks set far upstream. Citizens are governed less by their elected representatives than by the technocratic meshwork of foundations, corporate boards, NGOs, and algorithmic enforcement tools.

This is the emerging model of planetary governance: legitimacy outsourced to institutions no one votes for, policies drafted behind closed doors, and narratives managed through centralized communication channels. COVID didn't create this model. It revealed it - and it made compliance its own form of contagion.

The concept of the so-called "15-minute city" is marketed as a breakthrough in sustainability and livability - an urban utopia where everything you need, from groceries to healthcare to entertainment, sits within a short walk or bike ride from your home. On paper, it sounds harmless, even progressive: fewer cars, less pollution, stronger local communities. But beneath the glossy branding and sustainability rhetoric, the framework carries a far more significant agenda - the integration of IoT-managed urban compliance systems into the everyday structure of human life.

The true function of the 15-minute city isn't about convenience. It's about control through infrastructure. Once you centralize resources and services into tight, algorithmically defined "urban cells," you also centralize the ability to monitor, restrict, and manage movement. IoT sensors, facial recognition cameras, smart meters, license plate scanners, digital payment systems, and biometric IDs converge into a single data layer. Every transaction, every journey, every interaction within the zone becomes measurable. And once it's measurable, it's manageable.

The narrative of environmental responsibility is the carrot. The stick comes later - carbon scoring, mobility permits, and programmable access. In a fully digitized 15-minute zone, compliance isn't enforced by police patrols; it's automated at the infrastructure level. Want to drive across your designated boundary? Your permit is approved or denied instantly based on your personal carbon quota or ESG score. Want to attend a stadium event? Your digital ID must validate your vaccination status, credit profile, and biometric match before your QR code opens the gate. Think of it less as "urban planning" and more as a programmable city operating system - a software layer over physical reality where permissions are determined upstream, enforced invisibly, and updated in real time.

This isn't theoretical; the groundwork already exists. Smart city initiatives across Europe, North America, and Asia have quietly embedded IoT monitoring at scale. In places like Oxford, Barcelona, Toronto, and Paris, municipal partnerships with global consultancies, the WEF, and Big Tech companies are deploying dense networks of connected devices: energy-use trackers in homes, real-time traffic monitors, environmental sensors, and citizen-behavior dashboards tied to centralized control centers. Public-facing justifications emphasize sustainability, congestion relief, and improved public health, but in the backend, these systems create a unified data spine mapping the city in real time - and everyone inside it.

The danger lies in coupling this infrastructure with digital ID frameworks and programmable finance. When your identity, mobility, and transactions are all tied to interoperable systems, control can shift seamlessly from nudges to restrictions without public debate. Access to roads, buildings, or services becomes conditional, not guaranteed. Cross a boundary without permission? Your automated toll doubles. Exceed your personal carbon allowance? Your payment app rejects the gas pump. Fail to comply with health mandates? Your biometric credentials flag you for restricted travel.

The 15-minute city model positions itself as voluntary, but once implemented, opting out becomes impossible. Physical layout is designed to make leaving your zone inconvenient; digital systems make it expensive; algorithmic enforcement makes it effectively forbidden. And because the system operates through code and policy frameworks rather than explicit legislation, democratic oversight erodes by design. Decisions about permissible behavior migrate from public institutions into opaque governance layers - city planners, private consultants, unelected NGOs, and machine learning models trained on "population optimization."

This dovetails directly with broader supranational agendas. ESG scoring systems, carbon markets, CBDCs, and WHO-backed digital health credentials converge neatly within 15-minute frameworks, creating programmable compliance zones where movement, energy use, spending, and even social participation can be throttled in response to centralized mandates. Cities become nodes in a planetary network, each running its own software instance but drawing on the same cloud-based governance infrastructure built by the same unelected actors - the WEF, UN agencies, Gates-aligned foundations, and their corporate partners.

The social conditioning is already underway. The message pushed relentlessly: "If you oppose 15-minute cities, you oppose sustainability, fairness, and progress." But hidden inside the messaging is an unspoken inversion: in these "open, walkable" neighborhoods, your freedom exists only insofar as it aligns with upstream policy objectives. Cross the algorithm, and the city closes around you silently - not through violence, but through denied permissions, disabled access, and invisible geofencing.

This isn't urban planning in the classical sense. It's governance by infrastructure, with IoT networks functioning as the real enforcers. Once implemented at scale, the 15-minute city becomes less about where you live and more about what you're allowed to do. Your neighborhood stops being a place and becomes a managed zone, with compliance automated and dissent engineered into irrelevance. The streets remain open, but only to those who are cleared to walk them.

COVID normalized the first layer of this infrastructure: digital credentials, movement restrictions, and population-scale behavioral conditioning. The 15-minute city folds those lessons into physical design and permanently embeds them into the architecture of urban life. It isn't about reducing traffic; it's about hardcoding governance into the grid itself, where cities evolve into programmable platforms and the citizen becomes just another managed endpoint.

Digital identity frameworks are the linchpin holding together the emerging technocratic control grid. Without them, the 15-minute city, social credit scoring, programmable currencies, and ESG-driven behavioral compliance remain fragmented systems. With them, they fuse into a single architecture capable of governing populations at planetary scale - invisibly, algorithmically, and without democratic consent. At their core, these frameworks are designed to replace traditional concepts of citizenship, rights, and anonymity with conditional access tied to a unified, interoperable ID. Your existence in the system becomes verified, measured, and managed through code.

The public narrative is seductive: security, convenience, efficiency. Digital IDs promise seamless access to banking, healthcare, education, travel, and government services through one credential - no more passports, no more multiple logins, no more bureaucracy. But beneath the sleek marketing lies the foundational shift: your rights and permissions become programmable. Identity stops being something you hold and becomes something granted, revoked, and modified in real time depending on your alignment with upstream policy objectives.

Every major institution is moving in lockstep to normalize this infrastructure. The World Bank's ID4D initiative seeks to bring interoperable digital IDs to the billions of people without formal identification. The UN promotes "legal identity for all" as part of its Sustainable Development Goals under Agenda 2030. The World Economic Forum has published repeated white papers describing "a trusted digital identity system" as essential to future governance and finance. Big Tech companies like Microsoft and Mastercard are partnering with consortia like ID2020 to create frameworks where identity is tied directly to financial, health, and mobility credentials. None of these entities are elected. None of them answer to you. Yet together they are defining the scaffolding for your participation in society.

Once implemented, the potential for conditional access becomes limitless. Want to buy groceries? Your carbon footprint is checked automatically before your payment clears. Want to cross a city boundary? Your ID is pinged against mobility permissions tied to 15-minute city policies and climate quotas. Want to open a business loan? Your ESG compliance rating, political affiliations, and medical history determine eligibility. If you fall outside the accepted thresholds, the rejection doesn't arrive in the mail. It happens instantly, at the point of transaction, enforced silently by the infrastructure itself.

This is governance shifting away from law and toward code. Traditional political systems operate in public: legislation is debated, policies are challenged, and decisions can be appealed. Digital identity collapses that transparency by embedding rules directly into the infrastructure of daily life. Your rights are no longer enshrined in constitutions; they're defined by APIs, cross-checked in real time by AI-driven systems that make automated decisions about who you are, what you're allowed to do, and where you're allowed to go. The very concept of a citizen evolves into that of a managed user in a global compliance platform.

The COVID response accelerated this shift dramatically. Vaccine passports normalized the idea that access to society could be conditional, revocable, and digitally enforced. "Health passes" became the perfect Trojan horse, integrating identity, mobility, and permissions into a single interface. Once populations accepted that QR codes could determine whether you enter a restaurant or board a plane, the foundation was laid for expansion into financial, environmental, and behavioral realms. These frameworks didn't vanish when mandates lifted - they evolved. Interoperable IDs are now quietly being piloted across Europe, Canada, India, and parts of Africa, tied to banking rails, carbon reporting systems, and biometric verification tools.

The architecture is global by design. National governments manage deployment, but the standards are set by supranational networks - WEF, IMF, World Bank, BIS, WHO - whose priorities are increasingly aligned through ESG scoring systems, carbon markets, and predictive compliance dashboards. Each node in this network manages a piece of the infrastructure, but none of it exists independently. Digital IDs become the universal key, unlocking every gate in the system, while simultaneously binding your participation to a constantly updated profile.

Here is the most critical point: once digital identity becomes mandatory, opting out ceases to exist. Without a compliant ID, you cannot transact, travel, or even verify your existence within essential systems. Even "basic rights" - food, shelter, healthcare - become contingent upon verified credentials. What was once voluntary becomes structural. The social contract flips: access is no longer presumed; it is earned through compliance.

And because the system runs on code, not debate, appeals vanish by design. You don't petition a judge; you debug your permissions. If the algorithm denies your access, there is no courtroom to argue in, no elected official to lobby, no collective bargaining to fight for your rights. Sovereignty dissolves into automation.

The push toward digital identity is framed as modernization, but its function is consolidation. It unites finance, mobility, health, reputation, and even citizenship under a single control layer. Combined with IoT-managed cities, carbon scoring, programmable currencies, and centralized policy alignment, it becomes the skeleton key of a planetary technocracy. Without it, these systems remain disjointed experiments. With it, the grid locks into place.

The infrastructure is being built now, in real time, sold as progress, safety, and sustainability. But the true cost isn't convenience versus inconvenience. It's autonomy versus automation. In a fully integrated digital ID ecosystem, freedom isn't revoked with force. It simply expires when the system decides your profile no longer qualifies.

23

Conclusion - Breaking the
Algorithm

Democracy didn't die in a single moment. It wasn't assassinated on the steps of a parliament or drowned beneath mobs of dissenters. It was eroded - piece by piece, process by process, replaced by an entirely different operating system of governance built on unelected power. What we live under today still carries the symbols of democracy - the flags, the ceremonies, the elections - but these are façades. The real decisions shaping the direction of nations, economies, and societies are increasingly made far from public chambers, drafted behind closed doors by networks of technocrats, bankers, NGO boards, and private consortia that answer to no electorate and fear no accountability.

The shift began quietly, with the gradual migration of policymaking away from local and national governments into supranational structures. Central banks like the Federal Reserve, European Central Bank, and BIS determine economic reality for billions yet operate independently of democratic oversight. Institutions like the IMF and World Bank dictate sovereign policies through conditional lending agreements, forcing entire nations into compliance with frameworks their populations never voted on. The WTO, OECD, and other trade bodies set the rules for global commerce, and governments simply ratify what's already been decided. In this arrangement, democracy becomes a theater while power concentrates in bodies immune to its reach.

Corporate capture accelerated the process. Through lobbying, regula-

tory partnerships, and public-private task forces, multinational conglomerates and financial giants rewrote the social contract to serve markets, not citizens. BlackRock and Vanguard hold controlling stakes in
companies across nearly every major industry, influencing not just corporate governance but also the policy directions of governments dependent on their capital flows. The World Economic Forum's "stakeholder
capitalism" framework gave CEOs political power without electoral accountability, embedding corporate objectives into government policy
under the guise of global collaboration. By convening heads of state, regulators, and billionaires on neutral ground at Davos, the WEF normalized the transfer of decision-making authority from elected parliaments
to closed-door technocratic councils.

The rise of NGOs and philanthropic foundations masked this centralization beneath a veneer of humanitarianism. Gates, Rockefeller,
Wellcome, Ford - their influence reaches into public health, education,
environmental policy, and beyond. They fund scientific research, shape
WHO recommendations, and steer the agendas of international forums, yet they are accountable only to their boards and benefactors. By
positioning themselves as "partners" in global governance, these entities
bypass democratic scrutiny while embedding their interests deep within
policy pipelines. What looks like collective action is, in reality, coordinated influence, where private capital determines public outcomes.

Technology completed the capture. Where parliaments once debated
policies openly, code now executes them silently. Big Tech platforms,
through partnerships with governments and intelligence agencies, have
assumed control over the flow of information. Algorithms decide which
narratives dominate and which disappear, creating manufactured consensus while suppressing dissenting voices in the name of safety, misinformation control, or public health. During COVID, entire
populations were conditioned to accept platform-driven censorship as
natural, unaware that much of it was coordinated directly between unelected elites, WHO directives, and technology monopolies operating
beyond national jurisdictions. Policy enforcement is no longer about

passing laws; it's about rewriting the conditions of visibility and participation in the digital public square.

What makes this structure resilient is its decentralization. There is no single institution to overthrow, no tyrant to depose, no parliament to reform. The power web is distributed across foundations, think tanks, supranational bodies, private corporations, and data-driven enforcement systems. No one person appears in charge, yet every lever of control converges into the same outcomes: centralized policy alignment, automated compliance, and diminishing citizen sovereignty. Democracies simulate choice through elections, but the agenda transcends parties and persists across administrations. The machinery runs uninterrupted regardless of who appears to lead.

The deeper tragedy is psychological. Citizens are conditioned to believe they participate in governance while their influence shrinks to irrelevance. Voting gives the illusion of agency, yet the major levers - financial regulation, energy policy, security infrastructure, technological standards - are set far upstream by committees and boards hidden from public view. Governments become service desks implementing protocols written elsewhere. "National sovereignty" becomes a slogan used to pacify populations while the real authority flows through pipelines of capital, data, and cross-border governance frameworks designed for durability, not debate.

This isn't accidental. The erosion of democratic systems was engineered gradually through crises - financial, environmental, biological - each one used to justify the concentration of decision-making into the hands of "experts" and "trusted authorities." COVID made this plain. Overnight, public health bureaucracies aligned globally, empowered to suspend freedoms, restructure economies, and implement population-wide restrictions without electoral consent. Emergency declarations became executive pipelines for unelected power, setting precedents for how future crises - climate, cybersecurity, energy - will justify deeper centralization without accountability.

Democracy didn't collapse; it was rewritten. What we are left with is governance by networks, not nations. A planetary operating system where legitimacy is manufactured through branding, where "global consensus" replaces public debate, and where sovereignty is reduced to managing populations within constraints decided far beyond their borders. Elections happen, but policy is programmed elsewhere. Citizens speak, but their data, not their voices, shape outcomes.

The rise of unelected power is the endgame of technocracy. When decisions are framed as too complex, too scientific, too urgent for public input, governance migrates permanently into the domain of experts, coders, and financiers. This is not democracy; it is management. And the managed have no seat at the table.

Sovereignty was once understood as the right to govern oneself - the authority of individuals, communities, and nations to set their own paths without interference from external forces. But sovereignty in the digital era is dissolving, not through conquest or invasion, but through architecture. What's emerging in its place is a new form of digital feudalism, where access, opportunity, and autonomy are mediated by centralized platforms, unelected networks, and algorithmic enforcement layers that function above governments and beyond borders.

In the old feudal system, power was concentrated in the hands of a few landowners. Kings granted authority to lords, who managed territory and extracted labor and taxes from serfs in exchange for protection. It was an explicit hierarchy: everyone knew their place. Today's feudalism is less obvious but far more pervasive. The "lords" are no longer monarchs; they are the owners of data, infrastructure, and financial rails. The new vassals are nation-states themselves, stripped of autonomy as they integrate into digital ecosystems controlled by supranational institutions and private entities. And ordinary citizens, once imagined as free participants in democratic societies, are being recast as managed users within a planetary compliance grid.

The shift begins with infrastructure dependency. Modern governance relies on systems it no longer owns: payment rails controlled by private banks, cloud networks owned by Big Tech, global trade standardized by transnational bodies, and security architectures coordinated through intelligence-sharing alliances like Five Eyes and NATO. When governments no longer control the backbone of finance, data, energy, and communications, sovereignty becomes ceremonial. Policy-makers sign agreements, but the real enforcement power rests with platforms that dictate the conditions of participation - Amazon for logistics, Google for information flow, Microsoft for enterprise infrastructure, BlackRock for capital access. States no longer govern directly; they manage populations within frameworks dictated elsewhere.

Central bank digital currencies (CBDCs) will cement this dependency. Once money itself becomes programmable, access to economic participation can be instantly granted or revoked based on behavioral compliance, carbon scores, or ESG alignment. This is feudalism without castles: a system where citizens do not "own" their assets so much as they are granted conditional usage rights through profiles embedded in digital identity frameworks. National currencies are being rewritten into interoperable ledgers managed through standards set by the BIS, IMF, and other unelected entities. The sovereignty of money - the foundation of political autonomy - is evaporating, replaced by code that reports to systems far above the jurisdiction of any single government.

Digital IDs are the binding agent. In this emerging hierarchy, your existence within the system - your access to banking, healthcare, mobility, and even citizenship - is tethered to a singular, interoperable profile. This profile lives in databases controlled by alliances between governments, NGOs, and private corporations, operating under standards drafted by global institutions. Lose alignment with those upstream frameworks, and your permissions vanish. You are technically "free," but without a functioning ID or compliant score, you cannot transact, travel, or access essential services. What feudal lords once enforced through armed guards is now handled by software - silent, instantaneous, and unquestionable.

Even nation-states are being transformed into vassals. Supranational frameworks like the UN's Agenda 2030, the World Bank's ID4D, the

WEF's "stakeholder capitalism," and WHO-backed health governance programs dictate policies that ripple downward through national systems. These agreements are rarely debated in legislatures and never subjected to public referendum, yet they define the operational boundaries within which nations must function. Financial dependency locks in compliance: IMF loans, carbon credit markets, and ESG-driven investment flows create leverage points where dissent carries economic punishment. Governments don't resist these frameworks because they cannot afford to - their survival is tied to the platforms, funding mechanisms, and technologies managed elsewhere.

This is the essence of digital feudalism: authority migrates upward, while responsibility for enforcement flows downward. Nations act as administrative zones, enforcing policies they did not create on populations who never consented to them. Individuals become assets in a managed network, their behaviors tracked, scored, and incentivized through predictive analytics. The lords no longer need armies; they have algorithms. Compliance doesn't require violence when denial of access to food, travel, money, and information achieves the same result with less resistance.

Sovereignty in this environment survives only at the edges - in the spaces where systems fail to integrate or populations refuse to comply. But those edges are shrinking rapidly. IoT-driven smart cities, interoperable CBDC networks, and biometric digital IDs are stitching together a planetary architecture of control that transcends borders and elections alike. It is governance without consent, enforced invisibly through infrastructure dependencies and financial chokepoints.

To reclaim sovereignty in such a system requires rethinking what autonomy means. It's no longer about political independence on paper but about decoupling from infrastructures designed to mediate every interaction. If you do not control your money, your data, your identity, and your ability to transact, your sovereignty exists only as metaphor. Digital feudalism thrives by selling convenience while embedding dependency so deeply that opting out becomes impossible without exiting society altogether.

This isn't coming. It's here, incrementally installed beneath the language of progress, sustainability, and inclusion. The walls aren't visible because they are coded into the architecture itself. The castles have no gates; the lords don't wear crowns; and the serfs don't yet realize they've been bound.

Self-reliance in the age of digital feudalism is no longer a romantic ideal; it's becoming a survival strategy. The infrastructure being built around us - digital IDs, programmable money, IoT-controlled cities, predictive policing, carbon scoring - is designed to centralize control while removing the individual's ability to opt out. The illusion of choice persists, but in a system where access, mobility, and participation are mediated by upstream policy frameworks, autonomy can't be handed to you by law, elections, or committees. It has to be reclaimed, rebuilt from the ground up, and defended at every layer of life - physical, digital, and psychological.

The first step is rejecting dependency on systems designed to condition compliance. The less reliant you are on centralized infrastructure, the less leverage those systems have over you. Food, energy, finance, information - these are the four pillars where autonomy begins and where technocratic control seeks to concentrate power. If your food supply flows entirely through corporate chains monitored by carbon dashboards, scarcity can be manufactured instantly by flipping a policy switch. If your energy comes from grids tied to ESG compliance frameworks, your consumption can be throttled remotely in the name of "sustainability." If your ability to transact depends on programmable CBDCs linked to your identity profile, one decision far upstream can freeze your economic life in seconds. And if your understanding of the world is mediated solely through filtered, algorithmically curated information streams, then even your perception of freedom isn't yours.

True resistance starts by decentralizing these dependencies. Local food systems, independent power generation, community-based trade networks, and analog alternatives to digital choke points are not luxuries anymore - they are shields against enforced conformity. A garden becomes political in a world where carbon quotas dictate grocery access. Offline tools and cash reserves become defensive infrastructure when every payment is logged and scored. Skills once dismissed as obsolete - mechanical repair, hunting, foraging, natural medicine, community governance - transform into assets when automated platforms dictate who gets served and who gets locked out.

But autonomy isn't just material; it's informational. Predictive governance thrives on managing perception, manufacturing consensus, and isolating dissenters. To resist it, you need parallel channels of communication and trusted networks outside algorithmic control. Independent media, encrypted peer-to-peer platforms, and physical meetups bypass systems designed to score, monitor, and throttle "noncompliant" narratives. The ability to speak freely is inseparable from the ability to organize, and organizing will increasingly happen off-platform as censorship deepens and visibility itself becomes conditional on obedience.

Psychological sovereignty may be the most overlooked battleground. Technocratic systems function by manipulating fear - fear of exclusion, scarcity, or punishment. But the tools of predictive control rely on compliance patterns, not courage. When populations self-censor, self-restrict, and self-police, enforcement becomes invisible and cheap. Breaking this cycle starts with recognizing manipulation for what it is: narrative framing, crisis amplification, false binaries, and weaponized empathy used to manufacture consent. The more conscious you are of these levers, the less power they have over you. An unafraid, informed individual resists at a frequency no algorithm can predict.

Self-reliance also means building parallel economies and micro-sovereignties wherever possible. Local exchange systems, cooperatives, barter networks, and community currencies provide insulation from digital chokepoints like CBDCs and ESG-compliant financial rails. Open-source technologies, mesh networks, and decentralized communication infrastructure preserve freedom of information when mainstream platforms close ranks. At scale, these approaches don't dismantle the emerging technocratic grid directly, but they weaken its leverage by creating alternative ecosystems that operate on principles of consent rather than automated coercion.

Resistance doesn't mean chaos. It means deliberate, strategic decentralization. It means refusing to surrender agency to unelected networks, even when doing so feels convenient. It means understanding that every integration - every digital credential adopted, every "smart" convenience accepted without question - is another hook into a system designed to govern without permission. Opting out entirely may be impossible for now, but insulation is possible, and insulation buys time. Time to organize, to innovate, to reconnect with the tools and traditions that make sovereignty something more than a slogan.

Above all, autonomy begins where obedience ends. This isn't rebellion for its own sake; it's survival in an environment where policy is no longer debated but programmed, and where consent is engineered through dependency. The less control you outsource to systems you don't govern, the harder it becomes to trap you inside their predictive models. The most dangerous thing you can be to technocracy is not violent - it's unpredictable.

The coming years will force individuals and communities to make a choice: remain integrated into a frictionless system that trades liberty for convenience, or accept the discomfort of rebuilding independence in exchange for retaining agency. That choice won't be offered openly; it will have to be taken, seized in the gaps while they still exist.

In a world of digital feudalism, self-reliance is resistance. And resistance is survival.

- James Watt - turned heat into leverage; patents + steam standardization birthed industrial energy monopolies and locked factories to owners' capital.
- Richard Arkwright - factory system architect; centralized labor, discipline, and time under mechanized looms; proto-platform power over human rhythms.
- Eli Whitney - interchangeable parts; early automation logic that decomposed craft into modules, preparing people to be treated as components.
- Isambard Kingdom Brunel - megaproject showman; rails, bridges, docks; engineered urban flow and taught empires to think in infrastructure.
- George Stephenson - rail standardizer; track gauge and timetables as soft law; logistics became policy enforced by steel and schedule.
- Cornelius Vanderbilt - rail and steam tycoon; private chokepoints over national movement; fares as governance before governance knew it.
- Andrew Carnegie - steel monopolist; scale + vertical integration; philanthropy doubled as narrative armor for concentrated control.
- John D. Rockefeller - petroleum emperor; trusts, rebates, and "efficiency" as weapons; shaped education and medicine to entrench the model.
- J. P. Morgan - banker-technocrat; consolidated rival firms and stabilized crises by decree; private balance sheets as public authority.
- Frederick Winslow Taylor - scientific management; stopwatches on bodies; reduced work into measurable motions, a template for algorithmic labor.
- Henry Ford - assembly line; humans as process units; wages as pacifier; mass production welded to social engineering.

- Nikola Tesla - rival energy vision; wireless and AC imagination; lost political backing to monopoly logic but seeded the electrified future.
- Thomas Edison - inventor-industrialist; patents as moats; direct-current showmanship turned labs into corporate research regimes.
- Auguste Comte - positivist priesthood; framed "science as the faith" and gave technocrats a theology of authority.
- Karl Marx - central planning imaginary; diagnosed capital yet normalized managerial supremacy via planned production schemas.
- Friedrich Engels - movement financier and theorist; rationalized industrial coordination as historical necessity.
- Herbert Spencer - social Darwinist gloss; naturalized hierarchy and elite stewardship under the banner of "fitness."
- H. G. Wells - Open Conspiracy utopian; scripted managerial world society and information unity long before databases.
- Sidney Webb - Fabian tactician; administrative takeover by increment; policy seepage into every ministry.
- Beatrice Webb - data-driven social reform; prototypes for technocratic welfare auditing and institutional capture.
- George Bernard Shaw - Fabian propagandist; moralized elite management as humane inevitability.
- Graham Wallas - psychological governance; crowd mind and consent cultivation for bureaucratic ends.
- Harold Laski - LSE power broker; trained policy clerisy for state-corporate fusion.
- Howard Scott - Technocracy Inc. promoter; energy accounting as currency; engineer's throne over economy.
- M. King Hubbert - peak oil prophet; "energy certificates" as programmable rationing; the spreadsheet before the chain.
- Franklin D. Roosevelt - New Deal centralizer; crisis as mandate to federate boards, codes, and quotas.
- Rexford Tugwell - Brain Trust planner; sectoral cartels reframed as recovery; blueprints over markets.
- John Maynard Keynes - macro policy priest; legitimized expert steer-

ing of demand and employment from above.

- Vannevar Bush - science-state broker; wartime R&D pipeline; permanent research bureaucracy after victory.
- J. Robert Oppenheimer - Manhattan Project director; scientific exceptionalism fused with state power.
- Leslie Groves - military manager of science; secrecy, compartmentalization, and timelines as ultimate control stack.
- Alan Turing - codebreaking pioneer; computational logic weaponized; birthed machine inference as state tool.
- Claude Shannon - information theory; quantified signals and noise; the math under every surveillance stack.
- John von Neumann - stored-program architecture; game theory for geopolitics; optimization as strategy for power.
- Norbert Wiener - cybernetics; feedback control across machines, markets, and minds.
- W. Ross Ashby - homeostasis theorist; adaptive management of complex systems as governance ideal.
- Stafford Beer - cybernetic management; corporate-state control rooms for live steering of economies.
- Jay Forrester - system dynamics; feedback simulation for policy; Limits-to-Growth math engine.
- Henry "Hap" Arnold - air power patron; seeded RAND; military foresight as permanent institution.
- Albert Wohlstetter - strategic stability modeler; quantified risk to guide nuclear doctrine and procurement.
- Herman Kahn - scenario futurist; normalized planning the unthinkable; systematized "what if" for policy.
- J. C. R. Licklider - man-computer symbiosis; ARPA patron of networks and interactive computing.
- Paul Baran - distributed networks; resilience logic that underwrote packet-switched governance.
- Leonard Kleinrock - queueing on the wire; performance math for the proto-internet.

- Vint Cerf - TCP/IP co-author; protocol as law; interop became jurisdiction.
- Bob Kahn - TCP/IP co-author; stitched networks into one internet, dissolving borders in code.
- Joseph Weizenbaum - early AI critic; revealed the seduction of authority cloaked as software.
- Marvin Minsky - AI maximalist; framed minds as machines, inviting engineers to manage them.
- Herbert A. Simon - bounded rationality; decision theory legitimized expert heuristics in bureaucracies.
- Allen Newell - cognitive modeling; encoded problem-solving for institutional automation.
- Julian Huxley - first UNESCO head; cultural engineering via education and science diplomacy.
- Gro Harlem Brundtland - WHO and sustainability chair; "Our Common Future" as mandate for global managerialism.
- Margaret Chan - WHO director; consolidated outbreak governance templates pre-COVID.
- Tedros Adhanom - WHO director; emergency declarations as global policy triggers.
- Harry Dexter White - Bretton Woods architect; IMF/World Bank levers over sovereign budgets.
- Robert McNamara - systems analysis czar; Vietnam metrics and World Bank conditionalities as governance by spreadsheet.
- James Schlesinger - RAND alumnus; energy and defense bureaucratization across agencies.
- Zbigniew Brzezinski - technetronic era theorist; surveillance + integration as destiny; Trilateral ideologue.
- Henry Kissinger - realpolitik simulator; secrecy, backchannels, and managed conflict as statecraft.
- Aurelio Peccei - Club of Rome founder; planetary limits as rationale for centralized planning.
- Alexander King - Club of Rome scientist; model-based scarcity as

global policy pretext.

- Maurice Strong - environmental technocrat; UN summits + carbon governance; public-private climate rails.
- David Rockefeller - banker-globalist; foundations + councils as unelected world cabinets.
- Peter Sutherland - WTO/Trilateral broker; border and trade integration via legal harmonization.
- Jacques Attali - planner-philosopher; portable supranational governance evangelist.
- Klaus Schwab - WEF founder; stakeholder capitalism to install CEOs as policy co-authors.
- George Soros - Open Society financier; NGO swarms shaping law from outside ballots.
- Larry Fink - BlackRock chief; ESG as capital discipline; allocations as private regulation.
- Christine Lagarde - IMF then ECB; austerity and then CBDC evangelism under one technocratic banner.
- Mario Draghi - ECB "whatever it takes"; monetary technocracy trumping parliaments.
- Jerome Powell - Fed chair; crisis facilities that socialize risk and consolidate central power.
- Janet Yellen - Treasury/Fed bridge; fiscal-monetary fusion under expert custodianship.
- Ben Bernanke - quantitative easing architect; normalized permanent emergency finance.
- Paul Volcker - interest-rate shock disciplinarian; independence myth shielding central bank power.
- Agustín Carstens - BIS general manager; CBDC clearinghouse and standards gatekeeper.
- Mark Carney - GFANZ and central banker; carbon markets fused to monetary rails.
- Kristalina Georgieva - IMF head; crisis conditionality dressed as resilience and inclusion.

- Jamie Dimon - JPMorgan czar; private infrastructure for public policy enforcement.
- Lloyd Blankfein - Goldman Sachs; crisis arbitration from trading floor to cabinet anteroom.
- Stephen Schwarzman - Blackstone; assetization of everything, including public goods.
- Henry Paulson - Treasury/Goldman; bailout choreography that entrenched private governance.
- Robert Rubin - Treasury/Citi; revolving-door template for financial technocracy.
- Larry Summers - macro consigliere; deregulation when rising, austerity when falling.
- Tim Geithner - crisis custodian; institutionalized "too big to fail" as doctrine.
- Warren Buffett - capital allocator as policy voice; crisis backstops crowned as wisdom.
- Michael Bloomberg - data mayor; technocratic urbanism at planetary scale via philanthropy.
- Rupert Murdoch - media empire switchboard; agenda bandwidth for elite consensus.
- Bill Gates - philanthro-industrialist; health, agriculture, education policy by checkbook.
- Melinda French Gates - foundation co-chair; gender and health levers aligned with platform goals.
- Nandan Nilekani - Aadhaar architect; biometric ID as gateway to services and finance.
- Ajay Banga - World Bank president; public-private rails for digital ID + finance convergence.
- Ngozi Okonjo-Iweala - WTO head; supply-chain governance cloaked as trade facilitation.
- Roberto Azevêdo - former WTO; dispute frameworks favoring scale over sovereignty.
- Ursula von der Leyen - European Commission; EU digital wallets

and green industrial policy alignment.

- Thierry Breton - EU digital czar; platform rules that entrench centralized ID and compliance.
- Margrethe Vestager - competition regulator; resets market rules while hardening digital oversight.
- Antony Blinken - diplomacy as platform; public-private foreign policy corridors.
- Jeff Bezos - Amazon logistics state; commerce operating system and cloud for governments.
- Larry Page - Google co-founder; search + ads as attention governance; maps as soft territory.
- Sergey Brin - Google co-founder; data accumulation as inevitable efficiency.
- Eric Schmidt - Google chair; revolving-door AI policy and national security tech.
- Sundar Pichai - Alphabet CEO; planetary scale AI/ID integrations through Android and Cloud.
- Tim Cook - Apple supply-chain sovereign; privacy theater amid expanding device governance.
- Steve Jobs - design as persuasion; habit-forming ecosystems that prefigured digital dependency.
- Satya Nadella - Microsoft cloud empire; enterprise rails + OpenAI leverage into policy.
- Mark Zuckerberg - social graph governor; identity mapping and dopamine economics as control substrate.
- Sheryl Sandberg - ops + ads optimizer; scaled the behavior market into politics.
- Peter Thiel - Palantir + defense investor; data fusion for governments wrapped as startup grit.
- Alex Karp - Palantir CEO; predictive policing and logistics governance platforms.
- Stephen Cohen - Palantir co-founder; enterprise hooks into state information arteries.

- Elon Musk - Starlink/Neuralink/SpaceX; orbital internet + brain interfaces as dual-use infrastructure.
- Sam Altman - OpenAI + Worldcoin; AGI governance + biometric money experiments.
- Ilya Sutskever - AI lab priesthood; frontier models as justification for centralized control.
- Greg Brockman - OpenAI organizer; productizing frontier AI into platform dependencies.
- Dario Amodei - Anthropic co-founder; "safety" as governance scaffold for AI policy.
- Daniela Amodei - Anthropic co-founder; compliance-centric AI operating guidelines.
- Demis Hassabis - DeepMind; reinforcement learning scaled inside health, energy, and science stacks.
- Mustafa Suleyman - Inflection/Microsoft; AI assistants as population mediators; now policy conduit.
- Shane Legg - DeepMind; long-termist risk narratives that centralize AI oversight.
- Geoffrey Hinton - deep learning pioneer; alarm siren that still legitimizes elite control.
- Yoshua Bengio - AI leader; ethics frameworks that route power to expert boards.
- Yann LeCun - Meta AI; open-ish rhetoric inside a walled attention economy.
- Andrew Ng - MOOC + applied AI; labor automation packaged as upskilling.
- Fei-Fei Li - ImageNet; vision datasets that normalized mass labeling of human life.
- Mira Murati - OpenAI product; model rollout cadence as de facto public policy.
- Reid Hoffman - LinkedIn + venture; social graph + capital shaping governance narratives.
- Gilman Louie - first In-Q-Tel head; venture pipeline from intelli-

gence priorities to startups.

- Norman Augustine - In-Q-Tel godfather; defense boardroom fused to Silicon Valley funding.
- John Poindexter - Total Information Awareness; blueprint for population-scale data fusion.
- Michael Hayden - NSA/CIA; bulk collection normalized under national security branding.
- James Clapper - DNI; "metadata as truth" doctrine across agencies and platforms.
- Alex Pentland - social physics; behavioral telemetry for policy nudging at scale.
- Tom Inglesby - biosecurity voice; tabletop exercises aligning public-private pandemic playbooks.
- Neil Ferguson - modeling authority; scenario outputs as policy triggers.
- Jeremy Farrar - Wellcome/WHO; research funding vector to global health mandates.
- Richard Hatchett - CEPI; vaccine R&D finance steering the pipeline and priorities.
- Seth Berkley - Gavi; procurement leverage tying nations to supranational terms.
- Albert Bourla - Pfizer CEO; blockbuster public contracts as corporate policy power.
- Stéphane Bancel - Moderna CEO; mRNA scale-up entwined with state logistics.
- Pascal Soriot - AstraZeneca CEO; global supply under emergency harmonization.
- Uğur Şahin - BioNTech; platform biotech inside geopolitical procurement.
- Anthony Fauci - NIAID; domestic gatekeeper of research funding and mandates.
- Soumya Swaminathan - WHO science lead; consensus manufacture via "evidence" arbitration.

- Zhou Xiaochuan - PBOC; digital yuan groundwork; central bank identity meets currency.
- Mu Changchun - PBOC Digital Currency Institute; e-CNY pilot architect; programmable money proof-of-concept.
- Xi Jinping - centralizes "informatization"; social credit as governance doctrine at scale.
- Jack Ma - Alibaba/Ant; payments + scoring infrastructure braided into state priorities.
- Pony Ma - Tencent; WeChat super-app as daily life gateway and policy lever.
- Robin Li - Baidu; search + AI within the national data stack.
- Ren Zhengfei - Huawei; telecom backbone underpinning data sovereignty and exportable control tech.

World Economic Forum (WEF) - Unelected alignment hub connecting heads of state, CEOs, and NGOs under "stakeholder capitalism." Sets global policy templates that flow downstream into national legislation via Davos declarations, bypassing democratic processes entirely.

World Health Organization (WHO) - Positions itself as neutral science authority but functions as the central node of global health governance. Emergency declarations trigger coordinated mandates worldwide, funded heavily by private foundations and corporate actors with vested interests.

Bill & Melinda Gates Foundation - Philanthropy as leverage. Uses funding power to steer global health priorities, education frameworks, agricultural models, and climate initiatives, embedding its policy preferences into WHO, Gavi, CEPI, and countless governments.

Gavi, the Vaccine Alliance - Founded by Gates, Gavi negotiates global vaccine procurement and distribution while binding nations into contractual frameworks. Operates above domestic health authorities, conditioning access to medicine on alignment with upstream mandates.

Coalition for Epidemic Preparedness Innovations (CEPI) - Vaccine R&D finance mechanism co-founded by Gates and WEF. Funds proprietary biotech pipelines and fast-tracks vaccine development, consolidating control of intellectual property under private-public consortia.

COVAX - Coordinated by Gavi, CEPI, and WHO, this program allocates vaccine access globally. Markets itself as equitable but creates dependency structures that lock developing nations into pricing frameworks set by corporate suppliers.

Bank for International Settlements (BIS) - Central bank of central banks. Sets monetary policy rails, oversees CBDC integration, and manages cross-border settlements. Functions above any national jurisdiction, dictating financial infrastructure standards governments must comply with.

International Monetary Fund (IMF) - Sovereign leverage engine. Uses debt-based conditionality to force nations into structural reforms aligned with supranational frameworks, effectively dictating economic policy while bypassing legislatures.

World Bank - Primary architect of global infrastructure funding, ID4D digital identity integration, and development frameworks. Its financing agreements reshape governance models in the Global South under the banner of modernization and inclusion.

International Finance Corporation (IFC) - World Bank affiliate funding private-sector initiatives tied to global policy targets like digital identity, green infrastructure, and ESG compliance. Channels capital directly into technocratic transformation projects.

World Trade Organization (WTO) - Global rule-setter for trade, harmonizing regulations across borders. Functionally strips national sovereignty over trade policy by embedding enforcement through arbitration and dispute resolution mechanisms.

Financial Stability Board (FSB) - BIS-affiliated risk regulator. Shapes systemic banking frameworks, crypto policies, and capital allocation standards, giving private capital unprecedented influence over state fiscal decision-making.

Basel Committee on Banking Supervision - Sets banking compliance standards globally. Embeds risk metrics, reporting requirements, and capital frameworks directly into domestic banking laws via international "agreements" drafted behind closed doors.

Financial Action Task Force (FATF) - Anti-money laundering and anti-terror finance watchdog used to justify surveillance of all financial transactions. Global KYC/AML frameworks harmonized through FATF allow unprecedented monitoring of individual behavior.

International Organization for Standardization (ISO) - Generates technical standards that become de facto law. Through ISO 20022, rewiring the global payments infrastructure for interoperability and programmable transaction metadata.

United Nations (UN) - Uses "sustainable development" as a vehicle for harmonized governance. Agenda 2030 ties environment, health, and infrastructure under centralized policy objectives executed via subordinate agencies.

UNESCO - Controls educational, cultural, and scientific frameworks. Influences curriculum, narrative formation, and population conditioning under the guise of global literacy and progress.

UNDP (United Nations Development Programme) - Funds "resilience" projects aligned with Agenda 2030 targets, conditioning infrastructure financing on ESG, DEI, and digital identity integrations.

UNEP (UN Environment Programme) - Sustainability-driven enforcement body pushing carbon markets, consumption quotas, and biodiversity credits, shaping economic behavior via environmental pretexts.

UNICEF - Originally humanitarian, now instrumental in pushing digital ID pilots tied to child health and education records. Tests early frameworks later scaled into adult identity systems.

World Trade and Economic Forums (multiple regional) - Replicate WEF's stakeholder capitalism model on continental scales, harmonizing resource allocation and tech integration strategies across blocs.

OECD (Organisation for Economic Co-operation and Development) - Generates policy templates for tax harmonization, AI governance, and financial transparency adopted directly into domestic law without democratic debate.

European Commission - Unelected EU executive drafting frameworks like the European Digital Identity Wallet and carbon border tax systems. Operates outside direct voter influence but controls policy execution for 27 nations.

European Central Bank (ECB) - Monetary policymaker for the Eurozone, accelerating programmable CBDCs and green bond markets while bypassing member-state fiscal sovereignty.

Trilateral Commission - Founded by Brzezinski and Rockefeller, this private policy group integrates U.S., European, and Asian elites into unified economic strategies. Policy recommendations bleed into G7/G20 platforms.

Council on Foreign Relations (CFR) - U.S. foreign policy pipeline connecting academia, think tanks, and corporate power into synchronized geopolitical strategies adopted across administrations.

Chatham House (Royal Institute of International Affairs) - UK policy hub that coordinates energy, security, and finance agendas for Commonwealth and EU elites under strict non-disclosure frameworks.

Bilderberg Group - Annual off-records convergence of political leaders, central bankers, and corporate executives. Not policy-setting officially, but aligns narratives and objectives informally at the highest levels.

RAND Corporation - Designs predictive models, war-gaming simulations, and behavioral steering systems. Its methodologies underpin DARPA, surveillance infrastructures, and digital twin population mapping.

DARPA (Defense Advanced Research Projects Agency) - U.S. innovation pipeline for dual-use technologies: drones, ARPANET, AI, biotech. Acts as the R&D arm for surveillance capitalism and algorithmic control.

IARPA (Intelligence Advanced Research Projects Activity) - Intelligence community DARPA-equivalent, focused on predictive analytics and cognitive modeling for population-scale data fusion.

In-Q-Tel - CIA's venture arm seeding startups like Palantir, Keyhole (Google Earth), and biometric surveillance firms. Ensures intelligence objectives are baked into consumer technologies from inception.

Palantir Technologies - Government data fusion contractor integrating predictive policing, logistics optimization, and population-scale analytics into law enforcement and military operations globally.

OpenAI - Positioned as an AI lab but functions as a governance hub shaping international AGI regulations, access controls, and safety frameworks - locking smaller players out while consolidating AI into elite hands.

DeepMind (Alphabet) - Focuses on advanced machine learning and reinforcement systems, building models now embedded in healthcare, energy management, and experimental policy optimization platforms.

Anthropic - AI lab building "aligned" models with governance-compliance frameworks embedded, collaborating with governments to draft AI legislation that benefits the largest players.

Amazon Web Services (AWS) - Operates as a sovereign infrastructure provider. Hosts defense clouds, health databases, and financial platforms, giving Amazon silent leverage over entire economies.

Microsoft Azure - Runs government clouds globally and integrates OpenAI into enterprise deployments, making Azure the backbone of both AI governance and state digital transformation programs.

Google Cloud - Hosts health, education, and population-level data; also coordinates AI regulatory influence through WEF and OECD channels, positioning Google as policymaker by infrastructure.

Meta Platforms - Social identity layer tied to political manipulation, data harvesting, and algorithmic influence strategies. Facebook's partnerships with WHO and WEF show its integration into behavioral compliance systems.

Tencent - WeChat super-app serves as China's population management backbone; now exporting this infrastructure globally through fintech partnerships.

Alibaba / Ant Group - Anchors China's payments ecosystem and supplies biometric scoring systems used in social credit pilots; expanding digital ID/payment frameworks across Belt and Road nations.

Huawei - Global telecom backbone provider for 5G/6G networks, supplying data sovereignty chokepoints embedded with exportable surveillance capabilities.

Club of Rome - Ideological architect behind "Limits to Growth" models justifying managed scarcity, resource quotas, and population control frameworks later absorbed into UN, WEF, and IMF agendas.

GFANZ (Glasgow Financial Alliance for Net Zero) - $150 trillion coalition chaired by Mark Carney, uses climate targets to redirect global capital flows and force ESG compliance on corporations and states alike.

ID2020 - Digital identity consortium led by Microsoft, Gavi, and Rockefeller Foundation; integrates health records, financial credentials, and biometrics into programmable identity wallets.

The Commons Project - WEF-affiliated NGO piloting CommonPass and digital health credentials; gateway project for global biometric mobility frameworks.

Agenda 2030 - UN's master plan sold as sustainability and inclusion, embedding ESG compliance, carbon tracking, and digital identity into national laws without voter consent.

Agenda 21 - Predecessor to Agenda 2030; reframed environmentalism into policy harmonization across municipalities, laying the foundation for globalized governance through local zoning laws.

Public-Private Partnership (PPP) - Corporate takeover disguised as collaboration. Governments outsource infrastructure, policy, and enforcement to private actors who aren't elected and can't be held accountable.

Stakeholder Capitalism - WEF's model replacing shareholder-driven companies with firms acting as unelected policymakers. CEOs gain power equal to regulators while bypassing democratic processes.

Global Public Goods - Framing device used by the UN, WEF, and WHO to justify supranational policy over health, climate, and infrastructure - often stripping sovereignty in the name of "collective benefit."

One Health - WHO-backed integration of human, animal, and environmental health governance into a single framework, enabling cross-sector control over medicine, agriculture, and population policy.

Global Resilience Frameworks - Crisis-preparedness programs designed to harmonize emergency response across borders. Marketed as safety measures; functionally create mechanisms for policy lockstep.

Harmonization - Bureaucratic euphemism meaning national laws are rewritten to match supranational mandates, bypassing local debate entirely.

Finance, Money & Control Mechanisms

CBDCs (Central Bank Digital Currencies) - Programmable state-backed money tied to digital IDs. Enables real-time enforcement of policy, spending restrictions, and carbon allowances directly at transaction level.

Programmable Money - Currency coded with built-in rules on how, where, and when it can be spent. Not yours - licensed for conditional use.

BIS (Bank for International Settlements) - "Central bank of central banks" based in Basel. Sets the standards for monetary policy, CBDC infrastructure, and payment interoperability above national authority.

IMF (International Monetary Fund) - Uses loans as leverage to force nations into structural reforms and policy compliance aligned with global financial governance.

World Bank - Finances infrastructure projects and ID systems worldwide. Its "ID4D" program links biometric identity, digital payments, and financial inclusion narratives into global control rails.

ISO 20022 - Global payments standard enabling interoperability across banking, CBDCs, and digital wallets. Framed as efficiency; actually builds universal traceability into transactions.

KYC (Know Your Customer) - Verification system marketed as anti-money laundering but weaponized to enforce financial surveillance and pre-screen participation in the economy.

AML (Anti-Money Laundering) - Regulatory pretext for monitoring all transactions. Gives supranational bodies jurisdiction over private financial flows globally.

ESG (Environmental, Social, Governance) Scoring - BlackRock-driven compliance regime disguised as "ethical investing." Redirects capital flows toward policy-aligned corporations and penalizes dissenting sectors.

GFANZ - Glasgow Financial Alliance for Net Zero, chaired by Mark Carney. $150T finance bloc enforcing ESG adherence across corporate and national economies.

Carbon Markets - Trading systems for carbon allowances, converting consumption behavior into trackable tokens that tie directly into ESG scoring and programmable money.

Bail-In Mechanisms - Financial frameworks allowing banks to seize depositor funds to stabilize themselves, legalized globally after the 2008 crash.

De-Dollarization - Global central banks re-engineering financial rails to bypass the USD, using CBDCs and cross-border settlement frameworks governed by BIS.

Digital Identity, IoT & Social Control

Digital Identity Frameworks - Interoperable systems linking biometric ID, health status, financial credentials, and ESG scoring into a single programmable identity profile.

ID2020 - Gates-, Microsoft-, and Rockefeller-backed initiative creating unified global digital identity frameworks for healthcare, banking, and travel.

CommonPass - WEF-affiliated pilot for digital health credentials, later evolved into vaccine passport systems and tied directly to digital wallets.

Vaccine Passports - Introduced under COVID, normalized biometric-based access permissions. Expanding now into "unified ID wallets" integrating finance, health, and mobility.

Digital Twins - Real-time virtual simulations of cities, supply chains, and individuals used for predictive modeling and automated policy interventions.

Geo-Fencing - Invisible digital borders controlled by IoT and GPS. Denies movement or triggers penalties when you enter or exit zones without permission.

IoT (Internet of Things) - Global sensor web collecting real-time behavioral data through connected devices, appliances, meters, and wearables.

Smart Grids - "Energy efficiency" systems that monitor and control home consumption, enabling automated rationing tied to carbon scoring.

15-Minute Cities - Marketed as sustainability and livability but enable

IoT-managed mobility zones, geofenced permissions, and algorithmic restrictions on travel.

Surveillance Capitalism - Business model converting behavioral data into predictive products sold to governments, advertisers, and security agencies.

Social Credit Systems - Algorithmic governance frameworks pioneered in China that score citizens based on "trustworthiness," conditioning access to finance, mobility, and services.

Predictive Policing - AI-driven law enforcement targeting individuals before crimes occur, embedding pre-crime governance into urban IoT infrastructure.

Health, Pandemic Governance & Biosecurity

Event 201 - WEF-Gates-Johns Hopkins pandemic simulation in 2019, piloting policy coordination frameworks later mirrored almost exactly during COVID.

COVAX - Gavi- and CEPI-run vaccine distribution hub controlling procurement contracts globally, binding countries into standardized health compliance.

Emergency Use Authorization (EUA) - Legal mechanism bypassing safety and liability protections during crises, later normalized for routine approvals.

Biosecurity Governance - Policy alignment linking health mandates to mobility, digital ID, and programmable finance. Positioned as safety; functions as enforcement infrastructure.

One Health - WHO narrative tying human, animal, and environmental health together to justify global agricultural, food, and medical governance.

Gain-of-Function Research - Engineering pathogens to enhance transmissibility or lethality. Publicly debated in science, privately tied to biosecurity centralization.

Digital Health Passes - Unified credentials linking personal identity to vaccination status, insurance, and mobility permissions.

AI, Automation & Algorithmic Governance

AI Alignment - Framed as ethical guardrails for artificial intelligence, but centralizes power among elite consortia, excluding smaller players from innovation.

AI Safety Boards - "Independent" oversight councils packed with corporate partners, establishing top-down control over model deployment thresholds.

Anthropic Principle (AI Context) - Narrative positioning AGI development as existential risk to justify consolidating AI governance under aligned private-public alliances.

MLOps (Machine Learning Operations) - Back-end systems for deploying predictive models across populations; enables invisible scaling of algorithmic governance.

Reinforcement Learning from Human Feedback (RLHF) - AI trained on curated "ethical" datasets, embedding elite-approved values into systems determining what information reaches the public.

Digital Thought Policing - Suppression of narratives through algorithmic content moderation and deplatforming driven by AI "trust and safety" frameworks.

Deep Learning Safety - Industry euphemism for access control. Prevents unauthorized labs from competing while securing control over AGI research directions.

Narrative Management & Psychological Operations

Behavioral Nudging - Predictive analytics driving choices subtly via algorithmic targeting - manipulation disguised as personalization.

Misinformation Governance - Global partnerships between Big Tech, WHO, and WEF to define and censor "unapproved" narratives at scale.

Trusted News Initiative (TNI) - BBC-led alliance coordinating narratives across mainstream media and social platforms, harmonizing messaging across countries.

Agenda Framing - Strategic selection of crises, data, and imagery to manufacture public consent for predetermined policy solutions.

Consent Architecture - UI and behavioral design techniques that guide populations toward policy-aligned "choices" they believe are self-directed.

Narrative Harmonization - Synchronizing messaging across institutions, NGOs, corporations, and governments to ensure unified perception management.

Climate, ESG & Resource Management

Carbon Quotas - Personal consumption caps enforced through carbon scoring, tracked in real time via digital ID-linked transaction logs.

Personal Carbon Allowances - Next phase of ESG integration, assigning each individual a finite carbon budget embedded into programmable money systems.

Biodiversity Credits - Financial instruments monetizing natural ecosystems; traded like carbon allowances, expanding ownership of planetary resources.

Green Transition - Framing energy restructuring as moral imperative; drives rapid dependency on IoT-linked energy grids managed by centralized authorities.

Just Transition - Redistributes industries, labor, and capital flows to ESG-compliant sectors under climate governance frameworks.

Security, Intelligence & Control Infrastructure

Five Eyes Alliance - Intelligence-sharing consortium that extends surveillance reach across five nations beyond local legal limits.

In-Q-Tel - CIA's venture arm funding tech startups like Palantir, Keyhole, and biometric identity companies to bake surveillance into commercial products.

Palantir Gotham - Predictive policing and military intelligence platform fusing personal, financial, and geospatial data into unified decision engines.

DARPA - U.S. defense innovation hub funding dual-use technologies from ARPANET to AI, shaping the infrastructure of control under national security branding.

Cyber Polygon - WEF-backed simulation training for global financial "cyber attacks," laying groundwork for digital ID-linked emergency protocols.

Core Theme Definitions

Technocracy - Governance by unelected experts, engineers, and algorithms - legitimized through "science" while circumventing democratic consent.

Algorithmic Governance - Rules hard-coded into infrastructure, enforced automatically by systems rather than debated or voted on.

Digital Feudalism - Structural dependency where individuals and even governments act as vassals to unelected global platforms controlling finance, mobility, and information.

Sovereignty - Formerly self-determination; now increasingly conditional, mediated through compliance with supranational frameworks.

Opt-Out Mirage - Illusion of choice offered to populations while critical infrastructure forces default participation in centralized systems.

1750–1830 | The First Industrial Revolution
• 1750s - Coal-powered mechanization begins in Britain; energy concentration seeds early monopolies.
• 1769 - James Watt patents his improved steam engine → standardizes industrial energy use.
• 1771 - Richard Arkwright pioneers the factory system → centralizes labor, births time discipline.
• 1793 - Eli Whitney invents interchangeable parts → automation logic emerges.
• 1804 - First rail networks laid; early logistics become power levers.
• 1825 - George Stephenson's Stockton & Darlington Railway launches → rail standardization as governance.

1830–1900 | Industrialization, Data, and Corporate Empires
• 1837 - Telegraph patented → information control enters policy architecture.
• 1851 - Great Exhibition in London flaunts mechanized dominance and imperial industrial power.
• 1865 - Cornelius Vanderbilt consolidates U.S. rail infrastructure → private chokepoints over public movement.
• 1870 - Rockefeller's Standard Oil founded → vertical integration + monopoly dominance.
• 1876 - Alexander Graham Bell patents telephone → global data transmission begins.
• 1886 - J. P. Morgan begins consolidating finance → banking becomes governance.
• 1890 - Sherman Antitrust Act passes but monopolists adapt → trusts evolve into coordinated networks.

1900–1930 | The Technocratic Seedbed
- 1901 - U.S. Steel formed under J.P. Morgan and Carnegie → first trillion-dollar corporate structure.
- 1913 - Federal Reserve Act creates U.S. central bank → private consortium controls money issuance.
- 1919 - League of Nations created → precursor to supranational governance.
- 1927 - First synchronized economic modeling attempted at LSE under Fabian influence.
- 1933 - Howard Scott launches Technocracy Inc. → energy-based economy vision at Columbia University.
- 1935 - Social Security Act passes in U.S. → identity numbering introduced as governance infrastructure.

1930–1950 | Crisis as Catalyst
- 1939–1945 - WWII accelerates R&D; Manhattan Project fuses science + state power.
- 1944 - Bretton Woods Agreement creates IMF and World Bank → global finance centralized.
- 1946 - RAND Corporation founded → predictive modeling begins shaping policy.
- 1948 - UN established → policy harmonization at global scale.
- 1949 - NATO founded → cross-border military alignment embeds sovereignty trade-offs.

1950–1970 | Cybernetics, Cold War, and Systems Control
- 1953 - Watson & Crick map DNA → biological data enters the governance equation.
- 1958 - DARPA founded → military-industrial innovation pipeline begins.
- 1961 - First predictive policing experiments tested in Chicago.
- 1965 - Gordon Moore predicts exponential chip growth → data

dominance begins.

- 1968 - Club of Rome founded → "Limits to Growth" narratives emerge.
- 1969 - ARPANET goes live → proto-internet built for defense, later repurposed for surveillance.

1970–1990 | Neoliberal Integration & Supranational Governance

- 1971 - Nixon ends gold standard → fiat regimes empower central banks.
- 1971 - Klaus Schwab launches WEF → CEOs enter policymaking arenas.
- 1973 - Trilateral Commission founded → U.S., EU, and Japan policy convergence begins.
- 1974 - Privacy Act establishes centralized data collection frameworks in U.S.
- 1980 - BIS Basel Accords begin standardizing banking globally.
- 1987 - Montreal Protocol sets precedent for climate-linked supranational policy.
- 1989 - Tim Berners-Lee invents the World Wide Web → digital governance inevitable.

1990–2010 | The Digital Integration Era

- 1994 - NAFTA launches → free trade embeds corporate arbitration above national courts.
- 1995 - WTO established → trade sovereignty ceded to supranational frameworks.
- 1999 - Glass-Steagall repealed → Wall Street fully fuses with governance.
- 2001 - 9/11 reshapes global security → Patriot Act legalizes mass surveillance.
- 2004 - Facebook founded → identity mapping accelerates.
- 2008 - Financial collapse triggers coordinated bailouts → "too big to fail" entrenches private dominance.

- 2010 - IMF, BIS, and WEF converge on CBDC frameworks behind closed doors.

2010–2020 | AI, Biosecurity & Predictive Control
- 2012 - Deep learning breakthrough accelerates AI integration into health, defense, finance.
- 2015 - Paris Agreement aligns carbon policy globally; ESG pipelines quietly activated.
- 2016 - ID2020 formed → biometric identity + finance frameworks merge.
- 2017 - China begins live deployment of Social Credit System → first planetary beta test for algorithmic governance.
- 2019 - Event 201 simulates pandemic → policy coordination rehearsed.
- 2020 - COVID-19 declared global emergency → planetary governance model stress-tested.

2020–2030 | Lockstep Integration Phase (Projected)
- 2021 - Vaccine passports normalize digital credentials tied to access permissions.
- 2022 - BIS, IMF, and WEF pilot interoperable CBDCs across 80+ central banks.
- 2023 - AI governance frameworks drafted by OpenAI, DeepMind, and Anthropic, bypassing legislatures.
- 2025 - First widespread rollout of programmable money tethered to carbon quotas.
- 2027 - WHO legally empowered to trigger binding global health mandates.
- 2028 - ESG enforcement reaches individual-level carbon scoring integrated with CBDCs.
- 2030 - UN's Agenda 2030 fully deployed: ID-linked, IoT-managed, AI-optimized compliance grids operational in all G20 economies.

2030–2050 | Full Convergence Scenarios

- 2032 - WEF-led AI Council formalizes AGI governance; "alignment" protocols become planetary law.
- 2035 - Digital twin simulations integrate urban planning, social credit, and predictive policing at citywide scales.
- 2040 - Majority of personal transactions mediated via programmable currencies; cash effectively extinct.
- 2045 - First post-national "sovereignty zones" formed - governance shifts to networked platforms entirely.
- 2050 - Autonomous governance fully operational: machine-led policy enforcement replaces democratic negotiation.